Praise for

DANCING WITH
THE DEVIL IN
THE CITY OF GOD

"A powerful work of reportage. Eloquent, heartfelt, and thorough, Barbassa is a brilliant guide to the underside of Brazil's showcase city. If you want to understand twenty-first-century Rio de Janeiro, read this book."

—Alex Bellos, author of *Futebol: the Brazilian Way of Life*

"Returning to Rio after years abroad, Juliana Barbassa takes the reader on a journey of urban exploration beyond the tourist clichés of Ipanema and Carnival. Her book, *Dancing with the Devil in the City of God*, seamlessly melds deep reporting with nuanced memoir, providing an insider's guide to a global city of immense energy, appetites, heartbreak, and danger. To understand Rio's prospects for the twenty-first century, come with Barbassa on her voyage of inquiry and rediscovery. It's a trip worth taking. I savored every moment."

—Ambassador Derek Shearer, director of the McKinnon Center for Global Affairs, Occidental College

"Juliana Barbassa has written a beautiful yet unflinching meditation on one of the world's great cities during a moment of profound change. Her book is a moving examination of the immense charms, staccato violence, and unfulfilled promise of the marvelous city and of the heart of modern Brazil.

—Michael Deibert, author of *In the Shadow of Saint Death: The Gulf Cartel and the Price of America's Drug War in Mexico*

"A timely tour-de-force . . . Drawing on the city's history, geography, social structure, culture, political intrigues, and economic disparities, Barbassa has written a multidisciplinary masterpiece. This splendid and accessible narrative is must-reading not just for the journalists, spectators, and athletes who will be in Rio for the Olympic Games, but for anyone who has visited Rio—or not—and has been caught up in the magnetic attraction of this spectacular and complicated city."

—Dr. Robert Maguire, director of the Brazil Initiative
at the Elliot School of International Affairs,
George Washington University

"Frank, fluid dispatches . . . Energetic, intrepid reporting by an insider."

—*Kirkus Reviews*

"[A] fascinating urban chronicle . . . [readers] will come away with a sense of having been there."

—*Publishers Weekly*

"The book is exquisitely written, a blend of a memoir and some of the best reporting you will find on Rio de Janeiro. Some parts are heartwrenching (see the chapter on the mudslides), and some parts are laugh-out-loud funny (don't miss the anecdote about the Mexican entrepreneur and how he got his Brazilian visa). Not only does she get into the nitty-gritty of security, gentrification, evictions, environmental degradation, and mega-event preparation, she digs deep into the history of Rio's ongoing conflict."

—*Rio Gringa*

DANCING WITH THE DEVIL IN THE CITY OF GOD

RIO DE JANEIRO AND THE OLYMPIC DREAM

JULIANA BARBASSA

TOUCHSTONE

NEW YORK   LONDON   TORONTO   SYDNEY   NEW DELHI

Touchstone
An Imprint of Simon & Schuster, Inc.
1230 Avenue of the Americas
New York, NY 10020

First Touchstone trade paperback edition July 2016

TOUCHSTONE and colophon are registered trademarks of
Simon & Schuster, Inc.

For information about special discounts for bulk purchases,
please contact Simon & Schuster Special Sales at 1-866-506-1949 or
business@simonandschuster.com.

The Simon & Schuster Speakers Bureau can bring authors to your live event. For
more information or to book an event contact the Simon & Schuster Speakers
Bureau at 866-248-3049 or visit our website at www.simonspeakers.com.

Interior design by Akasha Archer

Manufactured in the United States of America

10 9 8 7 6 5 4 3 2 1

The Library of Congress has cataloged the hardcover edition as follows:

Barbassa, Juliana.
    Dancing with the devil in the city of God : Rio de Janeiro on the brink / Juliana
Barbassa.
        pages   cm
    "A Touchstone book."
    1. Rio de Janeiro (Brazil)—Social life and customs.   2. Rio de Janeiro
(Brazil)—Social conditions.   3. City and town life—Brazil—Rio de Janeiro.
4. Social change—Brazil—Rio de Janeiro.   5. Social problems—Brazil—Rio
de Janeiro.   6. Rio de Janeiro (Brazil)—Description and travel.   7. Barbassa,
Juliana—Travel—Brazil—Rio de Janeiro.   8. Economic development—Brazil—
Rio de Janeiro.   9. Rio de Janeiro (Brazil)—Economic conditions.   I. Title.
    F2646.2.B37   2015
    981'.53—dc23   2014042530

ISBN 978-1-4767-5625-7
ISBN 978-1-4767-5626-4 (pbk)
ISBN 978-1-4767-5627-1 (ebook)

For my *Cariocas*—Gabriel, Clara, Marina, Henrique, and Rafael

The drums, like thunder, drummed the tremulous hour.
—Fernando Pessoa, *The Book of Disquiet*

CONTENTS

INTRODUCTION: OR, IS GOD BRAZILIAN?

It started as a persistent tapping, like impatient fingers on a tabletop: tah-cah-TAH tah-cah-TAH tah-cah-TAH.

I was on deadline, hunched over my desk in the back corner of the Associated Press newsroom in San Francisco, trying to block out the perennially ringing phones and the reporter chatter. This was October 2009. President Barack Obama's plan to reform health care was the news of the day, and my editors in New York wanted an article on what it meant for immigrants. I had a couple of hours to make something coherent out of the reports strewn on my desk.

On my screen, sentences refused to coalesce into paragraphs. Through the office din I heard that pulse, faint but insistent: tah-cah-TAH tah-cah-TAH tah-cah-TAH . . . TAH TAH. TAH TAH. Then it clicked. I knew that pattern: it was the call and response of *surdos*, the bass drums that drive a Brazilian samba beat. The sound was so out of place in the air-conditioned newsroom that my eyes flew up to the TVs that hung in clusters from the ceiling, tuned to the news. I walked over.

One of the tech writers was already there, craning his neck to watch, curious about the commotion. There was the long sweep of Copacabana Beach, the cobalt of the Atlantic. The white sand was thick with people, tens of thousands, skin glistening as men stripped off their shirts on the warm spring day and women danced, arms widespread, the whole crowd flashing Brazil's green and yellow colors and heaving to the syncopated beat.

This was the day. Brazil—Rio de Janeiro—was in the running to host the 2016 Olympics, up against Tokyo, Madrid, and Chicago. The announcement would be broadcast live on massive screens raised on the beach.

This wasn't the country's first try. It had bid two times before and failed. But this run was different. Brazil was different. A copy of *The Economist* sat on my desk under the health care reports, folded back to an article on vast oil finds just off Rio's shore. There had been other intriguing headlines recently. Brazil was lending money to the International Monetary Fund, after years of failing to pay its debt. Its middle class had grown by a population the size of California's in less than a decade. Something remarkable was happening in this southern giant. Financial papers had picked up on it, even if to most foreigners it was still a place of poverty and parties, samba, soccer, and favelas.

The country's recent good fortune and its Olympic bid made for good copy; as a journalist, I knew that. But my interest wasn't just professional. I was born in Brazil, although I'd spent most of my life rambling from country to country, first as the daughter of an oil executive, and later as a reporter with a chronic case of wanderlust. Over time, the roots connecting me to my home country had grown long and thin, but I'd kept them alive through annual visits and by collecting news articles such as the ones that littered my desk.

Recently, I'd noticed a change in these articles. What had been occasional pieces, mostly short briefs about a burst of violence or a presidential election, came more frequently, and in greater depth.

The world had begun to pay more attention to Brazil. The Olympic vote could push it right into the spotlight.

I watched as in Copenhagen the camera panned to Brazil's president, Luis Inácio Lula da Silva, a stocky man pumping a few more hands in the moments before the cities made final presentations to the International Olympic Committee. Brazilians affectionately shortened his name to Lula, as if he were one of the family. Being chosen to host the Olympics would give Brazil—the Brazil crafted during his tenure—an unprecedented vote of confidence, a gold star to show that this forever-emerging nation had finally arrived. The International Olympic Committee had played that role before: Tokyo won the 1964 bid as Japan rose from the devastation of World War II. Seoul hosted the 1988 Games just when Korea was taking off, and China got the 2008 Olympics right as it was flexing its muscles on the international stage.

In the week leading up to the IOC decision there had been a scrum of press conferences with presidents and campaign trail stunts, making the run-up feel like something between a high school popularity contest and a political summit. The Madrid team flew in a liveried plane; Oprah Winfrey shilled for Chicago.

Still, as the Olympic Committee members gathered there was no clear favorite. Tokyo was a safe, functional alternative. Madrid already had most of the venues built. In a last-minute twist, Obama said he would deliver the U.S. pitch, becoming the first American president to address the IOC. His perfectly timed trip swayed the bookmakers. On the day of the vote, the money was on Chicago.

Whichever country won, it would face scrutiny and tremendous expense. The Beijing Olympics the year before had cost an astounding $40 billion, removed 1.5 million people from their homes, and left behind empty stadiums. The torch relay had sparked huge protests over China's human rights record; I'd helped cover the marches in San Francisco.

Spain and the United States were mired in a global recession;

Japan's economy was faltering. And yet the contest was more intense than ever. Staging the world's biggest sports bash was expensive, but voters loved it; it also gave the host country tremendous leverage to promote a particular agenda, whether it was fostering rapid urban renewal, picking up a lackluster economy, or showing off new political and economic might.

The problems with Rio were obvious even from afar. Security came first, then transportation, with old airports and roadways that flooded with every major storm and gridlocked hopelessly every rush hour. There were not enough hotel rooms for the millions of expected visitors, and the proposal to stash them in the dilapidated port area made the whole plan seem rather improvised. Official estimates said that preparing the city would cost more than $11 billion. That was three times more than the second most expensive proposal that year, from Madrid.

But the Olympics had never been held in South America, and Brazil's Lula had thrown himself into the campaign. He visited London's Olympic Park and spoke on the topic over months, making it clear that Rio's bid was the nation's bid, with support and funding guaranteed from the top. There had been protests in Chicago, where residents worried that hosting the Games would mean budget overruns, corruption, or neighborhoods razed to make way for Olympic projects. Brazilians, on the other hand, were eager to host, Lula said.

The president's personal magnetism made him a powerful salesman for brand Brazil. But his life story spoke more eloquently for the country than any of his speeches. In his well-cut suit, he represented something unheard-of in Brazil's history: a rise from abject poverty to absolute power. He had set his meaty shoulders against the odds—his birth in the parched northeast, a childhood shining shoes and selling peanuts on the street, his years as a steelworker and then a union leader in the country's industrial guts—and he'd made it.

This was startling in a country of entrenched hierarchies, in which one's niche in society was determined by a complex calculus involving class, race, geography, and income. By those measures, Lula should have never left the factory floor. And yet, there he was: an equal among presidents of some of the most powerful countries in the world.

After coming up through the labor movement, he helped found the Workers' Party, which defended the rights of the poor and working classes. He ran for president—three times—and lost. By his fourth run, in 2002, he'd trimmed the bushy, revolutionary beard. The ink-black hair that had crowded his brow had softened into gray and lay back in brushed waves; his suits no longer looked borrowed, tight in the wrong places. He took on a businessman as running mate, reassuring the upper classes and foreign investors that his radical days were over. This time, he won. Four years later, with a stable economy and a broadening middle class, he won again.

This was the Lula who went to Copenhagen: a man who drew on his rank-and-file background to charm, with an informal, back-slapping manner that could sometimes startle heads of state, but was cordial, disarming, and very, very Brazilian. The country he promoted was a profitable place to invest, a growing power, and a real democracy in which men like him could become president.

None of this was lost on the International Olympic Committee that October day as he sat, dark jacket, gray beard, waiting.

After the informal greetings and handshakes, the candidate cities' presentations started. Chicago was the first to make its case. Michelle Obama, in yellow with big TV hair: "I was born and raised on Chicago's South Side. . . ." She talked about family and about her dad, who taught her to "throw a mean right hook." Barack picked it up from there: he wanted to welcome the world "into my neighborhood." It was the Obama two-step—graceful, polished. They did it well. Chicago looked like a winner. Tokyo was up next, with something about green Games. I went back to my desk, to health care reform and my deadline, all but giving up on Rio after the Chicago performance.

Then, there was the drumming again—louder. I looked up. There was the beach at Copacabana, the swarming crowd, the Olympic anthem floating over the masses. There was IOC president Jacques Rogge at the podium, lean, staid, aristocratic, so European. There was Lula in the front row of the auditorium, fidgeting and crossing himself for good luck.

Joseph "Sepp" Blatter, president of FIFA (Fédération Internationale de Football Association, the world governing body of soccer) and one of the IOC's voting members, sat across from the Brazilian president, watching him. Blatter poked other IOC delegates, mimicked Lula's superstitious gesture, shook his head, and cracked a grin as if to say, "Can you believe this guy?"

Rogge thanked the candidate cities. He lifted the envelope with the five rings. He fumbled, then pulled out the card.

"Rio de Janeiro," he said, stumbling on the hard Portuguese *J* and giving it the soft, aspirated Spanish sound: Reeow day Haneirow.

No matter. Lula, Pelé, the whole Brazilian contingent jumped from their chairs and fell into each other's arms as if they had just scored the winning goal in a World Cup final. They cried, they kissed, they bounced around like popcorn. Lula barreled over to the Spanish delegation. The eighty-nine-year-old Juan Antonio Samaranch, former president of the IOC and a big campaigner for Madrid, had been sitting quietly through the chaos. Lula pulled him in for a big kiss on the forehead.

Next he went for José Luis Zapatero, the Spanish head of state. Lula wrapped him in a hug, yelled something in his ear, then he turned around, heading against the human current with a green and yellow Brazilian flag in his hand. Someone started singing "Cidade maravilhosa . . ." and Lula led the chorus of Rio's informal anthem, belting out, along with the Brazilians in the room, his love for the "marvelous city of a thousand graces, the heart of my Brazil." Protocol was in shreds. IOC president Rogge looked uncomfortable.

But Lula was unstoppable. He now wore the flag like a cape, an unlikely superhero from the global South. Photographers went in for the shot, and flashes of light brightened Lula's way as his security guards huddled around and pushed with him through the crowd.

The cameras cut back to Copacabana. The air quickened with flags and flying confetti, fireworks. CNN's Shasta Darlington, reporting from the beach, tried to talk over the racket. She described a party expected to last all night.

Watching the raucous celebration on TV, I knew the exhilaration was fueled by much more than the Summer Games. Brazil was on the brink of something exceptional.

Other countries suffered through bloody battles for independence, civil wars, revolutions—the sort of historical junctures that can reconfigure a nation's character. Brazil had experienced few great ruptures. Independence was granted without a fight, there was no upheaval to end slavery, no communist insurrection. The scaffolding that propped its wealthy and powerful had never been challenged; these structures lay like bones under the surface, hardening over centuries, shaping Brazil into one of the most unequal countries in the world.

Now powerful and overlapping circumstances—local and international, social, political, and economic—were forcing those old bones to shift and, perhaps, settle in new configurations. For the first time in generations, possibly ever, there was money and political will for change. The possibilities were tantalizing.

Lula himself was a symbol of this potential. He'd lost a finger at eighteen, crushed in a lathe during a late-night shift at a steel mill. When he used his hands to make a point—which was often—there it was, the reminder of how far he'd come. The man himself embodied this moment when everything seemed possible. That's what the crowd on the beach was celebrating. It was Brazil's turn. The Olympics in Rio would give it a stage and a spotlight.

This is when it struck me: it was time to go back.

I was three years old when my family first left Brazil, following the whims of my father's job. For the next seven years or so, we moved around the Middle East and the Mediterranean, changing cities more often than most families change cars. This hopscotching left me a perennial outsider, a bookish kid with glasses and a halo of curly hair who spoke a home-baked Portuguese sprinkled with English and Arabic, and who felt out of place anywhere but in a library. My sense of the country named on my passport was patched together from conversations, the outdated magazines that reached us, and yearly visits to our vast extended family when I'd lose myself among dozens of cousins, watching and listening, trying to grasp what it meant to be Brazilian.

Each time we landed in Rio, there would be a moment after we left the airport when I'd roll down the taxi window and let in the city's humid embrace. It was the first sign I was home.

In these visits I'd take my fill of the hothouse atmosphere, letting it gush though my senses. After the spare vistas of the Middle East, with their limited palette of sand, stone, and sky, I always returned hungry for Rio, where green shoots pushed from every crack and thick-petaled flowers bloomed year-round, saturated with color, rich with scent. The people thronging the streets, bare-chested men and women in short-short-tight-tight everything, walked with a fluid grace as if on well-oiled joints. They talked a lot and laughed out loud, the rounded vowels of Brazilian Portuguese tumbling out like marbles.

After a year surrounded by the discreet monochrome of Muslim women's concealing chadors and the men's loose *jalabiyahs*, the physical exuberance and informality of Brazilians was always shocking at first. This was a place where life happened at close range. Apartments were small, stuffed with too many relatives, and breathless on hot afternoons, so much of what elsewhere was private was conducted outdoors in Rio: people kissed, drank, danced, even groomed themselves in full view. Accustomed as I was to the high walls and modesty of Muslim society, the people of Rio de Janeiro—the Cariocas, as they are called—seemed almost obscene and entirely fascinating. But our visits were always too short, and before I could grasp what it meant to be of this place, we were on our way to the airport again.

Now this city that had mesmerized me for very personal reasons was drawing attention of a different sort in a world where the power balance was tilting, making a little more room for up-and-comers.

Brazil was living a unique moment in its history. It was forging an independent foreign policy with stronger ties to other emerging nations, and demanding a voice at the world's important round-tables, including a permanent seat at the United Nations Security Council. But the biggest novelty was the economy. China's appetite for Brazil's main exports—iron ore, soy bean, sugar, meat—seemed endless. Foreign investment was pouring in. As Brazilians emerged from poverty, they began to buy everything from stoves to cars to flights abroad. Suddenly flush with cash and credit, they were going on spending sprees in New York and Miami. Those who'd moved to other countries during the lean years were going back home, where there were not enough engineers, architects, or accountants to meet demand. Brazil was on its way to becoming the world's sixth-largest economy.

Petroleum was a big part of this boom. A huge new discovery showed there was enough of it trapped underwater, 180 miles

beyond Rio's coast, to heave the country onto a higher geopolitical echelon. A big spread in the *Wall Street Journal* brought over
by one of the AP business editors lay on my desk: Brazil had long
teetered on the edge of energy self-sufficiency, but this find could
catapult the nation into the top tier of energy producers, making it
an exporter—and an international force to be reckoned with.

"God is Brazilian," Lula said, celebrating the oil discovery with
a popular saying that refers to the country's natural bounty.

The country had already been chosen to host the 2014 World
Cup. Now it had the Olympics, too. The enthusiasm was catching—
I felt it from California.

But what did all this mean? From afar, the whole thing seemed
to veer between a well-founded optimism and a giddy sky's-the-limit
euphoria. Good news came in daily and by the handful. For the
first time in generations, there was money and political will to
push through substantial reforms. The World Cup and the Olympics gave Brazil—and Rio in particular—concrete deadlines and a
long to-do list; social and economic change was transforming the
landscape and the expectations of the population.

This was a unique experiment. Its results mattered—not just to
me as a Brazilian, but to me as a reporter. Urban chaos, poverty,
pollution, and an indifferent government were not exclusive to
Rio. Other megacities in the developing world faced these same
challenges. Would Rio find original answers within the high-
pressure crucible of the next few years? Or would it crack in unforeseen ways?

There's a Brazilian expression for something that's only a façade: *para inglês ver*, or "for the English to see." It comes from the
years after England abolished slavery and campaigned to end the
human trade. Brazil signed an international treaty and passed a
law promising to stop, but the traffic continued. The laws were
meant for the English to see—a nicety for foreign eyes. Would
the changes of the next few years be just *para inglês ver*, or were we

looking at a transformation that would go to the core, reforming the violence and inequality that had historically hobbled the city? Whatever the case, I didn't want to just read about it in the news.

I applied to be the Associated Press's Rio de Janeiro correspondent and got the job. Within three weeks, I rented out my apartment, sold my car, gave away my books. On November 4, 2010, I checked in at the United Airlines counter in San Francisco with a one-way ticket to Brazil. After twenty-one years, I was going home.

CHAPTER 1

RIO, HOME

The plane banked and dipped for descent. I pressed my forehead against the tiny window, taking in the vast bay below, its surface broken by scattered islands. When Portuguese explorers first found shelter here in the early 1500s, they thought they'd hit the mouth of a great river—the River of January, Rio de Janeiro.

The name eventually settled on the city itself, which spreads along the bay's west side. From the airplane, Rio was ethereal: a smear of white separating sky and water, anchored by great granite mountains blanketed with emerald green. There were no noises, no smells, no people, just water and mountains, possibility and light.

As the abstract elements below arranged themselves into familiar forms—beaches and buildings, highways, the crosshatch of tiny shacks seen from above, then the international airport on the largest of the islands—I felt the pull of this postcard city, with its palm trees and white sands, its languid heat. For years I'd kept this image in mind, retreating to it when I felt drained, cold, out of place.

Once I stepped out of the airport's air-conditioned recesses and pulled onto the highway, the real Rio pressed in, an immediate assault on the senses.

To the left there was Guanabara Bay. Dense vegetation crowded the water's edge and curled over it. The debris disgorged by this metropolis of 13 million people wreathed the shore: old couches, a bashed-in television set, unrecognizable plastic bits snarled in decaying plastic bags. I rolled down the window and the cloying scent of sewage filled the car.

A vast patchwork of favelas stretched out on the right. Boxy houses of unfinished red brick, stacked like kids' building blocks, bristled with exposed rebar and hugged the highway's shoulder. High acrylic barriers rose on both shoulders of the expressway. Their decorated panels replaced a view of the favela with enticing previews of the best Rio had to offer: samba musicians playing tambourines, children flying kites, the graceful outline of the Sugarloaf Mountain. Some of the acrylic panes were pocked with bullet holes.

Many of those exiting the airport locked their doors and rolled up their windows at this point, heeding those travel guide warnings that started with "To reduce your chances of becoming a victim . . . ," and then settled into the safety of their air-conditioned cocoon, thoughts speeding ahead to their own picture postcards, the places they came to see: Copacabana, Ipanema, Lapa, Leblon, their very names rhythmic and evocative of summer, sunshine, and good times.

But leaving the airport that day I wanted all of Rio, its hot, humid breath, its extremes. I was home. I rolled the words around in my mind, trying them out: Rio, home.

I settled into a hotel in Ipanema, a few blocks from the ocean. This was the Rio most foreigners came looking for: upscale but still casual, its streets lively with eateries that spilled onto the sidewalks. Just down the street was the corner bar where, back in 1963, a poet and a composer talked music, nursed their whiskeys and watched for a local girl who made the sun shine a little brighter when she walked by, "tall and tan and young and lovely," on her way to the sea. The pair, musician Tom Jobim and poet Vinícius de

Moraes, would cull the intimate sound of bossa nova from those long, sultry afternoons, and distill that quintessential Rio tune, "The Girl from Ipanema," from the deceptive simplicity of the young woman's gait.

Ipanema still had this easy charm, this ability to catch the eye. No matter that buses now stopped and huffed their air brakes by the open-air bar where musicians once scrawled lyrics on the back of napkins, or that troupes of young, shirtless men now played a few rushed cords and did capoeira backflips during traffic stops, hoping for some tourist change. Ipanema still had that levity, like the girl whose glance once filled the world—or at least one grimy corner bar—with grace.

I'd arrived in November, almost at the beginning of the South American summer. On Sundays, the beachfront road was closed to cars and thronged with people. I dropped my bags at my hotel and pushed through palm-draped lanes packed with kids on bikes, skateboarders, couples, bodybuilders, grandmothers with their broad-brimmed hats, a river of bodies tangling and touching in the golden light. Rio's denizens, the Cariocas, feel at home in a crowd and don't mind brushing past strangers. This comfort with closeness left a thin film of other people's sweat on my bare arms and shoulders.

Ipanema is slender, narrow at the waist, with only seven blocks separating the Atlantic to the south from a lagoon, the Lagoa, to the north. Forested mountains rise behind the lagoon's dark mirror and hold aloft the white stone statue of Christ the Redeemer—just Cristo to the informal Cariocas.

In this gorgeous little strip of land, burdened as it is with ungainly buildings, the frenetic hum of the city slows down. I felt it as soon as I stepped out of the hotel. It is hard to take anything too seriously when locals flip-flop around in Havaianas, board shorts, and post-beach dresses over still-damp bikinis, the flimsy fabric slipping off bronzed shoulders just so.

From the edge of the sidewalk I surveyed the beach. To my right, the sand ended at the granite flanks of massive rock outcroppings. On that hillside, perched above the ocean, was the Vidigal favela. Two massive boulders jutted out behind it: the Dois Irmãos peaks, the name meaning Two Brothers for their closeness. To the left was Arpoador, a park of immense granite formations that tumbled into the ocean and where Cariocas liked to gather for a sunset beer. The name harked back to a time when whales were harpooned off this coast. Now fishermen cast their lines from the base of the rock and surfers swarmed the break at its feet like sharks.

Vendors in numbered shacks, or *barracas*, claimed the space between the sidewalk and the water. Burnished by decades in the sun, these men kept a close eye on their realm, offering prospective customers a sun umbrella or beach chairs, ice-cold water or a beer. In time, I'd pick a favorite spot on the beach, get to know them by name, and be recognized by them in turn.

I bought a fresh coconut, which the *barraqueiro*, the vendor, fished out from a Styrofoam cooler and hacked opened with three expert chops of the machete. The *agua de côco* inside was sweet and cool, the perfect balance to the heat of the day and the tang of sweat and sea spray. I sat on one of the concrete benches facing the sea and reveled in it: coconut, sun, ocean breeze.

This was the Rio I'd dreamed of for years, and there was a deep satisfaction in feeling the present layer comfortably over my matching memories. Volleyball players rose and curved their bodies into perfect arcs above the net, supple in the honeyed light. Down near the water, gaggles of girls lay facedown on their sarongs, side by side, rows of perfect bums to the sky. Hawkers slung with ice chests, coolers, grills and other paraphernalia trudged by calling out their wares: peanuts, sodas, beer, caipirinhas, fresh shrimp, grilled cheese.

Never mind that my legs had the indoor pallor of white asparagus and I was alone, disconnected from the clumps of Cariocas, a stranger to the vendors. I was home. Perhaps it would be this easy. Perhaps all it took was repeating it a few times, like a prayer or a spell, and it would start to feel that way.

Rio de Janeiro had always been a port of entry into Brazil, a place of connections, deals, and trade. Ships coming from Africa disgorged onto its dock the enslaved men and women who'd wrench the country's fortune from its plantations and mines. When the Portuguese royal family fled from Lisbon in 1807, just ahead of Napoleon's invading army, they'd sailed to Rio and made it the seat of their empire.

For my family, too, Rio was a threshold. My parents were born in Minas Gerais, a Texas-sized state of coffee and cattle, rolling hills and baroque churches. Rio was their gateway to the world beyond; it was where they started their married life, staying just long enough for my mother to have three children and for my father to start working for the Brazilian oil company, Petrobras.

It was from Rio that we left for Saddam Hussein's Iraq in 1977. When he waged war against Iran in 1980, we hid under the stairway to escape the air raids that shattered windows along our dirt street in Basra. My father had to stay behind to close up the office, but my mother crammed her three children onto a school bus and, along with other Petrobras families, headed toward Kuwait. Bombs rained down on oil rigs along the way, turning them into furious towers of fire whose roar could be heard for miles.

We took only what we could carry—a change of clothes and food for the unknown road ahead. Along the way we had to stop. I didn't know why, or where we were. The road shimmied under the sun, a long asphalt ribbon that unspooled over the desert, equally forbidding in either direction. We sat on the dirt ground under a white-hot sky for what seemed like hours, surrounded by other dazed evacuees. Iraqi and foreign, we were all trying to escape the war. Unlike us, many of the local families were walking. There were children, goats, sheep, all equally round-eyed with fear. A hand snuck into the bag that held our food for the trip, making off with the hard-boiled eggs. My mother shrugged it off: "They need it more than we do."

In Kuwait, a five-star hotel allowed us and other Brazilian families to sleep on pool mats scattered around their ballroom. Eventually, we found our way from that Kuwaiti ballroom to my grandmother's house in Minas Gerais. For months we waited for my father and hung on to the news for reports of the war. As soon as he rejoined us we were on the move again, this time to Malta, a dot in the Mediterranean. A year later we moved again to Libya, where national television featured the public hanging of political dissidents, and the square-jawed profile of a young Muammar Gadhafi loomed on massive outdoor billboards and in nearly every home.

After years of flirting with Brazil, we moved back in 1984. I'd wanted to go back; still, the landing was rough. I was excruciatingly shy. Attending an international school run by oil companies in Tripoli had not prepared me for junior high in Rio de Janeiro.

My private school classmates had all been raised in the city's new gated communities. They'd been honing their tastes for years, and even their pencil cases had brands. I was all wrong: kinky curls that my mother treated like topiary, trimming into a perfect circumference; glasses in pink, shatterproof plastic so they'd last the year, and then, oh yes, a retainer. My sneakers, from the government-run store that carried Tripoli's few consumer goods, had no brand at all. They were green, the color of Libya's flag, with orange trim. On their sides, where other kids' shoes said Reebok, mine had the country's official name: "Socialist People's Libyan Arab Jamahiriyah."

But I was finally in Rio and curious about this place where everyone spoke the Portuguese we used only at home, and where I was supposed to—finally—belong. I threw myself into it the way I knew how: reading. After school I would grab the newspaper, spread it over my bed, and try to make sense of the turmoil wracking the country.

After two decades under a military regime that had seized power in a 1964 coup, Brazil was transitioning to democracy. The first civilian president, chosen by an electoral college, faced emergency surgery the day before taking office and died of septicemia. The vice president was inaugurated in his stead, but what should have been a moment of celebration was tense and uncertain, weighed down by national mourning.

I'd watched the funeral from my grandmother's house, with cousins, aunts, and uncles all clinging to the television. My grandmother broke into tears. It all seemed so frail, this transition, the new government. Everything was shifting at once—political allegiances, business connections, power relations, even the amount of nudity on newly uncensored television.

Disastrous economic policies crashed one recovery plan into another. Brazil would have six currencies between 1986 and 1994. With each new set of bills, the government slashed zeroes from numbers that inflation had made so large they no longer fit on printed money. Prices went up so fast that shoppers tried to snatch up the day's groceries ahead of the supermarket employee with the mark-up gun, grabbing soap or a bunch of bananas before he had a chance to put on the new price tag.

Even to my young eyes, the country was an unmoored disaster. The city of Rio was no better.

Rio de Janeiro had once been the seat of empire, and after independence from Portugal, it became the capital of Brazil. It lost that status to Brasília in 1960, along with federal jobs and money. As the country's economy slipped into years of instability and hyperinflation in the 1980s, the city's decadence continued. Genteel neighborhoods fell apart. Squatters took over abandoned warehouses on Avenida Brasil. The once-grand shipyards disintegrated in the salty ocean air. Giant cranes, visible from the highway that looped around the port, held up their heavy heads for years like the last survivors of an ancient race, then crumpled as rust ate at their joints. Downtown, entire buildings went vacant, their rows of darkened windows reflecting the hopelessness of the moment.

The economic disarray and escalating violence squeezed the population. Business executives were targeted for kidnappings. The rest of us worried about carjackings and holdups. My brother came home wearing only shorts one day, robbed of his T-shirt and sneakers by kids not much older than himself. Women covered their car windows with dark film so as not to look like easy targets, and no one stopped at streetlights after dark. Those who could afford it retreated behind barred windows, into gated communities and bulletproof cars. Many left the city or the country altogether.

My family had settled in one of the gated *condomínios* then sprouting in the sparsely populated west. Barra da Tijuca was gorgeous—a long strip of marshy flatland hemmed in by green mountains to the north and miles of white sand and the Atlantic to the south. Rivers streamed from the heights and collected in lakes and lagoons. The new condomínios, watched over by an army of uniformed doormen and private security guards, filled up as fast as they were built. I lived in one of these new communities, called Nova Ipanema, and went to school in another, Novo Leblon, names that suggested new versions of the old Rio neighborhoods and promised a life that could no longer be found there.

Far from the heart of Rio, I sought out that city as I could—in occasional visits, and always, through the news. I read about the favelas that clung to steep, unstable hillsides, and the hard rains that inevitably sent dozens of their homes tumbling down into the mud.

By the 1980s, drug lords had taken over these shantytowns,

turning them into fortresses nearly impenetrable to police. This new power was put on spectacular display when Escadinha, a drug kingpin with Robin Hood pretensions, was hoisted out of his maximum-security prison by fellow gang members in a helicopter. The cinematic escape was all over TV. He gave interviews, boasting about the help he offered the favela that harbored him and his gang, the Comando Vermelho, or Red Command.

Turf wars between gangs or with the police meant shoot-outs. The press at the time coined a phrase, *bala perdida*, or lost bullet. The unintended victims of these stray shots often made headlines: the young mother killed while sitting at home with her two-year-old on her lap, the kid with a book bag caught by a bullet on his way down the hill, his bloody public school uniform displayed in the nightly news.

This Rio I read about in the newspapers brushed up against me on occasion, in spite of my sheltered condomínio life. Once, it left an indelible impression. It happened in 1989, while I was walking on Ipanema beach on a Sunday afternoon. I felt a jab in my side. Turning, I looked right into the jaundiced eyes of a drugged-up kid, no more than nine or ten years old, his nose crusty with snot. Gaggles of these children roamed the streets back then, sleeping in doorways and under overpasses. This was before crack hit Rio. They'd huff shoemakers' glue for a cheap high. Sometimes you'd catch the chemical smell on their breath.

This kid held a jagged piece of a beer bottle against my side, mugging me for whatever I had in my pockets. He stood close, mumbling his words.

"Tia. Trocado, pra comer." Change, for food, he said, half begging in spite of the sharp glass pricking the soft flesh beneath my ribs.

I was only fourteen, but he was calling me *tia*, aunt. This is a very Brazilian expression, part affection and part respect, that kids use when talking to the grown-up women in their lives—their teachers at school, their friends' parents. I was a child being threatened by a child. It was heartbreaking and revolting.

A few months later, in August 1989, we left Brazil again for my father's next assignment: Houston. I went back to a sporadic relationship with Rio. The image of that kid stayed with me as a reminder of what the city had become—something broken, abandoned, its decay more tragic because of its promise, like fruit that's picked too green and rots before it ripens.

More than two decades later, I was back. The country's prospects had changed, and the city was shaking off the torpor of decades. But the clock was ticking. Rio had less than four years to go until it hosted the World Cup, and six years until the Olympics. The challenges were clear from the moment I landed in Rio's old airport, with its perennially broken elevator, and drove past the polluted bay and the favelas alongside the highway. A massive overhaul of long-neglected infrastructure was in order; stadiums needed to be refurbished, new Olympic venues built from scratch.

The biggest challenge, though, was security. Rio's Olympic bid had promised "a safe and agreeable environment for the Games," but this would not be easy. Gangs like the Red Command, which I remembered from my time in Rio a generation ago, had taken over favelas the size of small towns, marking their territory with graffiti tags scrawled on walls. From these safe havens they targeted the neighborhoods below. The police were poorly trained and ill-equipped at best, corrupt and lethal otherwise. Disputes between them, or turf wars between gangs, meant shoot-outs with a high body count.

Rio would have to confront all this under the scrutiny of national and foreign media, which had the city in its crosshairs. In this era of social media and Internet activism, Brazil's international standing would be measured in quantifiable terms such as gross domestic product, but also in the buzzwords that were becoming the yardstick of a country's status in the twenty-first century: human rights, equality, justice, environmental sustainability, and quality of life.

As I unpacked that Sunday night, getting ready for my first week of work, I wondered what lay ahead for me, for Rio, and for Brazil.

CHAPTER 2

THE RISE OF THE RED COMMAND

The city didn't leave me time to settle.

The first sign of unrest was easy to overlook. It came on Tuesday, November 9, my second day on the job, just a short news brief tucked into the crime pages of *O Globo*, Rio's main newspaper. It told of a violent carjacking in Jacarepaguá, a neighborhood in the far west of town. Four men armed with shotguns and pistols used their Peugeot to force a man in a Volkswagen to pull over. It was 7 a.m., and the driver, a pharmacist, was so scared he skidded up the sidewalk and smashed his car against a tree. He stepped out, as ordered. The men drenched the car with alcohol and set it on fire. Then they returned to the road and stopped the next motorist, a furnace operator driving a Chevrolet. They took the driver's cell phone from his pocket, doused his car, and set it on fire. The victims were baffled: "They didn't want to steal anything. They didn't even want my credit cards," the furnace operator said.

Within the next couple of days, the hit-and-run attacks began to show a pattern. On Wednesday morning at seven o'clock, five armed men stopped two drivers in northern Rio, took their cell phones, and torched the cars. That night, two men on a motorcycle threw Molotov cocktails into cars parked near the subway stop where I got off in the morning, on my way to the AP office.

This attack was close, but it was more worrisome for what it represented within the context of Rio. The neighborhood of Flamengo, a staid residential area on the south side of the city, was usually off-limits to warring gangs. A hit in these quiet street signaled this was not business as usual.

After the Flamengo attack, the gangsters began to strike all over town, first cars, then buses. The burning hulks were meant to snarl traffic and spread panic as the perpetrators melted back into the chaos. No one had died—yet. But the flames left the city on edge.

The experts I interviewed—former law enforcement officers, academics—said these attacks were likely a reaction the government's initial efforts to make Rio safer. Under a new security program, heavily armed police invaded gang-controlled favelas, but only after warning the population. This allowed gangsters to flee, but it also reduced bloodshed, in a radical break with the old approach—fast, guns-blazing raids that often left bodies in their wake. The biggest difference came once the officers were inside. Under this new program, they stayed, and set up permanent bases with round-the-clock patrols. These special policing groups were called Unidades de Polícia Pacificadora, or Pacification Police Units—UPPs for short.

The UPP program didn't end drug traffic, but it reasserted the state's presence in favelas where the gangsters had lived and run their businesses virtually unchecked. Nothing on this scale had ever been attempted.

When I landed in Rio in November 2010, there were twelve of these units in place and a thirteenth planned for the end of the month. They were a drop in the sea of more than one thousand favelas, but pinpointing them on a map made it clear that law enforcement had a strategy. The targets were in key areas, around the principal sports arena and the upscale parts of town. Most of the UPPs were in the city's south side, bracketing Copacabana, rubbing shoulders with Ipanema.

Now the gangs were pushing back.

I churned out the standard thousand-word articles for the AP about the attacks: the usual who-what-when-where-why, weaving in the requisite quotes by frightened residents, filing the story.

But as I sat alone in my office at night, staring at the scenes flashing on the small television—flames leaping from busted bus windows, the rictus of fear on the face of commuters—I was struck by how little I understood the forces tearing at Rio.

I knew the Red Command was first among these criminal networks in scope and power. I remembered its initial forays; the gangsters' bravado had left a strong impression on me as a teenager. About Rio's police I knew only enough to be wary of their methods. Now there were signs these forces were gearing up for a confrontation unlike any the city had seen.

Over the next three weeks, the conflict would leave dozens of people dead and more than a hundred buses and cars burning. In that short time I'd learn the peculiar Brazilian formula that determined which lives and which deaths counted and which would not be part of the tally, even when one of the bodies in question had just been heaped onto a gurney, warm and bleeding before my eyes.

Even as I covered the conflict, I realized that to really understand the balance of power in the city and to grasp what was at stake, I needed to fill in the gaps left by my years away. This meant reconstructing the history of the Red Command and of its influence on Rio, from the gang's origins to the moment when I returned and found buses on fire in public streets.

This mattered not only because of the November 2010 attacks, but because the gang's evolution was entwined with Rio's own. Its rise over the past forty years was intrinsically connected to the escalation of the drug trade and the armed violence that shaped this place, its culture, and its landscape.

This new UPP security program was a threat to the Red Command's core. The fallout would determine important aspects of life in Rio for years to come, years in which the city would host World Cup events and the Olympics. To understand what was at stake and gauge the consequences, I had to understand the Red Command.

This is the gang's story. In many ways, it is also the story of Rio.

The criminal organization that would one day strike terror in Rio was born in one of the most beautiful corners of the state: Ilha Grande, a pristine island of forested mountains skirted by beaches and fishing villages, about one hundred miles off Rio de Janeiro's southern coast. Even today Ilha Grande has few roads and cars. Abraão, the island's main settlement, barely registers as a town. It is a cluster of homes and pensions scattered along the dozen or so streets that spread at cockeyed angles from the dock.

It was on the island's ocean-facing side, where the waves are roughest, that one of Rio's most notorious prisons once stood. The institution that would later be known as Cândido Mendes Penal Institute was first established as a penal colony in 1903. Because it was so remote, it became a dumping ground for dangerous criminals and political prisoners.

Brazilian writer Graciliano Ramos, sent there in 1936 on charges of "communist subversion," described its filth and the violence in his memoirs. "Simple mention of the God-forsaken place froze conversations and darkened faces," he wrote.

Conditions were so loathsome inmates nicknamed it "the Devil's Cauldron."

By the time I moved to Rio, the prison had been shut down and its inmates scattered.[1] But one man could answer my questions about the gang's origin: William da Silva Lima. He was there at the beginning.

He did time in Ilha Grande starting in 1968 for robbing a bank, and was back again in 1974. Old mug shots and prison records show he was a slight man with a thick black beard, a receding hairline, and a long rap sheet. Beyond the bank robberies, he had convictions for kidnapping, extortion, and handling stolen goods. His calm demeanor and intellectual bent earned him the trust of other inmates; he wrote many of their petitions and letters and acted as their go-between with authorities. In return they gave him the nickname he still carries: Professor.

The Professor was seventy-one when we met. By way of introduction he showed me his scars, now spidery marks on his crepe-paper skin. The uneven knuckles on his left hand came from a time he was tied to his cell bars and beaten with a stick. The dent on the back of his head had the shape of a metal rod; it was the revenge of a guard after one of his many escape attempts.

"But I survived," he said, sitting down at a well-worn dinner table in his modest Copacabana apartment. "Many more didn't."

His body was broken from his forty-odd years in prison, his speech was slurred, but his mind held the stories I'd come for. These he spun with little prompting—tales of his first crime, an embezzlement carried off to perfection when he was fourteen, of famous cellmates, of his four prison escapes.

He also spoke of the prison—an overcrowded, disease-ridden

---

1 The prison compound was torn down in 1994. No one bothered to salvage its records, which were only dug up in 2002. I found them years later in the state archives, unsorted but rich in details. In 2009, a modest museum was raised where the prison had stood. It displays minutes of prisoner meetings, prison memos, and other documents from the Red Command's first few years, such as letters from gang members in prison to their "brothers" outside that signed off with "A family united will never be vanquished."

hell ruled over by authorities who made no pretense of reforming those who landed there. The food was never enough; there were no mattresses, no blankets, no uniforms, no cleaning supplies unless inmates bought these themselves. Men slept on the floor and fought off the rats that crawled from the open pits that served as toilets. Insects feasted on the naked flesh, leaving prisoners with swollen limbs and suppurating wounds. Guards, lacking enough guns and munitions and given free rein by distant prison authorities, improvised methods of keeping control. These included beatings, electric shocks, inventive forms of torture.

Guards terrorized the inmates, but so did other prisoners. Groups of inmates robbed and raped newcomers; prisoners killed each other over differences they brought from the outside, internal rivalries, or for pay. The inmates, the Professor said, were their own worst enemies.

It was within these perpetually humid cells, described by another former inmate as "walls that weep," that Brazil's military dictatorship stashed political prisoners found guilty of trying to overthrow the regime. Many were convicted under a catch-all Lei de Segurança Nacional, or National Security Law, passed in 1968, so prison records referred to them as the LSN prisoners, or simply, the politicals.

This group of convicts included student leaders, priests, academics, and union organizers; up to ninety-two of them were held at a time in the penitentiary's Gallery B between 1969 and 1975, alongside more than 850 common criminals. When a bank robber like the Professor was thrown into the same gallery, he found himself in daily contact with the firebrands who'd been advocating the overthrow of government.

The ideologues were impressive to the thieves and kidnappers with whom they shared quarters. They maintained within prison the same discipline they followed outside: a routine of regular study, collective decision-making, and obeisance to rules of conduct. Their presence began to change the prison: they curtailed robbery and rape, and led hunger strikes that gained the inmates better health care and better treatment for their visitors, who were routinely roughed up and shaken down by guards. They put the treats brought by their middle-class families into a collective pool and shared them.

These LSN prisoners brought more than lofty talk. Many were there for executing precisely planned bank robberies and high-profile kidnappings to finance their struggle against the military regime. They discussed the heists with the other prisoners as well. These conversations would later prove far more dangerous than the sticks the men sharpened into daggers on the rough concrete floor.[2]

From this stew of ideals, advice, and rebellion, the seeds of the Red Command began to germinate in Cândido Mendes's cells. At first, they were no more than a prison gang focused on improving conditions on the inside. Some of the earliest documents connected to this gang that would later terrify the city were poignant letters sent to "brothers" on the outside asking for donations to the prison Christmas Party and signed with their motto, *Paz, Justiça e Liberdade*: Peace, Justice, and Liberty.

As the dictatorship eased up, the political prisoners were transferred to prisons with better conditions; by August 28, 1979, the generals decreed an amnesty for those charged with political crimes. Just a month later, the incipient Red Command staged a coup within prison walls that left six rival leaders dead and secured its control of the penitentiary. In his 1979 year-end report, the head

---

2 The political prisoners also shared their books. Some of them offered inmates a new perspective on their lives; some taught the specifics of guerilla warfare. Among the publications apprehended within the prison were Portuguese translations of Wilfred G. Burchett's *Vietnam: Inside Story of the Guerilla War*, Ernesto Che Guevara's *Guerrilla Warfare*, and the *Minimanual of the Urban Guerilla*, by the Brazilian communist Carlos Marighella.

of the prison informed state penal authorities that "after the murders of September 1979 . . . the LSN phalanx or Red Command began to rule the prison of Ilha Grande and control organized crime in all of Rio's penitentiary system." His succinct account named the gang for the first time in an official document; it also recognized that they were no longer confined to the island prison.

The veneer of idealism that had inspired the gang's motto began to fade soon after the political prisoners were released. The men retained only the certainty that they were stronger together, and that they lived within a system whose rewards they couldn't hope to attain. Instead of fighting to change that system, however, the gang would organize itself in the years to come to wrench from it what it wanted: money, power, and visibility.

By the end of the 1970s, the Professor said, "what they called 'Red Command' could not be destroyed easily: it was a way of behaving, of surviving adversity."

The gang had risen within the penal system, but few outside the inner circles of law enforcement had ever heard its name. That changed on Friday, April 3, 1981, when the Red Command burst with a spasm of blood and bullets into Brazilian living rooms through the nightly news.

The police had been investigating a series of spectacular bank robberies—well-planned, precisely timed heists in which a group worked together to disrupt traffic, hit a string of banks, and melt away . . . the sort of thing the leftist guerrillas had pulled off in years past.

That April evening, a tipster pointed novice detectives to a north-side housing complex, saying the bank robbers had been hiding out there. The plainclothes investigation went dramatically awry. During the all-night shoot-out that followed—all of it covered on national news—a handful of men held hundreds of officers at bay. From their perch inside a third-floor apartment, the gangsters deployed a frightening arsenal and displayed an audacity that no one would forget.

Throughout the night, their leader shouted taunts at the cops below: "Come and get me, you bastards! This is the Red Command." He was José Jorge Saldanha, known as Zé Bigode, or Mustache Joe; at thirty-eight years old, he had twelve bank robberies to his name and had done time in Ilha Grande before escaping in 1980. An undated mug shot showed a man between black and white who looked at the camera through lowered eyelids, head tilted slightly back, with a dark mustache that hung over the top half of his mouth but left the lower, fleshy lip unguarded.

The standoff lasted eleven hours; by the time a 12-gauge bullet left a gurgling hole in Zé Bigode's chest, three officers were dead and half a dozen injured. Awe for the gang's skill and fearlessness breathed through the lines of the newspaper articles that ran the following day. To one downed officer's plea—"Get me out of here, please"—came Zé Bigode's mockery: "I've got a bullet for each one of you!"

The head of state security gave an interview that revealed the gangsters' arsenal was far beyond what the police could access. "We're in inferior conditions," he said. "Our weapons are only those allowed by law."

A photographer for *O Globo* captured the essence of that episode in one last photo of Zé Bigode. In the foreground was the body of the gangster, thin and shirtless, flung face up and arms akimbo on a dirt path of the housing complex lawn. The dark bulk of armed, uniformed police officers loomed over him. The episode became known as *quatrocentos contra um*, or four hundred against one.

This paroxysm of violence and daring became seared in the city's collective memory. It marked the public debut of the Comando Vermelho, or CV, an entity that would haunt Rio for years to come.

• • •

Over the next decade, the Red Command expanded its reach. One of Rio's particularities helped the group's spread: the favelas that climbed steep hillsides and blanketed stretches of suburbia. These communities, which often started as informal squatter settlements, were physically wedged within the metropolis and tied to it by the daily ebb and flow of residents who worked and studied beyond their borders, but they lacked access to even the most basic services. Residents rigged up their own electrical hookups and running water. Garbage collectors and mail delivery never climbed the *morro*, the hill; neither did the police, unless it was to look for suspects of crimes on the *asfalto*, the asphalt, slang for the formal city with its paved streets. Cariocas grew used to thinking of their city in these confining terms: the *morro* and the *asfalto*. Rio was the *cidade partida*, the divided city.[3]

Within these favelas, the Red Command found room to grow unchecked. One corner of northern Rio in particular brought together conditions that made it ideal as headquarters: the Complexo do Alemão, a cluster of fifteen communities that joined in a sprawling patchwork and spread over the hills.

This region had once been an industrial center. The first modest housing developments went up around the inauguration of the Curtume Carioca, the Carioca Tannery, a pretty Art Deco building with soaring windows and imperial palms along its sidewalks. It opened in 1920 and anchored industry in the area. From atop one of the granite peaks nearby, a quaint little colonial church, Our Lady of Penha, watched over the thriving working-class neighborhood below.

In the early 1950s, a Polish immigrant with a last name no one

---

3 The term *"cidade partida"* was further disseminated when it became the title of a 1994 book of reportage by journalist Zuenir Ventura.

could pronounce—Leonard Kaczmarkiewicz—and who owned some of this land carved up the property for sale. New arrivals called him the Alemão, the German, because of his European appearance and his tongue-twister of a last name. The settlement became known as Morro do Alemão, the German's Hill.

Fueled by federal policy, Brazil industrialized and urbanized at dizzying speed over the 1960 and 1970s. Buses arriving from the vast interior spilled entire families into Rio's streets. Without affordable housing available, they made their own. Favelas grew apace, including those around the Morro do Alemão. Over time, the nearby settlements merged, and the resulting conglomeration of favelas became known as the Complexo do Alemão.

This densely populated maze was nearly impenetrable to outsiders. Gangsters on the run could fall back into the conjoined favelas and disappear. Lookouts—the *fogueteiros*, boys on the lowest rung of the traffic hierarchy—would set off fireworks to warn their bosses should the cops or an aspiring rival broach the perimeter. In the investigation that followed the shoot-out with Zé Bigode in 1981, police found a large stash of guns and ammunition hidden in the Morro do Adeus (Good-bye Hill) one of the peaks that make up the complex.

Alemão had another advantage: location. This network of favelas ran right up to the city's main thoroughfare, Avenida Brasil, and sat less than ten miles from the port and the international airport. Later, when two new highways plowed over the landscape to ease the perennially jammed traffic—the Linha Vermelha and the Linha Amarela—the city's three main arteries formed a confluence within easy reach.

Inside these favelas, the Red Command was untouchable. From this safe base, the gang could stage robberies in the asfalto and run a side business in marijuana, which they sold in drug retail outlets within the favelas known as *bocas de fumo*.

Then cocaine came to town. The new drug hit Rio in the early

1980s; it upped the game and the stakes. Marijuana was cheap; cocaine was a highly profitable enterprise with international ramifications. Running it was a complex business that required transportation and distribution channels, packaging sites and sales points, plus a specialized army of lookouts, carriers, soldiers, and moneymen. It would change the Red Command and it would change Rio.

With more money to spend, and more money to be made, gangsters began to import weapons more powerful than any the police had seen, and to move aggressively into new territory.

Control of favelas was more important than ever. Local drug bosses often self-consciously stepped into the role that should have been played by government, securing the loyalty of residents and strengthening their grasp on the community. A Red Command man known as Pianinho described this to the *Jornal do Brasil* newspaper on December 10, 1984:

> *We, former bank robbers who have now entered the drug trade, educate the* favelados *and show them that the government isn't worth a damn, and won't do anything for them. Then we give them food, medication, clothes, school supplies, uniforms for the kids, even cash. We pay for doctors, for funerals, and we don't let the* favelados *leave for any reason. We even resolve fights between husbands and wives within the favela, to avoid messy situations that would require the police to come in.*

By the mid-1980s, little over a decade after the Red Command's origin in the Devil's Cauldron, nothing happened within a gang-controlled community without the gangsters' authorization, whether it was the construction of a soccer field with federal funds or of a child-care center by a nonprofit organization.

It didn't take long for the rest of Rio to realize something unprecedented was happening in the hills. There were vicious clashes in south-side favelas like Vidigal, Chapéu Mangueira, and Pavão-

Pavãozinho, which rose right by upscale neighborhoods like Copacabana, Leblon, and Ipanema. By the early 1990s, the taunt Zé Bigode had flung out of that third-floor window—"This is the Red Command!"—echoed around Rio; their tag—CV, for Comando Vermelho—was spread throughout hundreds of favelas.

Their headquarters were in Alemão, which made the favela complex a focal point of violence. By 2010, life expectancy within the complex was sixty-five—nine years lower than Rio's average.[4]

Back at the Professor's apartment, our conversation was winding down. It was nearing dinnertime and his family began to trickle in: his daughter, his grandkids, and his wife, an attorney he met in Ilha Grande when he was already an inmate and she was a young law school intern with perfectly arched eyebrows and a lot of idealism.

It was time to go, but I had one last question. What did he think of the Red Command now? As he described the values the gang espoused in its early days, I'd wondered whether there was any shred of connection left between this man and his once-upon-a-time group of jailbirds who organized Christmas parties and lived by the motto of Peace, Justice, and Liberty and the gang that held Rio in its grip decades later.

He shook his head. He no longer recognized the Red Command. It had morphed into a monster.

---

4 This was due in large part to fact that young men in the area died at a rate of 85 per 100,000. In Barra da Tijuca, the well-to-do western neighborhood of gated condominiums where my parents lived, the death rate for young men was 4 per 100,000.

CHAPTER 3

WHACKING THE WEEDS

As the Red Command grew, its identifying call—*É nóis!*—had become the statement of an uncontested power. This sharp jab of broken grammar conveyed a simple message: it's us. That was enough. Everyone knew who were the *donos do morro*, the kings of the hill.

That included Rio's police.

Mário Sérgio Duarte couldn't abide the short, taunting phrase; he spat out the words as he said them, upper lip curled back at their arrogance. He was a cop's cop, with a bristling salt-and-pepper crew cut and a square jaw, in the force since 1983. The gang had cast a dark shadow over his entire career.

When we first met, he was wearing in a black bulletproof vest and leading a battalion armed with semi-automatics. He'd barked orders then, and no one thought twice about obeying. But for this conversation, he'd invited me to his apartment in Grajaú, a middle-class suburb in northern Rio where he lived with his second wife and their twin toddlers.

The living room was cozy and unpretentious: a warm yellow blanket covered the overstuffed couch, and the sharp endpoints on the television stand had been padded with newspaper and tape.

The twins, Marco Aurélio and Maria Luíza, charged around in their onesies in the last minutes of play before bed. His wife, Viviane, blonde and reserved, also a police officer, brought us sweet coffee in tiny cups.

When I asked about his relationship to the Red Command, he'd leaned forward, his face hard, hands shaped into guns angled down at some imagined enemy, and repeated their boastful catchphrase: *É nóis!*

His disdain for the gang ran deep. The CV was behind more officer funerals than Mário Sérgio could count. He also blamed them for the degradation of the police force. As the drug revenue soared, relations between traffickers and the *banda podre*—the rotten half of the police department—became more promiscuous. There was the regular *arrego*, the payoff that dirty cops got for staying away from illicit business, but there were also officers who dealt in extortion and who sold guns and information to traffickers.

The CV had brought Mário Sérgio and the police force so many small, daily humiliations, so many public fiascos that over time, the frustration and the defeats had clearly distilled into something personal. He had defended the law in Rio for more than thirty years, and yet wherever he looked there were entire communities beyond his reach, visual cues of his powerlessness.

I repeated the question—what was his relationship with the Red Command? He took a deep breath, as if returning to the present moment, to the journalist sitting on his couch.

When he hit the streets fresh out of the police academy, the Red Command was one criminal enterprise among many. His first beat was in Niterói, across the bay from Rio, and he did the job with a .38 revolver on his right hip and a pair of handcuffs on the left, like real police, he said, working robberies, bank break-ins, armored car heists.

"We didn't worry about the *morro* then," he said.

Policing got in his blood; he was good at it, disciplined, and with a rigid sense of right and wrong that can be hard to find in a city known for its flexible approach to the law. By 1990 he was part of Rio's elite special operations squadron, now known as BOPE. The men in black get the best training and the biggest guns in the system; they are the front lines when police quell prison riots or push into favelas controlled by drug traffic. It is a fierce and fiercely loyal brotherhood. They make no excuses for their trucu-lence; their symbol is a human skull pierced by a dagger, superim-posed on crossed guns. Many of the men tattoo it on their skin: once a *caveira*, a skull, always a *caveira*.

By the late 1980s, however, the CV sported weaponry that no one, not even the *caveiras*, had ever laid hands on. Mário Sérgio re-membered the 1988 shooting frenzy that marked the public debut of semi-automatics in Rio. Traffickers let fly rounds from the roof-tops of the Rocinha favela; meanwhile, BOPE officers were limited to handguns and had one semi-automatic weapon per battalion for collective use.

That imbalance lasted until 1994, when Rio elected a new tough-on-crime governor, Marcello Alencar. With two changes in policy, he transformed Rio's police into one of the most lethal forces on the planet. First, he gave officers semi-automatics. Then he instituted raises for police who demonstrated bravery on the job—bravery as measured in the number of bodies left on the ground. This became known as the Wild West bonus: shoot, then collect. It was when Rio police really started aiming to kill. Ac-cording to Mário Sérgio, they had a lot of catching up to do.

"We had to whack the weeds that had grown too tall," he said.

The passage of that law doubled the number of suspects re-ported killed in gunfights with police, from an average of 16 per month before to 32 per month afterward. The law was revoked at the end of 1998. Researchers who investigated the deaths found most of the bodies bore signs of executions, not confrontations: there were no witnesses in 83 percent of cases, 61 percent had a bullet to the head, and 65 percent been hit in the back.

But taking the Wild West bonus off the books did not change the culture it had reinforced within police departments.[1] Killings by cops on the job continued to rise. These reports were seldom investigated; they became an institutionalized way for police to settle scores.

"We stopped being peacekeeping police and turned into troops at war," Mário Sérgio said.

I knew right-wing politicians and reporters often spoke of the conflict between the state and drug traffickers as a war. But hearing it from a career police officer made me uneasy. This was about more than semantics; it represented a dangerous shift in perspective.

Rio was not at war, I pointed out; and even if it were, wars have rules. I felt absurd, perched on the edge of his comfy yellow couch, balancing a thimbleful of sugary coffee on a saucer and bringing up conventions about wartime conduct. He rolled his eyes, made a flicking motion with his hand in front of his face, brushing my point away as if it were a gnat. Regulations, rules of conduct—these were formalities, refinements for those who could afford them. They had not applied to policing in Rio for a very long time.

I remembered precisely when I first saw that word, "war," applied to Rio: it was June 2002, and I was a graduate student at the University of California, Berkeley. I'd been doing research for my summer job at the Center for Labor Research and Education. Out of habit, I checked the Brazilian newspapers. The double-decker headline froze my fingers on the keyboard. Police had found the

---

1 Even after the measure was scrapped, the money continued to be paid out. A lawyer who represented a group of officers in their effort to keep their paychecks padded estimated 5,000 police participated in the program and saw salary increases of up to 150 percent.

body of Tim Lopes, a reporter who'd been missing for a week. Two gang members had been arrested. The story they told extrapolated the bounds of cruelty, even by CV standards.

Tim was a well-known figure, an investigative reporter with a white goatee, graying temples and a social conscience who'd been writing about Rio for more than thirty years. He'd disappeared while looking into the raucous *bailes* funk, massive favela parties fueled by Red Bull and whiskey, cheap cocaine, and the heavy bass beat of Carioca funk. There were allegations that gang members were pushing underage girls into selling sex in *bailes* in Vila Cruzeiro; he'd wanted to check it out.

According to the papers, Tim was kidnapped, tortured, and then executed, his body quartered and burned inside a stack of tires doused with gasoline—a gruesome device called a "microwave." The tale laid bare not only the extent of the gang's reach, but also the inability of authorities to intervene. Tim was kidnapped, tortured, and killed within Rio, and no one, not the police nor anyone in the city, state, or federal government, could do anything about it.

News of the reporter's death had run under an all-caps heading: A GUERRA DO RIO, Rio's War. After Tim's death, *O Globo* stopped referring to the Red Command by name; the organization became simply "the faction." And the way to deal with it, according to then-mayor César Maia, was "more police, bullets. And if criminals die, so be it: 100, 500, 1,000, however many are necessary."

As the gang and its offshoots grew stronger and bolder, state authorities, unable to curtail them, raised the body count. And yet for each trafficker shot down there were scores ready to replace him, as Mário Sérgio himself had said: "You kill one, there was another in his place, and what's worse, his nephew now hated you, his friend now hated you. . . . There was no end."

Leaving Mário Sérgio's house at the end of our meeting, I pressed the button for the elevator and, as I waited, I heard the click-slide-slide-click of a key being turned and then turned again in his front door. I'd have to cross two other gates before stepping out into the streets. I noticed these safety procedures not because they were unusual but because they were so familiar, as much a part of life in the city as the profile of Cristo.

Cariocas had lived for decades within a restrictive straitjacket of don'ts. I'd forget these commandments during my absences and then get chided upon my return: Don't talk on your cell phone in public, don't wear that watch, don't wear that ring, don't go out alone at this hour, don't open the window, don't stop at the light, don't forget to lock the doors. You're taking the bus, are you crazy? On a Copacabana sidewalk, a matronly madame with a helmet of frosted hair warned: don't pull out your wallet like that, *minha filha*, carry only the money you'll need. I was even scolded by a cabdriver once for climbing into his car without checking his face and his registration. Don't flag a taxi in the street, he told me, call for one.

Much may have changed in Rio, I thought, but the old precautions were still there—the nod to the security guard, the dark film plastered on the car windows, the thunk-thunk-thunk of the triple dead bolt on the door. They had practical value, but they were also rituals meant to soothe, much like doing the sign of the cross when passing a church or touching the little medal of Our Lady of Aparecida, Brazil's patron saint, which hung on rearview mirrors and necklaces. Even police officers needed their reassurance.

In spite of all the locks, gates, doormen, and intercoms, the many faiths and the countless superstitions that thrived in Rio under the tolerant gaze of its Cristo, there were moments when the population's vulnerability to violence was put hideously on display. It was during a visit in Christmas of 2006 that this fear became palpable to me, and I learned what it meant to live in a city under siege. The events of that year also laid the foundations for the conflict that would tear up Rio's streets years later.

By then, I was working with the Associated Press in California. After my usual San Francisco–Miami–Rio hopscotch, I headed to the city's bus terminal for the last leg of my personal pilgrimage: the eleven-hour bus trip to Uberaba, in Minas Gerais, where my grandparents still lived and the family gathered.

During peak holiday season Rio's squat, heavy-browed bus terminal funneled more than eighty thousand travelers into tens of thousands of buses destined to rumble over the back roads of this continent-sized country. Entire families of migrants who'd sought work in Rio camped out on the hard, bolted-down seats, surrounded by bags filled to bursting. This was their once-a-year trip home.

I got to Uberaba just in time for the big family dinner. In my grandmother's cramped house everyone squeezed thigh to thigh on the saggy leatherette couches, the fan overhead doing its best against the pressure-cooker heat of summer and too many relatives flushed with sweet wine. There was talk of the troubles in Rio—another dispute between police and gangsters. Armed men had shot up several police departments; a street vendor and her six-year-old had died from being at the wrong place at the wrong time. I was busy soaking up the syrupy comforts of my grand-mother's house—the candied fruit, homemade *doce-de-leite*, coffee that was three parts sugar, and I deliberately pushed Rio's ugliness out of my mind.

On the morning of the twenty-eighth I flipped on the tele-vision and the worst of it came pouring in: a bus taking holiday travelers between the states of Espírito Santo and São Paulo was stopped as it cut through the city of Rio on its main artery, Ave-nida Brasil. A band of a dozen armed men drenched it in gasoline and set it on fire—without letting the passengers out. What I saw that Thursday morning was the aftermath: seven charred bodies removed from the blackened metal frame, relatives crying, their holiday cut short by unforeseen terror of the most gruesome sort. Cops had gone looking for the suspects in Alemão and other favelas nearby.

There was no note or pronouncement from traffickers or from authorities, nothing that helped the terrified population understand. The governor had another three days on the job and was going to make a quiet exit. She had no comments. The new governor, Sérgio Cabral, would take office only on January 1, 2007.

All told, gang offensives and police raids during those last few days of December 2006 left nineteen dead, and the impression that no matter who happened to be sitting in Guanabara Palace, the seat of state government, Rio was defenseless in the hands of its criminal networks and inept police. These travelers had died right after Christmas, on Rio's main thoroughfare. Before the holiday was over, many thousands would make that same trip, including my family and me. There was no protection, no bars on the window, no dogs at the gate, no amount of touching the little medal of the Virgin of Aparecida that calmed the anguish we all felt.

This pall hung over the inauguration of the new governor a few days later. Governor Cabral had a doughy face, from which hung cheeks and a double chin that seemed to belong on a larger frame. These features dwarfed his small mouth and turned his eyes, when he smiled, into dark pinpricks in the mobile flesh. He'd run his campaign on the promise of putting more cops on the streets, investing in intelligence, returning Rio to its citizens. At the inauguration, Cabral spoke of law and order, promising revenge for these latest acts of terror: "These criminals, these cowards will get a response."

One of his first acts was to appoint a new "top cop"—the head of state security. This was one of the most influential positions in the state, and the governor's decision was unusual. Within the Brazilian government, choice positions are often used to reward political operators for their service; they come with juicy salaries, off-the-books perks, and the right to fill lower echelons with supporters. This turned many public service departments into Christmas trees of nepotism, each branch hung heavy with friends, connections, and cronies. But the man Cabral picked to lead the state security department was no politician; few outside elite law enforcement circles had heard of José Mariano Beltrame before he was tapped for the job.

Beltrame stood out in other ways. Rio is a place where tempers and voices rise quickly, where gestures are broad and faces expressive. He was as unreadable as the sheriff in an old western, with a trim runner's build, slate-blue eyes behind wire-framed glasses, and a habit of listening more than he talked. Furthermore, he owed no favors to the entrenched network of local cops; he'd come from the federal police, a better-paid and less corrupt force than that of the state. There he'd helped standardize investigations, introduced computer-based data analysis, and spent years pursuing organized crime on a national level.

In 2003, he'd relocated to Rio to establish a federal police intelligence center. During the next three years, Beltrame furthered his reputation for sobriety and dedication to the job by sleeping alongside his team within the gray Federal Police barracks, and never missing Sunday mass. These years also gave him a chance to study the city, to learn of the historic rifts between the neglected working-class suburbs in the north; the south, with its touristy beaches and trendy restaurants; and the fast-growing west side, with its gated communities and malls. He learned how drug traffic operated within the hills and saw up close law enforcement's own deficiencies, from decrepit equipment—patrol cars with bald tires, their hoods held down with wire—to their corruption and the involvement of certain factions of the force with organized crime.

Now this man with an avowed aversion to journalists, who'd built a career under the radar, scrupulously avoiding the public eye, had been given the state's most high-profile security job just as Rio was about to face unprecedented scrutiny. He took office in January 2007; within seven months the state would host its biggest international spectacle to date, the Pan-American Games. The opening ceremony was July 13. Construction of venues was running perilously late and ten times over budget. The police also had a lot of work to do. The federal government had sent funds to set up command centers and buy new patrol cars and communication equipment. This would be Brazil's test run on the world stage. It was up to Rio to get it right, and Rio was in Beltrame's hands.

One of his first decisions was to transfer imprisoned gang members to the far south of the country. Beltrame knew the attacks over the holidays had been ordered by CV leaders from within Rio's prisons. He was determined to break that chain of communication. Catanduvas Federal Penitentiary, in the southern state of Paraná, had been built on the mold of U.S. maximum security pens. It was just six months old, with 200 cameras and 208 individual cells. Red Command bosses would spend their next four months there in solitary confinement.

Then he turned to the sprawling complex of Alemão. In spite of the gang leaders' transfer—or maybe in revenge for it—gunmen had taken down two officers, tearing them up with thirty bullets in early May. Police went looking for the shooters and the conflict festered, devolving into daily gun battles that would leave more than two dozen dead. When there were arrests, officers would exhibit the handcuffed *traficantes* like trophies, their heads hanging low in front of the seized weapons and the drugs: piles of marijuana pressed into bricks, neatly tagged baggies of cocaine, rows of pistols and machine guns.

Still, the gang's firepower seemed endless. Then intelligence brought news: the Red Command had received a shipment of fifteen thousand cartridges and a load of new semi-automatic weapons. It was stored in an armory in Grota, deep within the complex.

With just weeks to go until the Pan-American Games, Beltrame had a potential disaster in his hands. Alemão was close to the highway leading to the international airport. The athletes, tourists, and journalists who would descend on Rio would all travel along that route.

"What was this ammunition for?" Beltrame asked when he told me this story, years later. We were in his hardwood-paneled office; an old-fashioned windup clock that he'd brought from his hometown in the rural south of Brazil chimed as if in response.

Beltrame had read the attacks as a demonstration of the gang's clout. In his estimation, the only way to fight it was with bigger firepower of his own.

"The equipment was in there," he said. "Either we took the risk and went in to get it, or we hid under the table to see what would happen."

Beltrame made his choice. On June 27, 2007, just sixteen days before the Pan-American Games' opening ceremony, 1,350 heavily armed police gathered at 5 a.m. at the base of the complex. Four hours later they stormed in with armored vehicles, helicopters, machine guns, and hand grenades, sights focused on Grota. They exploded into Alemão with a show of force the city had never seen.

Street-to-street fighting raged for the next seven hours. Beltrame was drawing a line: "We needed to take control."

As the day ended and the shooting wound down, the favela disgorged its wounded. The list of the injured was long and undiscriminating: Wesley Glauco da Silva, seventeen; Arlete dos Santos, forty-eight; Ivo da Silva, seventeen; Edvan Mariano de Souza, thirty-two; Carlos Henrique Matias Vitoriano, thirteen; Larissa Andrade da Silva, twelve; Karen Cristina Baptista Borges, twenty. The Getúlio Vargas State Hospital had become a national reference for treating bullet wounds because of its proximity to Alemão, though even its doctors had not seen a day like this one. By 4:30 p.m., armored cars started to ferry down the dead, among them boys as young as thirteen.

All told, nineteen people died in Alemão and nearby favelas that day. Autopsy reports would later show many of the bodies bore signs of execution: five had been shot at close range; eleven had been shot in the back, and two while lying flat on the ground.

Human rights organizations denounced the massacre in the hills. Philip Alston, the United Nations Special Rapporteur on Extrajudicial Executions, put it simply: "Murder is not an acceptable or effective crime-control technique."

Much of the population and the Brazilian media supported the action, in spite of the bloodshed. They were weary of gun battles and stray bullets, and shrugged off these deaths as the unfortunate collateral damage of Rio's War.

Rio's police also counted the offensive as a success. The load of seized weapons was impressive: fifty units of paste explosives with detonating devices, and a stash of rifles, submachine guns, pistols, mortars, a rocket launcher with its ammo, and two .30-caliber antiaircraft machine guns. More important to Beltrame was the point that his officers made: no community was beyond the grasp of Rio's police. They had pushed deep into Alemão, reaching areas they hadn't set eyes on in more than five years.

Right before the Pan-American Games, eight thousand soldiers from the National Force and the Federal Police flooded Rio to help out with any lingering security concerns. Altogether this made for a tense, but uneventful, July. The head of National Public Security, Luiz Fernando Corrêa, told a reporter afterward that in his estimation, the Games had been pulled off splendidly.

"The feeling of safety was great," he said.

Two months later, on September 13, 2007, Rio submitted its

official bid for the 2016 Olympics. In the following month, Brazil was awarded the World Cup. The final would be played in Rio.

The Pan-American Games went smoothly, but statistics for that year provide an X-ray of a police force out of control. In twelve months, uniformed officers on the job killed 1,330 people in the state of Rio; that's 3.6 people per day, every single day, according to their own records. Most of those deaths, 902, happened within the city of Rio.

The events of 2007 raised essential questions for Rio. When authorities spoke of making the city safe—safe for the 2014 World Cup, for the 2016 Olympics—whose safety were they talking about? How would it be enforced, and at what cost?

Once the Pan-American Games were over, Rio's security chief could look ahead. Beltrame would have to do better than the bloodbath of 2007 if he intended to bring a broad, sustainable sense of safety to Rio. The state would have to shed the image of a drug-ridden gangland perpetually torn between murderous police and well-armed traffickers. For that, he said, he had to end this war—not win it, as his predecessors had vouched, but end it.

It's hard to pinpoint just when the idea of reclaiming territory from gangs was first raised, Beltrame said. The idea was discussed among his staff during their long, informal lunches. It also drew on the knowledge he gathered while living in the federal police barracks, chatting with other cops and analyzing the gangsters' methods. It even owed something to the 2007 invasion of Alemão, which had been violent and short-lived, but had shown that it was possible to break into the Red Command's turf, he said.

Ticking off his points on his fingers, he laid out his reasoning: Take their guns, take their drugs, and they buy more. Arrest one gang member and there are others to take his place. But if you take their territory, the gangsters become vulnerable. It was within the favelas that they ran their business, stashed their weapons, and lived beyond the reach of law enforcement. Break their hold on these communities and they'd wither.

Beltrame started small, "eating porridge from the edge of the bowl," as he described it, ever the country boy in spite of his years in Rio. The first favela successfully brought under the program was Santa Marta, a community atop a vertiginously steep hill that shares views of Cristo with the high-rises that surround it in the middle-class neighborhood of Botafogo.

Santa Marta was a prudent choice. It was Red Command territory, but internal divisions had left it without a local gang boss. It was also small, with just over ten thousand residents, and had only two entrances: one at the top and one at the bottom of the hill.[2] It only took about one hundred officers to take it over during a heavy downpour on November 19, 2008. Only after the police were in the favela did Beltrame call the governor and explain that this time, he intended for them to stay. That phone call, he said, was the first time he used the word "pacification." The bases established within the favelas would be called Pacification Police Units—UPPs for short.

The UPP program piloted there was carefully orchestrated. Every step highlighted its difference over past approaches: the incursion was pulled off without the killing sprees of the past. Once the community was secure, a woman was appointed as commander—Captain Pricilla Azevedo. The 125 officers pulled into the round-the clock patrols were young, picked fresh from training before the soft rot of corruption set in. As the program spread, even the unit captains in charge of each operation were in

---

2 Santa Marta was also symbolic. In 1996, Michael Jackson came to Rio and wanted to use it as backdrop for the video of "They Don't Care About Us." Local authorities protested and refused access, but it backfired. Spike Lee, the video's director, called Brazil a "banana republic" for their bungled attempt to sugarcoat Rio. He and Michael Jackson shot the scenes anyway, their passage guaranteed by the local kingpin.

their mid-thirties at most. Beltrame reasoned that older officers came steeped in the old ways; many still had paychecks fattened by the Wild West bonuses of the 1990s. If this new plan was going to work, the police force had to change, to leave behind the ideology of war that held favelas as enemy territory, and favela residents as necessarily suspect. That was as essential, and as difficult, as changing favela residents' view of law enforcement.

The police would have to win the trust of the population, get involved, and ultimately, displace the gangster as the *dono do morro*, he said. In Santa Marta, a UPP post was built at the top of the hill, on the site of a day-care center that was never used by the community's children because the Red Command had liked its strategic location and seized it. By building their base there, the cops physically occupied the former headquarters of the *traficantes*.

The solution, Beltrame said, had always been there. Others had just been too afraid to face it.

"We did what everyone knew we had to do: go to those places where the state couldn't enter, and then stay. Cariocas knew this: taxi drivers knew this, sociologists knew this, politicians knew. We just did it."

To the public, he made it clear the new approach wasn't intended to be another battle in Rio's war. It was never intended to root out trafficking. The goal was less ambitious and therefore achievable: to rid each community of the heavily armed dealers who had long held sway, of open-air drug markets and the easy violence they spawned. Drug dealing still happened, as it happened anywhere else, but the permanent police presence broke the gang's exclusive control of the area.

Tangible results came fast. Within a year of the UPP's inauguration in Santa Marta, robberies and car thefts in the area were cut nearly in half, and there were no murders in the community. The boundaries of the favela, which had been impenetrable to anyone without gang authorization, were now porous. Cops could come in anytime. Anyone could: cable TV salespeople, garbage collectors, and technicians from the utility company.

The success at Santa Marta was trotted out whenever gringos needed proof that a new Rio was in the making. When Lula went to Copenhagen to defend Rio's Olympic bid, Captain Pricilla Azevedo went along, representing the transformative potential of this new program. Beltrame promised to inaugurate forty UPPs by 2014, reclaiming territory for the state, and most significantly, doing it "without a shot, without spilling a drop of blood."

This was when Beltrame pulled Mário Sérgio Duarte to his side. From beat cop Mário Sérgio had become elite police; by the time Beltrame was named head of state security, he'd been made leader of the elite battalion, BOPE. Since then, Mário Sérgio had moved over once more and was at the helm of a very different police institution—the Instituto de Segurança Pública, the Institute of Public Security, in charge of crime statistics. That was the position he held when Beltrame tapped him to be the 01, the head of Rio's Military Police.[3]

Beltrame wanted someone who could lead a police force that was under pressure, changing internally and externally at once. Mário Sérgio had a reputation for being clean. He also had the respect of many within the force, from the paper-pushers of the Institute of Public Security to the lethal skull-and-dagger battalion, BOPE.

Beltrame was an outsider, but when I landed in Rio in November 2010, his plan was winning over cynical Cariocas. The UPPs loosened the hold of criminal networks on favelas and brought crime down in the surrounding neighborhoods. In this city where even hospitals had bulletproof windows, some were starting to

---

3 The state police force is divided in two groups: the Military Police, which is responsible for maintaining order and first response to crimes, and the Civil Police, generally charged with investigations and forensics.

believe it might be possible to live without the fear of stray bullets and shoot-ups, without the daily dose of blood in the news. For the first time in decades, there was sense that real change, perhaps lasting change, was under way.

So, as I watched the CV spread terror in the streets in those first weeks of November 2010, I looked to Beltrame. The year of the Pan-American Games, 2007, was still fresh in my mind and in the memories of Cariocas. The last time the gang had staged assaults on the city, the response had been unprecedented bloodshed.

Rio had changed during its four years in Beltrame's hands, but there was also far more at stake. Winning the Olympic bid had cost nearly $50 million and a great outlay of political capital from local officials all the way to the country's president.

The international sporting competitions were meant to showcase Rio and an up-and-coming Brazil. Burning buses, a terrorized population, teenage gangsters who rested the butt of their semi-automatics against jutting hip bones and glared from the backs of motorcycles—this wouldn't do. Neither would a return to the old shoot-first approach to policing favelas. Under either of these scenarios, Rio lost. Was there another way out? Everyone speculated, but no one knew.

CHAPTER 4

FEAR AND HEAT

As tension mounted in the city in November 2010, I celebrated my birthday with my family. It was the first time in decades we'd been together on that day. In a retro-hipster restaurant of the sort that was popping up to cater to Cariocas' recent affluence, we arranged ourselves on vintage Formica chairs, picked out the wine, and ordered a half dozen tiny dishes with French names.

Like everyone in Rio, my family was following the play-by-play on the news as closely as they followed the prime-time soap operas. We discussed my younger sister's pregnancy—she'd just had the last ultrasound before birth—but the attacks in the streets dominated our evening. Something as simple as driving to a restaurant for dinner was a risk. My mother fretted; everyone's nerves were frayed. We ordered more wine.

Walking from the restaurant to the subway station after dinner, I saw television sets blaring the news from nearly every corner bar. Shirtless men at the rickety plastic tables leaned back from their beers to offer a stream of commentary. I stopped to listen. It didn't take much prompting for Cariocas who were sick of living with violence to advocate violence as a solution.

Kill them all, one of them said. *Bandido bom é bandido morto*—a good criminal is a dead criminal.

With each day that passed, fear and heat rose in tandem. The attacks escalated.

Gangsters on motorcycles zigzagged through traffic, ambushing cars, setting them on fire, and spreading panic in working-class suburbs, upscale residential neighborhoods, near the state government headquarters. In one confrontation, an air force sergeant scrambled out of his vehicle just in time to escape a grenade on the Linha Vermelha, the highway to the airport.

Out of a lifelong habit, I hung on to the news, looking to commentators and talk shows for the information and insights that could help me make sense of the chaos. I also got to work. This violence had meaning, and if I couldn't decipher it, there were people who could. I talked to anyone who would speak to me: taxi drivers, university researchers, cops who wouldn't give their names, local crime reporters who chain-smoked on the patio of the police headquarters, waiting for press conferences that were always hours late. That was where I first heard that the Red Command was still pulling strings from within the maximum-security pen. In spite of the expensive safety precautions, the gang's chain of command was unbroken.

What exactly the gangsters were planning, and how law enforcement would react, no one knew—not until those last days in November, when this simmering conflict exploded and forced those vying for control of Rio's favelas into actions no cop, gangster, reporter, or academic could have foreseen.

TUESDAY, NOVEMBER 23

Rio's top law enforcement brass filed into Beltrame's wood-paneled office at 5 p.m. sharp. Intelligence reports had confirmed what many of them suspected: the Red Command was behind the attacks. The UPP program and the transfer of gang leaders to the south were getting in the way of the gang's business. Prison officials had apprehended letters from the bosses behind bars to their soldiers in Alemão and Vila Cruzeiro, a favela physically connected to the complex. Their orders were to *zoar tudo*, to ravage the city.

The consensus that evening was that the state security apparatus had to come down hard, and soon. Mário Sérgio walked out with plans to stage aggressive overnight raids in nearly thirty CV-controlled favelas.

After the meeting, Beltrame called a press conference. It was time to break his long string of "no comments" and speak plainly. He spoke to us, journalists, and through us, seeking to reassure the Cariocas who were cowering at home, and the Brazilians who were following the conflict, aware of how much was riding on Rio. It was an uncharacteristically forceful speech; the sober head of security almost raised his voice to make his point clear: no matter the threat, the state would not back down.

"Anyone who crosses the path of the UPPs will be plowed under," Beltrame said, eyes focused steadily on the cameras.

Later that night, the gangs also made a statement of sorts. It came as a scrawled note left on a burning bus in Vicente de Carvalho, a north-side neighborhood: "If the UPPs continue, there will be no World Cup and no Olympics."

The author was unknown; there was no signature and no one was caught in the attack. But it didn't matter whether or not it was authentic. The threat it spelled out was implicit in the daily tally of burning vehicles. It confirmed what Beltrame had said: these strikes were meant to disrupt the state, to call into question the new security policy, and to destroy the vision of a secure new Rio.

WEDNESDAY, NOVEMBER 24

Reports of deaths and injuries from the overnight favela incursions trickled in as Beltrame slowly sipped his morning *chimarrão*, the piping hot, bitter tea he drank from a gourd, according to southern Brazil tradition. He'd given the previous day's intelligence report much thought. When his cell phone rang just before 8 a.m. with a call from the governor, the head of security was ready: "We are going into Vila Cruzeiro."

As Beltrame told it later, he knew this could be ugly. Rio state police had occupied favelas and installed a dozen UPPs, but never like this, in the middle of a live confrontation with gangsters. And Vila Cruzeiro wasn't just any favela. It was a redoubt of the Red Command, the main bunker beyond Alemão. Law enforcement hadn't been inside for more than a quick hit since 2007. The *movimento*, the movement, as the drug traffic was sometimes called, had spent the last few years fortifying its defenses. They'd be ready with turrets to shelter snipers, spiked metal barricades to protect access roads, and vats of oil and gasoline to pour down the steep pathways, plus years of stockpiled ammunition.

"We had no time to prepare, but we had no choice," he said. "We either put an officer on each corner of the city, or we went in and occupied Vila Cruzeiro."

The invasion would have to happen immediately. At noon, Beltrame headed to the Guanabara Palace, a cream-colored wedding cake of a building that is the seat of state government. He was meeting his chief of police, Mário Sérgio, and Governor Cabral for lunch. After the meal, they adjoined to a meeting room with supporting staff to plan their next steps. They had to consider strategy, such as how to broach a territory defended by men who knew each alley and who could count on the help of a population too scared or complicit to refuse. Now that Rio was under extra scrutiny by the national and international media, they also had to deal with prickly ethical questions of the sort Rio's police didn't often stop to ponder: How would such a high-risk operation appear to the population, to journalists? What was the acceptable cost in lives?

The only option not on the table was defeat at the gangsters' hands.

"If we failed, it would be seen as a failure of our entire security program," Beltrame said.

There was one more serious impediment to taking Vila Cruzeiro. Even with all of Rio's officers mobilized and with the Federal Highway Police lending support, law enforcement simply didn't have the manpower or the equipment to invade and hold the favela. Even the *caveirões*, the BOPE's black armored vehicles with skulls emblazoned on their sides, had weaknesses. Their tires could be shredded by bullets and would skid on the oil-slicked roads. The officials discussed this as they got up and walked out. The men were already standing by the door when the governor turned to Mário Sérgio with a question:

"What about the armed forces? The navy, for example. Would their tanks work?"

Tanks would cinch the deal, Mário Sérgio said; they had caterpillar tracks, revolving turrets, and steel bellies big enough for more than a dozen officers. The navy's weaponry included the M-113, which was being used by the U.S. Army in Iraq. Cabral called the justice minister right away. The go-ahead came that afternoon: the navy would back the operation with equipment and logistics.

Local news outlets were covering the conflict round-the-clock. This latest bulletin ignited discussions all over town.

A taxi driver named Bira drove me around often in those weeks when I was reporting on Alemão. He is a hulking man, with hands that cover half the steering wheel, and he took a hard-line stance against the traffickers.

"The government has to come down on these guys, break their back," he said, pounding a meaty fist on the wheel for emphasis.

No one could anticipate the cost of taking Vila Cruzeiro or the likelihood that it would work. Every housewife in line at the market and every suited-up businessman in the subway had an opinion. Mostly, they agreed with Bira, the cabdriver: authorities were raising the stakes, but they couldn't afford to lose this round.

Before going to sleep that night, I checked for an update. Over the past twenty-four hours, twenty-eight buses, vans, and cars had gone up in flames. Five passengers were injured in fires; one driver was killed for refusing to stop at an ambush. The stench of burning rubber wafted through the streets, a constant, acrid reminder of the pervading threat. In their raids, police had seized rifles, shotguns, submachine guns, grenades, homemade explosives, and a lot of gasoline.

They'd also killed fifteen suspects.

THURSDAY, NOVEMBER 25

The day dawned long and hot. I woke with the sunrise and dressed in a hurry, eyes on the news: a fleet of flatbed trucks had rolled down Avenida Brasil overnight with the military-grade armament promised by the justice minister. A crowd clapped and cheered as three M-113s maneuvered. The state had never prepared to take on the gang in this way.

Watching the tanks brought back my family's last few days in Iraq, when we hid under the stairs while shock waves from bomb blasts punched in the windows. I'd left with the faces of the neighbor's children in my mind. They'd climbed onto their front gate to see us go.

"They can't leave," my mother had said. "This is their country."

Rio was not Basra by any stretch, but the sight of men with assault weapons and tanks rolling down residential streets brought back the same nauseous, dry-mouthed anguish I'd felt as a kid. I went over to the balcony of the hotel room and slid open the glass

door to let in the ocean breeze. To the left, Cristo rose on Corcovado mountain's blue-green shoulders, his stark white face blank
and unreadable in the bright morning glare. Even the day's first
breath was heavy and humid. In spite of the warmth, a shiver ran
down my spine.

Behind me, the voice of the morning news anchor updated the
stats: There had been another fourteen attacks overnight. They'd
left six buses, a truck, motorcycles, and five passenger cars in
flames. There were now more than seventeen thousand police on
duty. Searches for suspects and weapons continued in favelas across
town.

Down in the lobby, I swallowed some coffee and scanned *O
Globo*. The paper had dedicated pages to its coverage, all of them
under the all-caps heading A GUERRA DO RIO, "Rio's War." This bel-
licose language permeated the reporting. There were maps that
indicated the sites of "battles." Articles referred to police as "com-
batants" and to the lanes of Vila Cruzeiro as "the front." Favela
residents were "civilians." Again, this incongruous talk of war.
When had a densely populated neighborhood become "the front"?

But there was no time for the paper, or breakfast. Bira was already waiting. Once out of Ipanema's drowsy streets, we headed
to Vila Cruzeiro along an eerily quiet highway. I don't remember
seeing a single bus that morning as we approached the favela,
although they usually choked Rio's thoroughfares on weekday
mornings. Later I'd confirm that about 115 bus lines had canceled
service.

On the way, we listened to the news. About ten public schools
and an untold number of preschools were closed. There were
around twelve thousand kids out of class. The population in favelas
was young—younger than in the city as a whole. On quiet days, the
lanes thronged with children. As far as I knew, no one had evacu-
ated the families. Then again, I'd never covered something like this

before. Maybe it was pro forma, a step not worth announcing, and I'd missed it.

I turned to the driver. "Did anyone tell parents to get their kids out? Have you heard anything about where families are supposed to go?" I asked.

He looked at me through the rearview mirror, the muscles in his forehead bunched above his heavy brow line. "What? No, no one said anything about kids."

Bira dropped me off in Penha, the working-class neighborhood that bordered Vila Cruzeiro and Alemão, as close as he could to the slope where modest two- or three-story buildings met the favela. Nearly five hundred officers and elite BOPE troops, plus some three hundred federal officers, were already milling about.

Flora, my colleague on AP's video side, was there in a bulletproof vest and boots, pulling equipment from the trunk of another taxi. Silvia, the veteran photo editor, and Felipe, a lanky twenty-five-year-old photographer who'd just started with the AP that year, had been there since before dawn. More than the print reporters, it was the photographers who tracked the action. By the end of the day, their bulletproof vests would be so soaked with sweat they'd lay them on the sun-baked car hoods to dry.

I looked around. Madness. I'd been in Rio for less than three weeks and was not equipped for what looked like urban combat. I had no vest and my thick-soled hiking boots were in my luggage, which would remain tangled in red tape at the port for six months. I wore the first thing I'd pulled out of my carry-on that morning—a bright green dress and purple sandals that made me look like an absurd parakeet among the camo of tanks, the black of BOPE.

My chest felt tight, shortening each breath. It wasn't fear; it was the sense of being so clearly out of place. This gang, this favela, this operation, these were things I'd read about or discussed in a handful of interviews. I'd rushed to Vila Cruzeiro because it was my job to be there, to watch whatever happened, gather information, write it up. It wasn't until I saw the police cars pull up bristling with artillery—the cops stuck the long black snouts of their weapons out the windows—that I realized how unprepared I was, how absurd in my highlighter colors and with my reporter's notebook. I would not head up the hill, that much was clear. Beyond that, I didn't even know where to position myself when the shooting started. I looked around: What here could stop a rifle bullet? A car? A brick wall?

I stayed busy filling my notepad with quotes. The conversations were clipped. There was an anguished mother cowering with two children under an awning, crying to whoever would listen, "What am I going to do? I can't go to work, I can't go home." There was a sixty-five-year-old retiree who gestured angrily at the tank outside his front door, saying, "This is no way to live!" A police officer no older than twenty-five was twitching for action. "We're going to flush them out," he said.

The warmth that was such a benediction in the beachfront south of the city turned vicious in these northern suburbs that stretched far from the open ocean and Cristo's embrace. The sun was an angry white eye glaring down from the sky. The heat weighed down my shoulders and rose in waves from the pavement, pressing against the skin. Sweat gathered in the small of my back and smudged the blue ink of my pen as I wrote.

Just past noon, the taut stillness finally broke with the clattering of tanks rolling uphill and the roar of police helicopters. Short staccato pops of machine gun fire greeted them. The sudden burst of movement and the explosions sent adrenaline flushing through my system; after a tense wait of nearly five hours, any action felt like a release. Conversations broke into a garbled stream of voices, noise. Interviews were useless now. I took refuge inside Getúlio Vargas Hospital and stared out the windows with other reporters, nurses, staff, watching and waiting.

• • •

Three blocks away from the hospital, inside a metal pod that served as her commercial kitchen, Dona Nilza moved her ample body closer to the television that sat above her refrigerator. Her eyesight forced her to squint an arm's length from the screen to follow as the police stormed Vila Cruzeiro.

It was from this tin-can space that she ran a van line—the extra-official transportation that served communities such as this one—and made lunch for the drivers.

A small plastic fan chopped at the air, swirling the steam around and stirring the tired pages of the Bible that always lay open behind the counter. On calmer mornings, neighborhood kids ran in for a kiss and some candy, calling out: Dona Niiiiilza! Dona Nilzaaaaa!

Not on that Thursday. The children were locked indoors, and Dona Nilza's thoughts turned to her own child.

To the police, the conglomeration of favelas was a fortress bristling with enemy soldiers; to people like Dona Nilza it was home. These alleys now swarming with men in flak jackets were playgrounds for their kids. She'd brought up ten children in Alemão, all of them crammed into a narrow, three-story house where rooms had sprouted organically, one on top of the other, as the family grew. She'd reared them all on the money from the van line and the teachings of the Assembly of God evangelical church, then set them loose in the world to find their way.

They'd all chosen the straight-and-narrow path—all except Diego, her second youngest. She'd lost him to "the life," as she put it, when he was a tall, spindly sixteen-year-old, timid for all his size. That was nine years ago. He'd be twenty-five now. He was up there, somewhere. This was why, when police and the army charged up the hill, she watched so closely.

"The bodies come down wrapped in sheets," she said. "You can usually see the feet sticking out. That was my biggest fear: recognizing my son by his feet."

That Thursday, she was also watching and waiting.

Once the shooting stopped, I walked out of the hospital. Across the street was one of the rickety wooden stalls that sold drinks and snacks—the convenience stores of communities like this one. I went over for some water. Nothing else was open. As I got closer, I noticed a man sitting on a short stool, taking deep drags on his cigarette. His hands shook and his outstretched leg was bandaged. His name was José Pereira, and he worked as an assistant at construction jobs. A stray bullet had lodged itself in his calf right around noon, when he tried to walk up to his shack in Chatuba, a favela bordering Vila Cruzeiro. After a cleanup at the hospital, he was released, the bullet still embedded in his leg.

It was nearly 3 p.m., and he was stuck there in a tank top and flip-flops, without money, without a phone to warn the wife who worked as a maid in the city and without a way to get back up the hill to the three kids who were home, waiting out the police invasion. Their school had been canceled for days.

I got him some water, offered my phone. He wanted Brazil's searing white sugarcane rum, *cachaça*. The leg was throbbing now. I had nothing else to give him. His broad face was set in a mask of pain. Talking cracked his resolve; tears found a path among the furrows that lined his face. He was a migrant from the Northeast, and spoke with the broad vowels and the hard *t*'s and *d*'s that set their speech apart from the Cariocas' soft, sibilant accent.

"They fight, but we're the ones who suffer," he said. He didn't know who'd fired the shot, and he didn't care who won. He wanted to be with his wife, his children, and to hold on to the job he had.

"What am I going to do now, like this?" he said, gesturing at the bandaged leg.

When I looked back up at the hospital, I saw six people shuffling in, holding on to the edges of a bedsheet. They leaned outward to balance the weight of the body in the middle; blood pooled at the bottom and dripped through the thin cotton, leaving a trail of lustrous red droplets. The bundle was heaved onto a gurney and gone before I could see if it was a man or a woman, young or old.

I hung around, waiting for the end, hoping to learn what was going on in the hills above. The temperature hovered in the triple digits. Time acquired a jagged quality: it jumped when the dead or wounded were carried down, and then it stalled. I heard bursts of gunfire, dry popping sounds that no longer startled me, and the deeper rumble of explosions. Plumes of thick, black smoke unfurled from different points within the hills. Otherwise—nothing. No information. The wait was dull and nerve-racking at once.

A police officer of some rank strode into the hospital at a fast clip. I didn't catch his title, but the cops stationed at the door made way for him as he passed. I caught him on his way out. I needed something concrete, numbers.

"How many people have been killed?" I asked.

None, he told me.

"None?" I asked. Again, that sense of bewilderment, of hearing but not understanding. "What about the bodies?"

"No one died," he said again. "Just criminals."

The officer turned his back on me and my half-formed questions. In the world I'd known, bodies such as the one I'd seen lugged down to the hospital would be named, their shooting investigated—maybe not fully or fairly, but investigated. Back in California, when transit police had shot an unarmed black man in the subway—Oscar Grant—there had been riots in Oakland. I'd helped cover them, had gone knocking on doors looking for the white officer who insisted he'd accidentally pulled out his gun instead of his Taser. In Rio, one man down in a favela—or a handful of them, or more, mostly black, sometimes white, always poor—didn't even count. Just criminals.

Rio's police killed hundreds every year. That much I knew. The law made no provisions for a death penalty, but somehow, having a rap sheet—being a bandido, a criminal, or just looking like someone's idea of a bandido—was enough to earn you a trial, conviction, and execution all in the fraction of a second it took to pull a trigger.

I knew it, had known it from years of following Rio in the news. But to watch it happen, to note the officer's shrug of the shoulder, to smell the dead and face the crackling anger of the living . . . all of it left me feeling queasy, off balance.

I turned my back and walked away from Vila Cruzeiro, toward the main road where the taxi drivers were waiting. I jumped into the cab and opened my laptop to write up the quotes I'd gathered and update the article published earlier. Deep into my work, I only realized the fighting was over when officers began to stream downhill and into the streets of Penha. A grinning BOPE officer gave me a thumbs-up. I stepped out of the car.

"Vila Cruzeiro is ours," he said as he ambled past the cars, loose-limbed and shaky from the win and the spent adrenaline. Others were still searching door-to-door in the favela above. The owner of a storefront bar rolled up the metal grate he'd pulled down during the shooting. Now that the fighting was over, he was open for business. The cops crowded in for a drink. I joined them.

It was sometime past 6 p.m., nearly twelve hours since police started gathering at the foot of the hill. The officers jostled and elbowed their way to the counter, their exhilaration palpable. On the television hanging overhead, I saw details of the operation that had unfolded, matching images to what I'd heard. News helicopters had caught the moment police troops had broken into Vila Cruzeiro. In attempts to stop their entrance, the Red Command had strewn concrete blocks across the lanes and set fire to a delivery truck that blocked one of the main access roads, but the police had pushed in.

Then came the aerial images that would loop on TV over the next few days and define the siege: the gangsters who had been stoking fear in Rio for days were running for their lives. There were nearly two hundred of them; some carried rifles or backpacks, others were shirtless, in nothing more than shorts and flip-flops. A couple of them were clearly injured.

They fled up a dirt road flanked by forest that cut across a hilltop between the smaller Vila Cruzeiro and Alemão. The men were falling back into the complex. As these images streamed on the TV overhead, a cheer rose from the policemen.

One of the men on the run, reduced to a tiny pixelated figure on the screen, took a bullet, stumbled, and fell. This drew laughter from the cops, and shouts of "Perdeu, playboy! Perdeu!" This was bandido slang, the jeering refrain Cariocas often heard when they were held up for a wallet or a phone: You lose, playboy! You lose!

The officers' reaction at the scenes left me confused at first. The gangsters were getting away. Didn't the police want to finish the job, bring them to justice? But I'd missed the point. The traficantes who'd been invincible within these hills were scurrying for safety like cockroaches while the whole nation watched. These cops saw themselves as the front lines in a war; they found real satisfaction in watching their enemy humiliated.

"I've been police for twenty years, and I feel like I'm finally doing my job," a heavyset BOPE officer with silver at his temples said.

I went back to work, wandering into the dusty streets of Penha for comments. Vila Cruzeiro was still off-limits, but this working-class neighborhood just beyond the favela's borders bore much of the burden when there was fighting between gangsters and police. Their schools shut down, their businesses lost customers, and their buses and van lines stopped running, leaving them without transportation.

Every television I saw was tuned to the news, and every news channel was playing the same footage. The scenes sparked conversation everywhere, and left residents in a state of nervous excitement that was equal parts hope, disbelief, and fear. I stopped at a twenty-four-hour funeral home and watched the gangsters' flight again while talking to the manager. He hadn't dared take out his car in ten days. His kids had stopped going to school, and his employees weren't showing up.

"We've been at their mercy for so long," he said. "Sometimes it's the police, sometimes it's the *traficantes*."

He paused, as if wondering how much to say.

"Now this," he said, gesturing at the endlessly looping track of men running down the dirt path. "They've really stepped on the anthill this time."

As I talked to other locals, I found that same caution tempering their glee. Tired as they were of the conflict, and eager as they might be to see it over, many could not believe that change would come so easily. They'd learned to *conviver*, to walk the fine line, coexisting with *traficantes* and a violent police force. They didn't trust either side. The only peace they'd known in decades was the uneasy stillness of a standoff. To them, the images looping on TV brought a moment of exhilaration—the bandidos were on the run!—but left a deeper apprehension. What now, now that the balance they'd known was irrevocably upset?

CHAPTER 5

IN THE HEART OF EVIL

Dona Nilza's son, Diego, was also watching the gangsters' flight on TV. He'd spent the day waiting inside a nondescript house on Rua Joaquim de Queiroz, one of the main access roads into Alemão.

At twenty-five he was a big man on the hill, second only to the boss, Pezão, and doing well off the revenue from the three *bocas*, drug retail outlets, he controlled. He was also agile on a motorcycle. His last straight job was as a moto-taxi driver, ferrying partiers to and from the *baile* funk high up on the hill. When his legs hugged the machine, he could maneuver it through the narrow passes as if it were part of his body. Seeing his comrades run and fall along that dirt road, some of them clearly wounded, he ached to race over and help.

But he stayed put. That was the plan. Any action they took would be coordinated. He paced and waited for a call from the boss, the room closing in, too small for the coiled energy of his six-foot frame. The call never came.

It would be a long, sleepless night—for Diego in his hideout, for his mother at home, for Cariocas who did not know what to expect from police the next day, or from the gangsters cornered within Alemão.

FRIDAY, NOVEMBER 26

It had rained overnight. Vila Cruzeiro awoke dank and crawling with journalists, police, cleanup crews. Tempers were frayed after a night of little rest.

Dozens of motorcycles had been abandoned by fleeing traffickers the day before; many were still strewn about the favela, clogging the way. The traffickers hadn't allowed trash collection within the alleys; the residents had to take their bags down to the bottom of the hills. With the shooting over the last few days, they hadn't been able to do even that. The wet lanes stank with days' worth of fermenting garbage.

Large stretches of the community had no electricity. The webs of wire that brought in pirated power had been severed in multiple places during the shooting, setting off small fires. The utility company had been afraid to send anyone for repairs. There was nothing, no cartoons, no video games to distract the cooped-up children. Schools were still closed, and kids had been locked inside the tiny homes for nearly forty-eighty hours.

The consensus was that with Vila Cruzeiro under control, law enforcement had to keep rolling over the gang's encampment. That made Alemão their next target, but the complex of favelas had a population of about seventy thousand—nearly ten times that of Vila Cruzeiro. It was also the heart of the Red Command. Taking it would require thousands of sharp, well-armed police.

The truth was, the state's cops were exhausted. Dozens of officers had spent the night in the community, sleeping in shifts. One of them joked he hadn't had a break in so long, he'd been wearing the same underwear for days. Police who hadn't participated in the assault on Vila Cruzeiro had been in a state of readiness since

Wednesday, stationed around town and sleeping in headquarters. There simply weren't enough of them in fighting shape to invade Alemão, even with the navy's tanks. I doubled back to the office, hoping for a quieter day in which to puzzle out Beltrame's next move.

The answer was in my inbox when I got there: the state police *would* invade Alemão. They'd do it with the help of Brazil's air force and the army. The navy had shared its tanks with law enforcement during the Vila Cruzeiro incursion, but this would be the first time all three armed forces lent men and weapons to a gangland operation. By evening, eight hundred troops would take up guard of the favela complex's forty-four entrances, with two additional battalions on standby.

With the World Cup and the Olympics on their way, what happened in Rio reflected on Brazil's international image. No one wanted to take any risks; support for the Alemão operation came from the top.

"Anything we can do for Rio, within the rule of law, we'll do," President Lula had said during a press conference.

I couldn't sleep that night, and stayed up late drinking the weak beer in the hotel mini-fridge, watching the news and obsessively checking the police website for updated stats: 35 people had been killed over the past five days. More than 30 had been wounded, including a Reuters photographer who took a bullet in the shoulder. The late news showed heavy shooting into the night. Tracer bullets drew graceful arcs above Alemão.

Mário Sérgio was up late as well. He thought back to the bodies and the damning human rights reports that followed the police's last invasion of Alemão in 2007, and fired off an email to the governor.

"Give me a chance to avoid a bloodbath," he wrote.

SATURDAY, NOVEMBER 27

Mário Sérgio got his answer first thing in the morning. The governor's reply hit his inbox at 7:34 a.m.: "Authorized."

It was worth a try. He called a press conference, and expounded his plan before a bouquet of microphones. It was a straight deal: any *traficantes* who wanted to surrender had to show up unarmed or with weapons held high, at the bottom of Rua Joaquim de Queiroz. The police chief couldn't give more details on the timing, but there was urgency in his voice.

"If anyone wants to turn himself in, do it now," he said.

He knew police would break into Alemão in less than twenty-four hours.

Dona Nilza was watching, still. Always. She had seen law enforcement take over one of the gang's most important bases of operations. Diego had survived that first assault. She didn't know where he was hiding, but as those scenes of gangsters on the run played over and over on TV, Dona Nilza knew the favelas were no longer a safe haven for men like him.

Walking past the favela complex, she eyed the police chokehold, the tanks grumbling at the bottom of the hill, the yard-long weapons soldiers held with both hands. She called on her God and weighed her options, praying and fasting, begging for a light. She had nine other children, plus grandchildren and great-grandchildren. They all depended on her. But she had one son who needed her the most.

That Saturday morning she was back at work in her kitchen, although there were few customers for her prepared lunches. Van drivers were also staying home during the conflict. Taped to the metal siding behind her stove, right next to where it said "Double portions!" was a poster printed with Psalm 29:11: "The Lord will give strength unto his people; the Lord will bless his people with peace."

She made up her mind. She shrugged off the lifetime of worry that rounded her shoulders and untied the heavy-duty plastic apron. She would find Diego.

"I couldn't stand by and watch my son come down wrapped in a sheet," she said later, returning to the image that haunted her. She called up three of her other sons, one of them an evangelical pastor, and told them it was time.

The favela's entrances were blocked, but she knew everyone living there and every alley. She found a way and walked into Alemão, huffing up the long flights of cement stairs, stopping here and there to catch a breath and ask about the man everyone else knew as Mr. M. It was a nickname Diego had always hated. It came from a corny magician who for years made regular appearances on *Fantástico*, a popular Sunday night variety show. The magician wore a black mask with white stripes. Diego was the darkest of her children; the name stuck. To her, though, he was only Diego.

He soon got word on his radio: his mom was looking for him. He was furious. What could the woman be doing in this place? Police could come up at any time. Diego had come to terms with the prospect of his own death. A neat round scar stood like a punctuation mark on his torso, amid the dark swoops and curls of his tattoos. There'd been other bullets, other times he'd been afraid. That was part of the deal. But he didn't want the burden of his mother's life on his back.

She'd done what she could to keep him out of the *movimento*, the game. After he dropped out of school in the fourth grade, he'd started hanging around the hill, running errands for the traffickers just so he could keep the change. The bonds tightened and complicated over time. There were friendships and bigger jobs: a bundle of money to stash, drugs to hide for some time.

"You don't even notice," he said. "You just slide into the life. Next thing you know you're carrying heat."

His mother had seen this coming and had countered in every way she could: she found him a spot in a state program where he got some stay-away-from-drugs lectures, plus basic training in computers and literacy. He was agile and coordinated, and she encouraged him to practice jujitsu at the community sports center. It wasn't school, but it was better than a lot of other options opening up to him.

In spite of her efforts, his prospects were dimming. At fifteen, he was a dropout who wrote with the grammar and spelling of a child. She gave him a job herself, something to keep him busy and in some cash. For fifty dollars a week he sat in a plastic chair, held a clipboard, and kept tabs on the van line that carried passengers around Penha, the No. 77. It was good money for a teenager, and Diego made a little extra driving moto-taxis late at night, when the more experienced drivers were worn-out. He liked to dress well and blew his money trying to stay on top of on the trends introduced by the *traficantes*.

The tipping point came on June 15, 2001, his sixteenth birthday. It was 5 a.m. and the *baile* was breaking up. Diego was at work, ferrying partiers down to the bus stops at the bottom of the hill, when police showed up. They often did at this hour, roughing up the strung-out teenagers, catching any drunks who'd found a quiet corner to piss in. This time something went wrong. Someone squeezed off some bullets, officers rounded up everyone for a search. Diego dropped the motorcycle, put his hands on the wall, legs spread wide.

Search over, an officer turned to him.

"Run," he said. "Get the fuck out of here."

"The motorcycle's not mine," Diego said.

"I told you to run," the officer replied, lifting his rifle.

Diego ran. But he turned back. The weapon was pointing at him. He felt a searing pain by his left knee; his entire leg recoiled, tucked up, useless now. Hopping on his right leg, using his hands to propel himself against the wall, he scuttled home.

His mother took him to Getúlio Vargas Hospital, where there was always police on duty to run the names of gunshot victims through the system. Diego was clean. A stray bullet, he told the doctor.

"It just fed my revolt. You grow up in the *comunidade*, you grow up hating the police," he told me later, his slight stutter making him repeat himself, giving an edge of frustration to his voice. "They rough you up in the street, smack you, call you a *vagabundo* if you're not carrying your documents . . . you grow up with lot of hate. That was too much, though."

He started within the CV as a motorcycle man, running errands from hill to hill. By 2008 he was Mr. M, one of Alemão's most wanted. The muscles he'd built in the martial arts classes and his low-key lifestyle made him perfectly suited to be the right-hand man of an aspiring *dono do morro*, Pezão.

A funk tune from the time marked the bloody putsch in which Pezão took down Tota, the former boss. Before the thump of the bass begins, a man's nagging voice rises in homage to Mr. M: "É só rajada de meiota, é só rajada de meiota . . . foi o Mister M que executou o Tota. . . ." "It's a hail of bullets, it's a hail of bullets . . . it was Mr. M who executed Tota."

A cell phone video leaked to police shows Pezão all done up in Armani presiding over the night-long open-bar party thrown in Largo do Coqueiro, an open square where there was a wholesale drug market, to celebrate Tota's death. In it, Diego danced, arms outstretched, baggy white T-shirt swaying around his lean frame. Other young men propped their semis on their hip or let them swing by their side so they could hold up their beer cans. A pretty young woman with jet-black hair and a white strapless top hugging her curves waved her hands before her face to show off the fat gold rings crowding her fingers.

The video ended up on television, part of a Sunday special on the gang. A frame froze around the face of Dona Nilza's son, capturing the flash of his smile and identifying him as the gangster Mr. M, rumored to have murdered the previous drug boss.

"Nobody knew me outside the complex until then. After that, I was done," Diego said. "Any ideas I had about leaving were over."

As Diego fell deeper into the *movimento* he withdrew from family life and traded day for night, taking care of business after dark while Pezão slept. He had his own semi, a Heckler & Koch G3 that he'd fire into the air during parties. But mostly he kept to himself, never leaving Alemão. When he wanted to blow some of the nearly five thousand dollars he made a week, he'd ask friends to hit the mall and pick up the entire new collection of a favorite stylist, mixing up the relaxed surfer look of Rio designers with the hoodies, basketball jerseys, and sneakers he saw in the hip-hop videos he loved. He was carving his own niche, setting the standard for the young kids, the runners and the *fogueteiros* who'd look up to him for style, for an example.

Seeing her son sink into this life nearly broke Dona Nilza. She couldn't stand to be in Alemão, where he lived a shadow life far from her eyes. She left the bustling three-story house where she'd raised her brood for a quieter one in Olaria, a blue-collar neighborhood nearby. A few times she heaved herself up the hill, asking the kids who ran the retail drug stands if she could talk to Diego. He'd never leave the life, he told her. Where would he go? What would he do? His face had been on TV, his name was dirty.

"I thought I'd only leave Alemão dead," he said.

Then that Saturday came. Dona Nilza walked past police barricades, asked around. This time, he let her find him, sitting by himself in his hideaway on Rua Joaquim de Queiroz.

By then it was clear his boss was gone and that his partners had run. He felt frightened and alone. She asked him to get down on his knees and pray with her. He did, and he cried. He thought of his two daughters, both growing up in the *complexo*, and about his mother.

"I'm ready," he told her. He rifled through his closet, picked out his favorite outfit: a sky-blue polo, slacks.

They still had to get out. Dona Nilza had no love for traffickers, but she also knew how cops would treat her son. She would not turn him in to just anyone in a uniform. They had to navigate the barricades and find the one officer she trusted: Seu Ferreira, who was now with the Sixth Police Battalion in Cidade Nova. He'd been the coordinator of the program Diego had taken part in when he was fifteen, before he was Mr. M.

Diego started walking down with one of his siblings; his mother went to get the car another son had brought.

The mayor had finally made provisions for the safety of residents. A shelter had been set up with food and mattresses to take in those who were afraid of staying home during the upcoming police invasion. Dozens of families streamed down the alleys, carrying supermarket bags of clothes, fans, pillows, television sets. The police tried to scrutinize the flood of people. Even the children were searched. But Diego slipped in with a large family laden with suitcases. As police went through their luggage, he walked away. It was as if God were clearing the way for him, he said.

He reached "A" Street at the bottom of the hill. He hadn't been out of Alemão in years, and his blood ran cold with the exposure. His mother was nowhere to be seen. Standing still, he'd be conspicuous. It was a matter of minutes, seconds perhaps, before someone recognized him. He kept walking, looking straight ahead. A bus stopped at the light, opened its door. He walked right in. He didn't care where he went. Anywhere. Away.

Minutes later, he used his cell phone to call his mother. She'd been stopped by police who recognized her as Mr. M's mother. The car was being searched. When she was released, she picked him up and they headed to the police department.

"My son is here to turn himself in," she said.

"Is that right," the cop on duty said, eyes darting between Diego's lanky form and the heavyset *senhora* next to him. "You're doing the right thing."

Within ten minutes photographers had their lenses trained on the handcuffed *traficante*. Gangsters who were arrested and dragged out before the cameras usually hung their heads, doubled down low to avoid having their faces stamped in newspapers.

In pictures from that day, Diego stood ramrod straight, shoulders thrown back and head cocked at an angle, in spite of the cuffs that brought his arms together up front. His gaze rested somewhere beyond the flash of cameras. He was down, but it was his choice. He had walked out.

Another trafficker was brought in by his father. The electrician Ivanildo Trindade walked his son Carlos to the police. "Better in jail, paying for what he did, than dead," he said.

There were just over a dozen who accepted the offer of a peaceful rendition. The deal was largely ignored. This, and the shooting overnight, heightened Beltrame's fear of a bloody resistance. The barricade held. We settled in for a wait—the reporters, the families up in Alemão, Cariocas, Brazilians. A slow drip of sleepless hours turned Saturday into Sunday.

SUNDAY, NOVEMBER 28

When the wait broke on Sunday morning and the tanks rolled up Alemão, I wasn't there to see it. I wasn't even in Penha, waiting inside the hospital for the dead to roll in.

I watched the action from within a hospital maternity ward. Early that day my sister had given birth to her first child. All the strain of the past few days, the tight knot of questions and anxieties that kept me up at night—questions about Rio, about the police action, but also about my place in this city—loosened when I saw Clara, with her crown of dark curls, through the window separating family from the newborns in their cribs.

This was also why I'd come back. I'd missed the birth of my first nephew, my brother's son. Now I held up the little boy so he could see his new cousin. He left smudgy handprints on the glass. My brother's wife was pregnant again—I'd be there for the birth of another niece in a few months.

My first three weeks in Rio had not been what I'd imagined; the first warm flush of recognition had given way to this landscape that oscillated, disconcertingly, between the comforting and familiar and the frightening unknown. But that Sunday morning at the hospital was a reminder: after decades of missed weddings, births, and funerals, I was where I needed to be, holding up my nephew, watching Clara sleep under the bright lights of the nursery.

Still, I couldn't stay long enough to see my sister, who was still recovering from the C-section. As soon as my brother-in-law came out of her room and gave us a thumbs-up, I ran back to Alemão.

It had taken 2,700 soldiers and police to seize the complex. They'd positioned themselves soon after dawn. The traffickers were also prepared; the first bullets flew just before 7 a.m. An hour later the police entered slowly, on foot. The airspace was closed to civilians, but military and law enforcement helicopters lent support to the men on the ground, flying low and returning fire. The armored tanks followed. Their caterpillar tracks rolled up Joaquim de Queiroz and into the favela, crushing the metal spikes cemented into the ground and the concrete boulders laid along the way by the gang.

After the weeks of planning and buildup, the takeover was smooth. There was no resistance other than the token shots after daybreak. This lack of resistance was unnerving; business as usual, even with the expected casualties, would have been more reassuring to the population. It was as if the gangsters had melted away.

Soon after 9 a.m., Mário Sérgio declared victory: "Vencemos." We won. He ordered the battalions to begin a thorough search of the more than thirty-one thousand homes within the Complexo do Alemão and the nearby favelas of the Penha complex.

When I arrived at 11 a.m., the iron gates that barred neighborhood businesses were still drawn tight, some studded by bullets. Spent casings littered the alleys. Trash was strewn everywhere.

Police pulled out tons of cocaine, crack, and marijuana, as well as the expected load of armaments: machine guns and submachine guns, dozens of grenades, homemade pipe bombs, rifles, handguns. More than 400 motorcycles were abandoned, along with 136 cars. There were 241 arrests and 275 people detained for questioning.

Once I walked up the hillside, now open to journalists and anyone else, what I heard was that those who could do so dropped their weapons and blended into the population. With a change of clothes and a Bible in his hand, a gangster without a rap sheet was indistinguishable from a hardworking *favelado* heading to Sunday service. Rumor had it that some even escaped inside one of the black armored vehicles emblazoned with the elite officers' skull and dagger. Evidence later surfaced that a few had managed an escape via Rio's massive storm pipes. Of the hundreds of Red Command gangsters authorities had expected to apprehend, only about twenty were arrested that day. Pezão was never found.

By 1 p.m., the Rio de Janeiro state flag and Brazil's yellow and green colors flew from the complex's highest point. This was the biggest accomplishment yet in Rio's effort to take back territory occupied by armed traffickers, and officials drove that point home in interview after interview. They spoke to the population in the familiar terms: this was a war, and they had captured the enemy's castle.

"Alemão was the heart of evil," Beltrame said at his press conference, summing up the tone of official comments.

Gradually, favela residents who'd remained ventured from their homes after days spent shuttered indoors. Many welcomed the police, offering them food or a drink of water. A woman took her seven-year-old grandson to see the tanks just outside Vila Cruzeiro. I asked her what she made of all this. Josiane remembered a time when there had been picnics and fireworks up at Our Lady of Penha. Over the past few years even the church's steps had been taken by traffickers, who used it as a lookout. She couldn't remember the last time she attended Mass there. The shoot-outs had made her grandson a startled child, afraid of firecrackers.

"Can you imagine raising a kid that jumps at every loud noise?" she asked. "I hope this will be the rebirth of this community. We have to hope."

I also heard a lot of skepticism. Three women gathered in a garbage-strewn plaza with a broken swing set. They smoked, kept their kids by their side, and laughed at the idea anything would ever be different.

"Look at these guys milling around. You think they're just watching the day go by?" one of them said, tilting her head toward the surly young men gathered at the edge of the park. "They're with the *movimento*, just waiting until they can go back to business."

Many in these favelas had grown up under the authority of drug bosses and had never been directly addressed by elected officials of any sort. When they needed something—money for a sick child, a job, justice for some slight—they went to the reigning chief. They had little reason to trust authorities and a lot of questions. The police had often come into their community shooting, ready to treat everyone as a suspect. Why would be any different now? Even if officers did change their ways, would they stay, or would it be all over after the Olympics?

Beltrame had promised that Alemão would get a UPP, but for

the time being there weren't enough trained officers. The military, untrained as they were for police work, would remain within the community indefinitely.

"We're trading one bunch of guns for another," another woman told me.

The state would have to earn the trust of women like these. It would not be easy. There were already reports of officers ransacking homes within the occupied favelas, shaking down residents for money, making off with cell phones, cameras, even a flat-screen TV. An ombudsman was appointed to comb through the accusations.

This was far from an unequivocal triumph. At least thirty-seven people died during that last week of November. We never learned their names. It wasn't clear exactly how many had been injured, but hospital officials told me the youngest person treated during the siege was two years old, and the oldest, eighty-one.

I was new to this Rio with its UPPs and its Olympic plans, but the declarations of victory seemed too early, too eager. They reminded me of George W. Bush's "Mission Accomplished" speech in 2003, when he made an action-figure landing on board an aircraft carrier and declared the United States had prevailed in Iraq. Most of the fighting and dying there happened after that moment of hubris.

Something was happening in Rio, that much was evident. There was a cracking and shifting of structures that had long been in place. But what city was being created here? And for whom?

CHAPTER 6

NOT FOR BEGINNERS

The apartment broker turned the key. The door didn't budge. He put his shoulder against the unit's front door, pushed gently. Nothing.

He put a little weight into it and the door gave way with a wood-against-wood squeak that echoed in the dim living room.

"It's the damp," he said.

His tone wasn't apologetic, just factual. I stepped in and felt the air brush against my face, moist and unwelcome like the breath of a stranger in a crowded bus.

Lights on, I could see the ad hadn't lied: newly finished floors in blond wood, spotless white walls. I also saw what it left out: the entire sixth-floor unit was face-to-face with one of the granite monoliths that surge against Rio's skyline. This was, indeed, an Ipanema apartment that would allow me to "walk to the beach!" as announced. It hadn't promised a view.

I approached the living room window. There were about six feet separating the apartment from the rock face; the gulf between them smelled of mulch and was lit by a diffuse, filtered light much like what you'd find at the bottom of a canyon. Looking up I realized I was indeed near the bottom of a deep crevasse formed by the twenty-story brick building and the mountain. Soft green moss and a delicate filigree of ferns covered the granite, fed by the humidity that condensed against the cool façade and trickled down in rivulets. Mold spores—abundant in much of Rio because of the tropical humidity and the nearby ocean—were already tickling my nose. In five minutes I'd be wheezing.

Further exploration revealed a bucket half full of dirty water with a submerged mop, testament to someone's good intentions toward the filthy kitchen floor, and missing faucets. They were gone from the kitchen and the bathroom, ripped out of the stone counters, leaving jagged holes.

I looked around for the broker—was this the right apartment? Two bedrooms, one bath, newly refurbished? Number 608? He had sagged in place by the door, all of his body language informing me he'd done enough when he left his air-conditioned office and met me, half an hour late, by the building's front gate with a key in hand.

"Yup," he said, thumb jabbing toward the "608" nailed to the open front door. He wasn't wasting words on the obvious. The missing faucets, the mold, the dirt? "I just open the doors, ma'am."

A month after my arrival there was a break in the news cycle, and I had begun to look for an apartment. This pushed me to confront another very volatile aspect of life in this city: the economy.

The apartment with the missing faucets was the twenty-fifth, or twenty-sixth, or twenty-seventh place I'd looked at; I lost track after the first couple dozen. It listed for the equivalent of $1,500 a month, plus $250 in condo fees and $125 in property taxes, which are the tenant's responsibility under landlord-friendly Brazilian law. With it, my search seemed to have hit a wall—a mossy, weeping wall of sheer granite.

The Brazil I remembered was affordable, at least to visitors who came bearing dollars. When Lula took office in 2003, one dollar went far, buying 3.5 Brazilian reais; when I arrived seven years later, one dollar bought 1.7 reais, and Rio no longer offered visitors a dose of exotic on the cheap. Bar tabs in those first few weeks rivaled any in San Francisco; a passion fruit caipirinha to take the edge off a long day could run upwards of fifteen dollars. Even a night drinking the local Antarctica beer in family-sized bottles and making do with some *bolinhos de bacalhau*, salted codfish croquettes, or *aipim com carne seca*, fried yucca and sun-dried beef—traditional bar food that dispenses with refrigeration—added up to an unhealthy sum.

Still, I started the apartment hunt with some confidence, secretly harboring images of ocean views, a porch with a hammock, flocks of parrots flying by. After all, I was moving from one of the most expensive cities in the one of the most expensive countries in the world. I knew how to handle hot markets; I was that person who showed up for an open house with a credit report, photocopies of my documents, and a nicely ironed shirt to beat out the competition. But I wasn't prepared for monthly rents that hovered between San Francisco and Manhattan for dank flats with no discernible natural light—or faucets.

Since then, I'd dropped the parrots and the ocean breeze from my wish list, and I'd jacked up my price range to a laughable two thousand dollars a month. The units that fell in that category included, in addition to the glorified cave with the mossy view, flats where the refrigerator purred like a big cat in the living room, and an apartment where the bathroom was so small the door only opened two feet before it hit the toilet. That shouldn't be a problem, that broker offered; I could just squeeze around it.

All of them included maid's quarters: claustrophobic little rooms with just enough space for a child-sized bed and microbathrooms so tiny that the showerhead was often above the toilet, so that the person showering had to straddle the seat below. Even one-bedroom apartments with kitchens barely large enough for a stove came with these brick-and-mortar testaments to the vast inequality that provided generations of middle-class Brazilians with a steady supply of nannies, cooks, and maids. Looking these over, I wondered if there was still room in this new Brazil for live-in help for anyone but the wealthiest. At the end of my first month in Rio, I was finding there was barely any affordable space for me.

Brazil was thriving. Back in 2008, when the U.S. subprime mortgage debacle had sent housing prices on a death spiral that would drag the economy down with it, Lula waved off worries, saying the crisis that had torn through the United States like a "tsunami" would be a little ripple, a "marolinha" when it reached Brazil.

His comment came the day after President George W. Bush signed a $700 billion financial bailout bill. Brazil would not have a similar package, Lula said, just specific measures: "Everything will happen in its right time."

Back then, many thought his remarks smacked of hubris, naïveté—or ignorance. Former president Fernando Henrique Cardoso, who as finance minister had captained the 1994 economic plan that changed the name of Brazil's currency to the real, had tamed hyperinflation, and later, as president, had stabilized the economy with austerity measures, gave his successor a condescending talking-to. "We have to say it: the emperor is naked," he said in a critical speech at the time. "Put your clothes on, President."

As it happens, Lula was mostly right. Reassured, the population went out and consumed. Banks in Brazil were in much better shape than in the United States, with tighter controls and far more conservative lending practices. Even as the U.S. economy tanked, Standard & Poor's became the first ratings agency to raise Brazil's foreign debt to investment-grade status; Fitch followed days later.

Brazil's economy hiccupped in 2009, but by the end of the year it had shaken off the downward drag of the crisis overseas. Foreign investment continued to grow as global money pulled away from what were traditionally safe perches—the United States and Europe—and landed in emerging markets like Brazil. By the end of the year, Rio had been chosen to host the Olympics; it seemed nothing could go wrong. The cover of *The Economist* in November 2009 nailed the optimism of the time: "Brazil takes off," announced the headline above an image of Cristo launching like a rocket into space.

As President Barack Obama took over from Bush, the American government would throw even more cash after that first bailout package in its attempt to stanch the bleeding. But by late 2010 the United States was still shaky at the knees, muddling through a jobless, joyless recovery, its suburbs littered with the abandoned homes of families who couldn't afford mortgages. Housing prices there had hit a trough and flatlined.

Brazil, on the other hand, was making good on that *Economist* cover. During Lula's tenure the stock market quadrupled, outperforming every other major bourse in the world. In 2010, when I made my move back to Rio, Lula was wrapping up his second mandate and the country had just elected his handpicked successor.

Dilma Rousseff, the daughter of a Bulgarian communist who immigrated and did well in real estate, had an entirely different background. In contrast to Lula's poverty she had an upper-middle-class upbringing, complete with French lessons and piano. Both presidents came of age under Brazil's military regime, which held the country in its grip for twenty-one years after deposing a democratic government in 1964. Although both resisted the generals' rule, their experiences forged entirely different political personas. Lula learned to be a leader by talking hundreds of thousands of autoworkers into strikes that paralyzed the heart of Brazil's industry, then by sitting down at the negotiating table to hammer out deals with the bosses. Dilma, as Brazilians would later refer to her, took up arms against the dictatorship.

She was sixteen when the military took power. Even as a teen-ager, she joined the opposition; by the time she was nineteen, she was part of an urban guerrilla group that advocated the regime's overthrow. In spite of her young age, former militants later re-membered her as a capable organizer and manager. In January 1970, at twenty-two years old, Dilma was detained. She would be tortured and held for nearly three years.

A photo taken in November of that year shows her sitting before a military court in Rio de Janeiro. She'd been subjected to twenty-two days of torture. She looks fragile, short-haired and thin, with a finely drawn mouth and delicate bone structure: arched brow, graceful jawline. But her eyes are narrowed to paper-cut thin slits. She looks up and away from the uniformed men in their ornately carved high-backed chairs. They are the ones who cover their face before the unknown photographer. A slump in her shoulders is her only concession to what she'd endured.

Lula at his best transfixed a crowd, pulled emotional strings; abroad, he sold the song and dance of Brazil. Dilma lacked his cha-risma and his *jogo de cintura*, his political ability to weave, dodge, and flatter. Even as a candidate she seemed wooden, unable to forge a personal connection with her audience. But she scored high in the polls. This was in part because she was Lula's protégé and would keep in place the social policies that had burnished his political halo, but also because she was seen as a wonk and a taskmaster, someone who could run Brazil more seriously, with less fanfare.

Many voters were ready to welcome a president with a less . . . flexible nature. Lula would step out of office riding high on the population's affection, but his administration had also engineered one of Brazil's most sordid political corruption scandals. The affair involved Lula's closest allies in an illegal campaign slush fund and a cash-for-congressional-votes scheme. Its nickname, *mensalão*, or the big monthly, came from the kickbacks of roughly twelve thousand dollars offered to smaller-party legislators in exchange for their cooperation.[1]

The scandal broke in 2005 and reached the highest echelons of the Workers' Party, tainting the head of Lula's cabinet, José Dirceu; the party's chairman, José Genoino; and its treasurer, Delúbio Soares. The media had a field day; the revelations featured scenes that seemed straight from a low-budget political thriller, including off-the-books payments in the Bahamas for the manager of Lula's campaign and the arrest of an aide caught boarding an airplane with $100,000 in his underpants and another $100,000 in Brazilian money stuffed in a suitcase.

That this far-reaching arrangement did not bring down the president was a tribute to Lula's charisma, but also a recognition that Brazil's Congress had been a dysfunctional cesspool of bribery and influence-peddling long before the *mensalão* came along.

Arguably, a more important factor in Lula's continued popularity was the economy.[2] Although his predecessor, Fernando Henrique Cardoso, had tamed inflation and brought stability to the country in the mid-1990s, substantial growth didn't come until about a decade later, fueled in part by China's increasing demand for Brazil's biggest commodity exports. This poured money into Brazilian coffers and helped create jobs and goodwill. It also created the conditions for Lula's real coup.

"It's cheap to take care of the poor," Lula often said. The words rang of genuine concern or populism, depending on the audience. They were also true. Once in office, he set about making good

---

1 Lula had won with 61 percent of the vote, but his party garnered less than one-sixth of Congress, where 21 parties vied for a share of power. Forming a coalition was essential to governance; the *mensalão* brought these parties into the fold.

2 This despite the fact that in 2006, his finance minister was brought down in another corruption scandal, revealing that he used a lakeside villa staffed with prostitutes in Brasília to entertain lobbyists and others in exchange for favors and information.

on campaign promises to eradicate misery. His first program, Fome Zero, or Zero Hunger, was a bungled mess. But in 2003 he launched Bolsa Família, or Family Purse, a cash transfer program that gave small amounts of money directly to the country's neediest. What he did essentially was unify a handful of existing programs, pump them with more funds, and give the money to the woman in the family. In exchange for the cash, recipients had to make sure the kids got their shots and went to school.

This was a roaring success on many fronts. The program didn't cost much: $10.5 billion, less than 0.5 percent of Brazil's GDP, and about 2.7 percent of all government spending (in 2013 numbers). The outlays averaged just under $70 per household. These modest amounts made a world of difference to the recipients. More than two-thirds of beneficiaries also worked; 90 percent said the money went toward food. It was one of the factors buoying the expansion of Brazil's middle class, which jumped from 66 million to 108 million within the decade.

The program sent a powerful message. In a country with a history of neglecting its needy, Bolsa Família was a stalwart ally of the working mother, of the father suddenly out of a job, and a monthly reminder that the state cared. Soon its bright yellow card was a fixture across Brazil. Bolsa Família started off with 3.6 million recipients; by 2009, the end of Lula's time in office, the number had quadrupled.

Because it went straight from the federal government to the recipient, the funds bypassed the trapdoors of corruption and misuse that inevitably funneled away resources sent through local governments. It also became indelibly associated with the president's image, and created a direct link between appreciative voters and Lula. Over time, Bolsa Família would become his biggest political asset, helping reelect him and then elect his successor.

In 2010, while Lula campaigned next to Dilma, Brazil appeared to be on an unstoppable winning streak. It was a great year. GDP grew 7.5 percent, the highest in a quarter century. The infamous gap between rich and poor diminished faster than in just about any other country as real wages rose for all. Most extraordinary, income went up the most for the poorest.

Brazilians wanted more of it. Dilma was elected the first female president of Brazil in October.

When she took over on January 1, 2011, the country was giddy with possibility. The cash-transfer programs had banished hunger from many quarters, and unemployment had dwindled to a record low. When the economy needed a little hand during the worst of the global recession, policy makers lowered select sales taxes and the historically high interest rates. The country went on a collective shopping spree, spending what it had and putting the rest on brand-new credit cards. After a lifetime of very limited access to credit on all fronts, from credit cards to car loans to mortgages, Brazilians were discovering something Americans knew only too well: the joy of consuming now and paying, well, later.

It worked. You couldn't pick up the paper without reading about another consumption record. There were record car sales, which would go on year after year straight through the toughest belt-tightening in the United States and Europe; record numbers of first-time flyers, with 11 million Brazilians boarding a plane for the first time in 2010; and record amounts of cash spent on trips abroad. In 2010, Brazilians were the biggest spenders of all U.S. visitors, dropping an average of almost $5,000 per person per visit.

In the customs line at the Rio airport I'd see couples weighed down by enough stuff to furnish a small apartment. I'd later learn this was, in fact, what they were doing. In 2010 nearly 1.2 million Brazilians flew to the United States—64 percent more than ten years previous. Altogether they dropped a whopping $5.9 billion on shiny mementos from America's consumer paradise—things like iPods, MAC lipstick, Victoria's Secret Gilded Pear Crème body lotion. They also brought home bigger-ticket items such as computers or high-end baby carriages, which could easily cost double in Brazil. If washing machines came with handles, they would have bought those, too. Travel agencies concocted tours that channeled these new tourists straight into outlet malls. Brazilians even bested their own waistlines. In 2010, 15 percent of the population was obese, up from 11.4 percent in 2006.

The newfound affluence was visible in the number of adults with metallic smiles, sporting the braces they could now afford, and in the proliferation of extravagant children's birthday parties. When a coconut vendor in Ipanema tried to make change for me while conducting a loud argument with his wife about redoing their kitchen through the smartphone cradled against his shoulder, I knew something had really changed.

This economic effervescence applied to real estate as well. New rules in 2005 made for more flexible lending by private and public banks, and many Brazilians could consider buying a house for the first time. The terms were still far from the American heyday of zero down and single-digit interest rates, but for those who had grown up in a country where buying a home was only for the wealthy who could pay up front and in cash, interest rates of 12 percent with 30 percent down looked like a fantastic deal.

A popular housing program for the lower-income brackets— Minha Casa, Minha Vida, or "My Home, My Life"—offered rates of less than 5 percent, opening up the market to families that had been entirely excluded. In 2009, when the program was created, one million families were promised their own homes within a year.

This didn't feel like the housing bubble I'd seen in the United States. The Brazilian surge was based on pent-up demand for credit and housing from a burgeoning new class of consumers.

This confidence was reflected in Rio.

To head up the state's finances, Governor Sérgio Cabral did as he'd done in public security; he chose in 2007 a chief economist with a technical background and a proven record instead of going with the business-as-usual approach of awarding choice positions to political supporters. His choice, Joaquim Levy, had served under President Lula and helped put the nation's fiscal and financial house in order before moving to Washington, D.C., as vice president for finance and administration at the Inter-American Development Bank. Cabral's offer drew him back to Rio.

"We had a wonderful franchise in Rio," said Levy, when I had the chance to ask why he came back. "We just needed to give people the confidence to invest."

The state's $200 billion GDP was substantial and very diversified, he said. But the lack of organization in the state's finances was such when he started that the doors were wide open to waste and outright abuse.

"The possibilities were there for corruption, absolutely," he said. "When I started, elephants would walk through; there was zero control."

He brought organization and transparency to the state's revenue and payments. It was basic, but no one had done it before. Investors followed. In March 2010, two years after Standard & Poor's had raised Brazil's credit rating to investment grade, the ratings agency gave the state of Rio de Janeiro the same status.

In the wake of the good news, the governor went to New York, promoting Rio and touting expected investments as high as $90 billion over the next four years.

The marketing budget for the governor's office is a good yardstick for its sales pitch: $69.4 million in 2008, $115.1 million in 2010. But anyone looking at Rio in those days would have caught the excitement: massive infrastructure projects to prepare the city for the World Cup and the Olympics brought construction companies, which drew architects, engineers, and managers from other states and abroad. The number of visas issued to foreigners broke records, and professional Brazilians who'd gone abroad in the 1990s after despairing of finding jobs were now returning.

There was all this, and then there was the oil, vast deposits of it discovered 180 miles or more beyond Rio's coast. This find alone had the potential to stimulate the economy in Rio and the country, creating jobs, attracting foreign investors, revamping the shipping and exploration industry, and bolstering national coffers.

Brazil had long teetered on the edge of energy self-sufficiency but this 2007 announcement by Petrobras, the company behind my itinerant childhood, could catapult Brazil into the top five oil producers in the world. Extracting it would require drilling through sixteen thousand feet of rock and salt, deep into the bowels of the earth, from platforms floating on the Atlantic—a risky and technically challenging proposition that would push the edge of ultradeep offshore exploration and require an investment of up to a trillion dollars.

As the first oil field started gushing, however, the promise of bonanza ahead prompted even the avowedly secular and notoriously stone-faced president Dilma to risk a joke and say the find was "strong evidence that God is Brazilian." The line is an old staple of Brazilian self-deprecating humor, but this time it was served up without irony. The pre-salt fields, as they're known, could bring the kind of wealth and geopolitical heft that could leverage Brazil into the big leagues.

By 2010, the announcement of deep offshore fields off Rio's coast had expanded the oil industry and attracted foreign players. Monthly rents on high-end offices jumped nearly 50 percent in 2010 alone, making Rio the most expensive market in the Americas. The building in which the AP had its office also housed corporate law firms and oil services companies. I'd often find myself boxed into a corner of the elevator by Japanese men in identical blue suits, a tall stand of Norwegians, or a particularly prominent Texas gut.

I should have known my dreams of beachfront living were in trouble when I saw a Nordic-looking man taking long-legged strides down the bike lane in Ipanema on what looked like cross-country skis on wheels. Of course. They wanted it, too, and they were flush with petrodollars. Asking prices in Ipanema had gone up nearly 300 percent over the last handful of years as multitudes flocked toward the golden sand. I felt like someone had taken the Brazil I'd known and sent it through an Alice-in-Wonderland rabbit hole. Nothing was as expected.

But I still needed a place to live. This time I would be more methodical. Instead of just plunging in, I wanted to make sense of the market. For that, I went to Leonardo Schneider, vice president in Rio of SECOVI, the biggest real estate association in the country and the source of reports that detailed price fluctuations across neighborhoods.

We met in his office and began our conversation by looking over graphs that outlined change over time. Oil was a factor, but there were others, he pointed out. The turning point was 2009, when the city got the Olympic nomination and the new favela policing projects, the UPPs, started to spread.

Going from graph to graph, he plotted out the ripple of higher prices through the city. It started in the sought-after south side. As Cariocas found out they could no longer afford the rent there, they began to consider neighborhoods in the working-class north, where new residential buildings were going up after a hiatus of decades, or the gated communities sprouting to the west.

"Before, we had whole areas where at night you simply wouldn't go. You had stray bullets, shoot-outs, traffickers, right?" he said. "There were whole sectors that were abandoned, with little value. And then we saw what happened with the first UPP— Santa Marta, in Botafogo. Buyers waited a little to make sure that this was serious, here to stay. Within seven or eight months we had people wanting to move to the area, rent, buy, anything. Soon the market was anticipating the UPP, and prices would go up even before the police came."

I thought of my sister and her husband, who lived not far from Santa Marta. They'd bought a two-story penthouse right under Cristo's armpit before there was any talk of UPPs. Two years later, refurbished and post-UPP, the flat was worth nearly three times what they'd paid. The favelas above Ipanema and Copacabana also had UPPs; that brought down petty crime in the area, but it also jacked up property prices and rent. It was inescapable; Leonardo had no secrets to share. If I wanted to live anywhere in the south side and near my job, I'd have to pay.

So, with my expectations readjusted to remove any thoughts of an ocean view, I went back to my search. Forty or so apartments later, I realized that cost wasn't my only problem. After dozens of duds pulled from the classifieds, I realized the apartments I was looking at were the worst of the lot, the ones left over for people like me—people who didn't know anyone.

Cariocas are, above all, connected. They value personal contacts and invest a lot of time into cultivating these relationships, often turning a simple operation, like ringing up purchases at the supermarket, into a ten-minute transaction. This was maddening to me, with my very American expectations of efficiency. But my failed apartment search had taught me all this chitchat wasn't a waste of time; these interactions were valuable ways of accumulating social capital. Without a friendly hand or a useful tip, one ended up as I had, looking at one flop after another.

It seemed the fewer traditional resources one had—money or power—the more important this web became. My problem was that I didn't have enough money to hire an apartment scout, who would use his network on my behalf for one month's worth of rent. I had no personal connections, either.

But I did begin to work at it. I walked down streets where I wanted to live and chatted up the doormen who spent all day perched on hard-backed chairs, solemnly buzzing in visitors, buzzing out residents. As Cariocas felt less safe during the 1980s and 1990s, *porteiros* had become ubiquitous.

Their salaries were part of what I thought of as Brazil's hidden cost of living: the extras you paid for twice, first through your taxes and then out of pocket. The police couldn't ensure safety, so you lived in a building with round-the-clock doormen or in a gated condo with private guards; public universities were top-notch and free, but a public high school education wouldn't get your kid past the entrance exam, so you forked out for private schools; the Brazilian Constitution enshrined the right of citizens to health care at no cost, but the hospitals and clinics were overburdened and underfunded, lacking essentials like gauze or saline solution. So, if possible, you paid for health insurance.

In my circumstances, the *porteiros* were the solution. No one knew the life of each building better than these men, generally migrants from the impoverished northeast who came south looking for jobs. As Brazil's regional stereotypes go, the *nordestinos* are tough, conservative, hardworking, and self-sufficient, perfect foils to the gregarious, life-is-a-beach Cariocas. By the second or third time I swung past my chosen streets, prying these taciturn men for news, I got nods of recognition. With some prodding, they would share tidbits about who was moving, which building offered better value, and which unit was torn apart by a divorcing couple on their way out (it was the *porteiro* who explained the mystery of the absent faucets in the weeping wall apartment).

This was how I eventually found a place. It was on the second floor of a slightly down-at-the-heels 1970s Ipanema building called Superstar, apparently without any irony. It was not yet advertised. I jumped on it after a quick glance.

It was well above my price range, with a view into the private lives of the elderly couple across the street, and right by an intersection of the neighborhood's main bus thoroughfare. The screech of brakes and deep rumble of revving diesel engines ricocheted off the concrete walls and into my bedroom, populating my dreams. When Carnaval rolled around, the acoustics brought the resounding bass of roving samba bands and the caterwauling of their drunken revelers right into my living room; I could sing along to the traditional *marchinhas* even in my sleep. The kitchen door came with a resident termite colony that had been breeding, unmolested, for years; the doorknobs came off in my hand.

The kicker I didn't learn until later: the bathroom window was inside the shower stall and opened onto the exhaust pipe of the restaurant below, which specialized in *picanha na chapa*—grilled meat served sizzling on a cast iron skillet. For the next year, each time I bathed I had the disturbing sensation I was soaping up with a chunk of medium-rare steak.

All these qualities would reveal themselves in the months to come. But when I first stood in that empty living room, I was so relieved to have found a place that was at least adequate that I raced to the real estate office handling the contract: I'd take it.

Apartment found, I thought, the hard part was over, and I could focus on making a home for myself. Right? No. Not even close.

CHAPTER 7

IT'S COMPLICATED, *QUERIDA*

If searching for an apartment had been a lesson in the cost of living in this new Rio, signing the lease was my introduction to Brazilian bureaucracy, a legacy of the Portuguese monarchy that stretched over centuries in a tangle of red tape that ensnared the simplest operation. Buying a cup of juice at the stand-up corner bar was a dance involving at least three people—a cashier, an attendant at the counter, and another in the kitchen, each playing out a specific role in a complex choreography. Why did I assume signing a lease would be a simple matter? Clearly, more of the United States clung to me than I had been ready to admit.

I should have guessed at the challenges ahead from the long look I got from the secretary, Maria José, or Zezé as we called her, when I announced at the office I'd found a place and would be in a little late the next day because I planned to sign the lease first thing in the morning. She had been a fixture of the AP in Rio for thirty years, nursing generations of correspondents through their wide-eyed enthusiasms, their first run-ins with paperwork, and their eventual deflation of confidence. It was the composer Tom Jobim who first pointed out that "Brazil is not for beginners," but it might as well have been the diminutive Zezé.

At just about five feet tall, she was the office's front line and drew from a bottomless well of forbearance to deal with the vagaries of the news cycle, the frantic demands of foreign management, and Brazil's maze of forms and stamps. She gave me a nod and a little Mona Lisa smile as I galloped out the door, absolutely confident that I'd be back contract in hand. And she was there, with her customary kindness and a demitasse of coffee, to prop me up when I returned, empty-handed, the next day.

The rental agency needed to see my Brazilian ID, not just the little slip of paper I was handed when I'd applied for it. Of course. Plus proof of income and of residence. I didn't have a bank account—I needed an ID for that—and so had no way of proving an income other than my old U.S. paychecks, which were not acceptable. I certainly didn't have a residence. To check my financial background they wanted last year's tax return and twelve months of bank statements, and since mine were in English, they needed them all translated into Portuguese by a certified translator, copied in triplicate, each page stamped by a notary.

The traditional Brazilian rental contract also requires a cosigner who owns at least one property in the same city and who is willing to put it up as collateral in case of default. So the rental agency also wanted the cosigner's documents, their proof of income, and their tax return—all, of course, in triplicate, notarized.[1]

By this point I was losing my mind. Each step I'd take toward completing a task I assumed would be simple—getting a local credit card, registering for health insurance, signing a lease— would instead reveal a myriad other smaller steps that needed to be taken first. The harder I ran, the deeper I found myself within this perverse hall of mirrors.

---

1 The cosigner requirement represents a particular hurdle for foreigners and Brazilians from other states, since they are unlikely to know property owners in the city who are willing to vouch for them.

This was when Zezé took pity and got the hotel clerk to write a letter giving that address as my official residence, opened an account for me with a bank manager she knew, and put me in touch with a notary from a local *cartório* who'd come to the office and stamp away for what seemed like hours while I worked. When we were done gathering the documents I stared in awe at the two-inch-thick bundle of stamped, signed pieces of paper we'd compiled. A city park's worth of trees went into that stack, plus enough notary stamps to guarantee his grandchildren a very merry Christmas, and it didn't even include the actual contract—which would have to come in triplicate, signed by myself, the cosigner, plus a witness, and notarized. Of course.

It was only years later that I was able to quantify the grip these *cartórios* have on Brazil. Although the United States has notary publics, to equate the two is to vastly understate the way Brazilian *cartórios* permeate, and strangle, the country's business, from contracts between multinationals to the simplest operations, such as renting an apartment. A survey by the National Justice Council, which oversees them, put the yearly earnings of the country's 13,803 *cartórios* at about $6 billion. Indeed, the profession is so lucrative its title was for a long time passed from father to son, in a sort of feudal inheritance system.

I began to feel as if this running in place were a test of my desire to call Rio home. Anyone can visit and dig their toes into the sand for a few weeks. But navigating the labyrinth of paperwork required to live and work in Rio while remaining calm took another level of resolve. Cariocas seemed to have an otherworldly ability to remain affable in the face of inefficiency, incompetence, or sheer indifference. They were also masters of the *jeitinho*, a certain tact that allowed them to bend the rules without breaking. This was a skill that started with the ability to charm and backslap, and, depending on individual style and the occasion, could range as far as proffering a bribe with grace and discretion, avoiding offense.

Fail to learn this dance—lose your temper, invoke your rights, threaten a lawsuit—and you could find yourself unable to get your cell phone to work or to ensure delivery of that fridge you bought for double what you'd pay elsewhere. Cariocas prize cordiality and go far to avoid confrontation, but they will say come back tomorrow, *meu amor*, you're missing a document, or it's complicated, *querida*, falling back on the infinite elasticity of evasion and spurious amiability, until you sink into despair—phoneless, fridgeless, and without an apartment.

I would take nearly a month of cold showers before I got the gas working. The new rules required a different kind of duct, something not revealed by the rental agency and which meant weeks of hosting a friendly but decidedly unhurried construction crew. At least moving in was easy: all I had was a suitcase. The furniture and personal belongings I'd shipped from San Francisco remained ensnared at the port. They would remain there, inside a metal container and baking in the summer sunshine, until I could rescue them six months later with another two-inch sheaf of stamped, signed, notarized documents. All copied in triplicate, of course.

Standing in my new home, keys in hand, I realized I'd signed up to pay more than two thousand dollars in rent to sleep, eat, and work on a flimsy camping pad in an empty, echoing apartment. And yet it felt like a victory.

Every morning I ran on the sand toward the great granite embrace of the Dois Irmãos peaks, and then swam back, flipping over to watch skeins of white clouds knitting and unraveling above. A balloon of happiness filled my chest and I knew this was right, in spite of Rio's angry heat and its ungainly apartment blocks, the honk and roar of its traffic, its lines and long commutes. From beyond the break, the city was beautiful again, reduced to a bright strip of buildings against a backdrop of green, to the idea and the promise of home.

Even as I struggled to get settled, I realized the trouble I had was far from unique. Bureaucracy and the sluggish pace of public service formed a bottleneck that choked all transactions and dampened growth even in this booming economy. In 2010, opening a business required 13 procedures and, on average, 119 days, if all went well and the documents were lined up. In the United States, this took 5 days; in India and Russia, 29 days, according to the World Bank. This red tape was a real burden, costing the country about $26 billion a year, according to a survey by an industry group.

And that wasn't the end of it. Once the company was up and running it came time to wrestle with another component of the "custo Brasil," as investors referred to the hidden costs of functioning in the country. This was the labyrinthine tax system.

Brazil has one of the world's highest tax burdens. It grew from 22 percent to 36 percent of its GDP over the last three decades, putting it on par with countries like the United Kingdom and Germany. The corresponding figure in the United States is 25 percent. Not only that, but the tax code is so complex that compliance requires firms to hire a cadre of dedicated specialists and takes companies an average of 2,600 hours per year. This puts the country dead last in a ranking of 185 countries produced by PricewaterhouseCoopers, the World Bank, and the International Finance Corporation. This was enough to give investors pause.

Still, the moment was such in Rio that there seemed to be no shortage of interest. There were new galleries, bars, restaurants, and boutiques. Downtown, old brothels were being turned into five-star hotels. In Ipanema and Leblon, new venues catered to the growing expat crowd and the newly traveled Cariocas who returned from their foreign trips looking for a taste of what they'd seen abroad.

One of these new places caught my eye—a little Mexican joint that opened in Ipanema soon after I got my apartment. It was stylish, with angular wood paneling, its handful of tables spilling onto the mosaic sidewalk. The first time I stepped in for a burrito and a margarita, the owner came over for a chat. Aglika, dark hair highlighting her alabaster complexion, had the fine features of a painted doll and liquid, emotive eyes.

The salt on the rim of the glass was Himalayan, she said. Later I'd find out the tortillas came from Texas and the peppers were packed into a shoe box and shipped to Miguel, the chef and Aglika's husband, by his mother in Mexico. This kind of careful sourcing was something any New Yorker would recognize, but in Rio, it stood out. Across the street was a food-by-weight restaurant like so many others, with rice, beans, vegetables and meat; next door was a *lanchonete*, Brazilian fast food, with the traditional array of juice, cold *mate* tea, and the chewy cheese-bread called *pão de queijo*.

Back in the United States, Miguel had been a chef. Aglika was a concert pianist who'd garnered acclaim for an energetic style that belied her birdlike frame. He was from Mexico; she was Bulgarian. They met in Chicago and led a charmed life in a city that appreciated what they had to offer: she had a university position teaching music; he worked at a renowned restaurant.

But there was something that cut short many of their plans. Miguel had gone to the United States like so many immigrants, with lots of ideas and no papers. Those who knew his skills didn't question his identification. But any time Aglika and Miguel contemplated a move or he thought of opening up his own place, there it was, chafing their progress.

In the United States they could open a restaurant under Aglika's name, but that would be . . . Miguel paused, searched for a word. We were sitting in the restaurant after the lunch rush. The kitchen was under control, so he could take a break. English was his second language; Portuguese was now the third. Our conversation wove together these two and Spanish, as did the tables around us.

"Frustrating?" I offer. He accepted. "Yes, frustrating." But it was more than that. I'd written about immigration in the United States and had seen too often how the lack of papers put a final period in lives where there should have been a new paragraph. Not having papers put a stop to his dream, any chef's dream, of having his own restaurant.

One night, during a distinctively Chicago variety of snowstorm, they curled up on the couch to discuss their options. There was one the solution to their quandary: they'd leave the United States and move somewhere warm, somewhere up and coming, and open their own restaurant. Their first idea was Spain, but Aglika's brother was already in Rio, doing well for himself renting furnished apartments to foreigners. He'd come in as a partner, offering them his knowledge of the location and business savvy.

Brazil has a generous immigration policy for those with cash to contribute. For a $300,000 investment in a business, anyone can get a visa and start a new life. Because it was Brazil, however, securing that visa took Miguel four months of visits to the Brazilian consulate in Mexico—"one more document, *querido*, one more copy, come back next week"—and a sit-down strike in which he refused to leave the building until the consul gave him that last required signature. But he got it and landed in Rio in October 2010. By January they had opened Azteka two blocks from Ipanema Beach, just in time to make a killing during Carnaval.

Miguel could pour his creativity into bringing to Rio authentic Mexican food with the flavors of his hometown, Acapulco. Beautiful Aglika circulated among the handful of tables that spread onto the Portuguese stone sidewalk, welcoming customers. The hole-in-the-wall was a hit. It wasn't cheap, at fifteen dollars or so for a sandwich, but nothing in this new Rio was. Most evenings, chatter in various languages mingled in the warm breeze. Tourists, Cariocas, and journalists from the growing number of countries interested in Brazil gathered there for the food, the conversation and the people-watching.

There were hitches, of course. Miguel was used to working in an all-organic restaurant and Aglika was a nut about health, but in Rio they had to make do with organic greens purchased at twice or three times the price of conventional and organic chicken. As for the other meats . . . some weeks there was organic pork, but the source wasn't reliable, so they had to give up.

Fitting in socially was easy, Miguel said. "Our cultures are very similar, Mexico and Brazil . . . very similar traditions, a way of being that is relaxed." The hard part was the work, he said. Deliveries came on Brazilian time, meaning maybe this week, maybe the next, with seldom a phone call of warning; staff cycled through by the dozen before he found dependable waiters and kitchen help.

"I was used to working with professionalism, you know? This was the hardest part," he said, talking about employees who failed to show, shipments of chicken that came late, or in which the supplier didn't have the parts he ordered and simply delivered what was available. "I used to think maybe because we are foreigners they were different with us, but no, not really, this is the way. Maybe it is too relaxed."

The rent was high and the place was small; their menu was limited to burritos, *tortas*, and tacos. But they knew they'd found a niche, and that Cariocas were open to what they had to offer. As I settled in, so did they. About 40 percent of new businesses in Brazil shut down within two years, crushed by the heavy load of laws, taxes, paperwork. But nearly three years after moving, they'd had a second child, a Carioca addition to their Mexican-Bulgarian-American mix, and were making plans to expand the restaurant, open up something more elaborate, with a real kitchen, furthering their bet on Rio.

The sense of opportunity and cost racing each other to the top that I had seen in Ipanema made me curious about how this was playing out across the city. In particular, I wanted to know what all this meant for the families living in Rio's favelas.

These informal settlements were the only alternative for many families. Even during the economic boom of the previous decade, the population of Rio's favelas had grown faster than of the city as a whole. How were those Cariocas managing within this mad real estate market? And what of the broader changes in the economy— were the rising cost of living and the better prospects noticed by the likes of Aglika and Miguel reaching Rio's poorest residents?

I decided to start with Santa Marta. It had been the first community with a UPP and was now a showcase favela, the example of transformation displayed to important visitors. Madonna had stopped by, escorted by the governor himself. Alicia Keys had visited. This community would let me gauge how the working poor were managing in this burgeoning economy and would also give a sense of how this new security program impacted everyday life.

Santa Marta was a ten-minute taxi ride from the AP's office. I got out across the street. The boxy, flat-roofed units were stacked against the vertiginous hillside in a tableau reminiscent of Mondrian, geometric and abstract. It was a small favela, contained on the right by the cable car line that took residents to the top and on the left by a brick wall nearly nine feet tall. At the very top was the UPP base.

I crossed the busy thoroughfare, passed the stand advertising community tours by local guides, and started the hike up along the Rua Marechal Francisco de Moura, where the favela meets the city. A for-sale sign in the window of a bare-bones building made me stop. I called on the spot. The asking price: $115,000. Here, too, it seemed real estate prices had lost their tether to reality. For that much you could find a modest home in any number of small towns across the United States, complete with your own little patch of lawn and a garage. In Rio it got you a basic two-bedroom apartment at the foot of a favela, with a view of a perennially congested road and officers strapped with semi-automatic weapons.

The road leading up was paved and wide enough for a car. Vendors crowded the shoulders with makeshift stands selling cell phone chargers, pork fritters, lacy underwear. A sign from a government agency advertised technical courses for electrical, plumbing, and metalwork. Farther up, a trailer without wheels played the part of a sports bar, its bulky TV blaring out a soccer game watched by patrons arranged around plastic tables cluttered with empties. Their eyes followed my progress without interest; visitors drew only the mildest curiosity these days.

I walked up the narrow alleys between homes that grew two, three, sometimes four stories high. It didn't take long to catch the nauseating scent of sewage, and to see the gray water washing down an open trough. Overhead, entwined bundles of cables thicker than a man's arm carried pirated electricity and cable TV up the hill. Water connections were also jerry-rigged, with PVC pipes snaking up, down, and around hurdles to feed the water tanks that squatted, heavy, atop the narrow buildings.

The tanks, blue or tan, were nearly always the same brand, Eternit; they were a precaution against the unreliable water delivery. I sounded out the name, giving it the sibilant Carioca pronunciation that turns *t*'s and *d*'s into soft fricative sounds— eh-ter-nee-tchy. Forever. Looking over the densely packed homes, built room by room as money was set aside for bricks, at the external pipes with their idiosyncratic paths, the gnarled wires drawing electricity from a friend of a friend down the way, it was clear that whatever improvements came with the police presence, much remained as it had always been, with the residents relying on their own ingenuity, their cobbled-together resources, and their network of connections to get even basic services.

Eventually I reached a small clearing ringed with businesses.

Here, closer to the street, were the most solid homes, well-finished residences with plate-glass windows fitted into aluminum frames and air-conditioning units sprouting out the sides. A duo of Dutch artists had painted the houses in lollipop colors—bright orange, green, blue. Yes, it was better than the unadorned cement gray that streaked black during the rains, but to me it gave the place the artificial gaiety of an amusement park.

On that Friday afternoon the public square was easing into the weekend's relaxed rhythms. Teenagers played Ping-Pong at a table in the middle of the plaza; smaller boys ran after a soccer ball in the outskirts, dribbling it through the table's legs. A tiny kid flew a kite from a rooftop, its span wider than his ribby frame. The sound of children at play, the occasional yelp of a stray dog, a hidden rooster crowing from the heights, the din of distant stereos, the slap and drag of flip-flops as women, tired from the day, carried up groceries for dinner brought to mind the cozy, your-business-is-everybody's-business feel of a small town.

A chattering crowd broke the peace and spilled out from the cavernous hall that opened up onto the square and housed Santa Marta's samba group. I wedged myself in to see dozens of adults get their junior high and high school diplomas. This was the first graduation of a state education program brought to Santa Marta after the UPP.

A state official said his piece about the long neglect of communities like this, about society's debt, but it was hard to hear. The stereo was turned up as loud as it would go, blaring a tinny, distorted rendition of Michael Jackson: "If they say why, why? Tell them that it's human nature. . . ." Women sang along with abandon, free of any allegiance to the original lyrics or the English language. The courses were offered in Santa Marta, run with the help of residents, and held before or after work hours. This made it a big draw with mothers who had to squeeze in studies between their jobs and their kids, like Kátia Castro. After the simple ceremony, she beamed over her plastic cup of syrupy-sweet Guaraná, balancing her three-year-old on her hip and swaying to the music.

This was her story, but change a few details and it could be the tale of so many other women there that afternoon. Born in Santa Marta, Kátia had started work at fourteen, scrubbing other people's homes for less than minimum wage. Then came kids, bills, a husband who left, more bills, more work . . . an avalanche that carried her along. She'd never had a chance to go back to school. Even now, she didn't know what she'd do with the degree—get a job, but what job? She wasn't sure. The broad smile ebbed for a moment. There was a break in the music. The speakers rattled with the bass line of a Carioca funk classic. Kátia shrugged off the heaviness of the questions and joined in the chorus: "Eu só quero ser feliz, andar tranquilamente na favela onde eu nasci. . . ." "I just want to be happy, walk peacefully in the favela where I was born. . . ."

Zé do Carmo took in the commotion from his barbershop. It was set at a prize spot in the square: against the back wall, with a commanding view of all that happened there and of anyone who climbed up the alleys. When Santa Marta was still in the hands of the Red Command, his regulars included the gang's soldiers and the drug users who came up for a fix and stuck around for five-dollar trims. All he asked was that dealers not flash their weapons around the shop. It scared away customers.

Above all, Zé do Carmo, full name José do Carmo dos Santos, was a businessman.

When I said I wanted to talk about the economy in Santa Marta, he gestured at a stack of empty beer crates at the entrance of the one-room barbershop.

"Sit down, sit down!" he said, and opened the fridge that stood behind the single barber's chair. "Beer, Coke, ice-cold water?"

Like so many favela residents, he'd come from the northeast, from the state of Ceará. He was two years old when the family settled in Santa Marta. At twelve he was working as a delivery boy.

He dropped out of high school but learned as he worked, jumping from job to job, until he became a store manager for a French clothing brand. In 1996 he opened up his own barbershop.

Since then he'd done so well a newspaper columnist had dubbed him "O Eike de Santa Marta," Eike from Santa Marta. Eike Batista was Brazil's celebrity billionaire, a maverick whose companies all had an *x* in their name for their ability to multiply cash, he said. At the time, he was the wealthiest man in the country and eighth richest in the world. The barber considered the comparison a good omen. Like Eike, reputed to consult astrologers, Zé do Carmo was a superstitious man and always wore at least one yellow piece of clothing to attract money. He wouldn't reveal the total he took home every month, to avoid the *olho gordo*, the evil eye of jealousy, but said if he were rich, he'd be on the beach.

"I still have a lot of hair to cut," he said with a grin that split his nut-brown face and tilted up the ends of a wispy, pencil-sketch mustache.

The UPP and the upturn in Rio's luck had been good for him. He was willing to give some examples: He'd nearly doubled the rent on the six houses he owned in the *morro* to $300. When business was brisk in the barbershop, he cleared more than $2,500 a month; and then there was the salon his wife, Mônica, ran just a few feet away. Unlike most entrepreneurs in favelas, who lived and worked informally, avoiding the maze of paperwork and taxes, he'd legalized his business and paid his share.

"Things are good and improving," he said. "We're integrating with the city in a way I've never seen. My clientele used to include a lot of addicts. Now I even get tourists who come up here to see the community and take advantage of our prices for a haircut."

A regular client came. Zé do Carmo continued to talk as he carved what looked like racing stripes into his close-cropped hair. The young man flicked his startling cat-yellow eyes at me in annoyance. He didn't want his barber distracted.

I left Zé do Carmo to his work. A walk around the square showed other enterprises had also traded an existence at the margins for legality. The head of Santa Marta's business association, Andréia Roberto, was having an end-of-the-day beer and poured me a glass as she pointed out the advantages of going legit: if you call for a truckload of beer, for example, the company has to bring it to your store. They can't just dump it at the bottom of the hill, at the favela's entrance, as they used to do when they knew locals couldn't complain. The grocery a few yards away took credit cards, only possible for those registered with the state.

But her husband was not convinced. He ran a little bar on the square and had seen a lot of bills and bureaucracy since he registered with the state, without enough new customers to make up for it. He'd had to unplug one of his two refrigerators, he said, now that he paid for electricity, but he still had to deal with blackouts. You can complain, he told me, but that doesn't mean they'll fix it. It just means you have to pay.

Glancing farther up the hill, it was clear this new affluence wasn't evenly spread. Above the square, up a cement stairway and deeper into Santa Marta, the homes were humbler. At the very top were frail shacks cobbled with wood and zinc, with sheets of plastic tacked to roofs and walls to keep out the rain. Along the way, alleys between houses narrowed and twisted, forming bottlenecks so tight the traffic was single-file. The air was hot and still within this maze, thick with frying garlic, Pine-Sol, and sewage. Around one bend I saw a woman resting her ample frame on a step outside her canary-yellow home. It was a bottom unit, the one closest to the slick granite; the inside was lit only by the blue, flickering glow of the TV set. The single room she shared with her six children had no windows.

Her name was Leidemar Barreto. She was raised on the hill, and she'd welcomed the police presence. Anyone who has children will be glad there are fewer drug users threading the lanes, she said, and fewer men flashing their weapons. But she hadn't counted on this: the violence had been a barrier between the favela and the sky-high rents beyond. In the past two years, since the UPP had come, her monthly payments had doubled to $180, eating up half of what she made selling lingerie from home.

As she talked, her six-year-old barreled out of the dark room, punching suddenly into the light then disappearing down the cement stairway. She stuck one leg inside the doorway, pressed a flip-flopped foot down on the plywood here, there, around the beams that supported the floor. The damp had softened the wood, rotting it in places; that made her sick with worry for the kids who ran in and out, heedless.

"I want to leave, but where can I go from here?" she asked. Her customers, her children's school, the friends who helped out when money was tight at the end of the month, the store where her word was credit . . . Santa Marta held all that. Every corner had its story, every face was familiar. She'd never lived anywhere else, and couldn't fathom a life far from its beehive heart.

Leidemar's family and her community came to represent in my mind the paradox of this new Brazil.

The plank holding Leidemar afloat was Brazil's broad poverty-fighting program, Bolsa Família. Its popularity had helped elect President Dilma; in turn, Dilma would quadruple its scope so that by 2013, nearly 50 million Brazilians benefited—fully one-fourth of the population. Although Brazil remained one of the most unequal countries in the world, programs like this, coupled with economic stability and the real growth seen over the past decade, had shrunk the gap between rich and poor to a fifty-year low.

This was visible in Santa Marta. Favelas that had been synonymous with grinding poverty and lack of opportunity now housed members of this new middle class. A 2012 survey of Rio's one thousand biggest favelas showed 66 percent of residents had officially reached that stratum, earning roughly between $500 and $2,050 a month.[2]

Zé do Carmo's success was exceptional among his neighbors, but not by much. Although he hadn't shared his full income with me, the little he told was enough to conclude that he fell into the 13 percent of favela residents who had climbed into a higher-income bracket, with earnings above $2,050 a month. A decade ago, only 1 percent of people living in favelas fit this category.

Santa Marta had free Wi-Fi and nearly half the homes had a computer. Cell phones were ubiquitous in the community, and credit cards common. Half the households had substituted the chubby old television sets for sleek flat-screens, and one-third had cable. In short, many of them had the stuff of the global middle class.

There was real pride in these possessions. The widespread use of computers and smartphones also pointed to another characteristic of this new middle class: three-fourths of them were better educated than their parents, and nearly all were more connected. But this visit also pointed out some of the glaring shortcomings of a purely economic definition of class. First, there were the parameters. The starting point for Brazil's class C—the middle slice of the country's A, B, C, D, and E socioeconomic classification system—was a monthly salary of $500. Moving the goalposts and decreeing that someone with that income was no longer poor but part of this other category called "middle class" did not make his wages go further at the supermarket. But let's leave the numbers aside.

A financial definition of middle class may describe important material changes, but it left out aspects that are essential to most anyone's definition of a middle-class existence. That community, as

---

2 Different organizations have their own parameters for what constitutes the middle class in Brazil. This is the definition used by the federal government.

the first UPP, had become a model and had been granted an unusual array of services. But its residents still lacked uniform access to essentials like safe and regulated electricity, water, and sanitation, not to mention quality education and transportation.

What did this mean? The ravages of hunger weren't as visible as they had been when I had last lived in Rio, twenty-one years ago. The punch-in-the-gut sight of a four-year-old begging at the traffic light was far less common in this new Rio. This mattered, immensely; it was one of Brazil's most tangible achievements.

But no matter what the statistics said, to members of Rio's traditional middle class, and to many of Santa Marta's residents themselves, the favela's residents were still poor because they lacked a middle-class quality of life. And Santa Marta wasn't unique. Its conditions were replicated all over Rio, around Brazil. Scratch the glaze of stuff and the old hierarchies remained the same.

CHAPTER 8

SAVING THEMSELVES

I was lingering in the office, taking advantage of the calm after dark to file expenses and listen to the evening news. It was January 2011, and in the few months since I'd returned, the city had sunk deep into the hot, wet Southern Hemisphere summer. Even the walls seemed to sweat. Outside my window, a hard rain fell in sheets that obscured the bay and the Sugarloaf Mountain, and turned the streets below into a congested river of red taillights.

A note of alarm in the announcer's voice made me look up at the TV flickering in the corner. There was trouble in the mountains that rose fifty miles or so north of the city. The downpour was loosening whole slopes in the craggy range, unleashing avalanches of mud and wiping out entire neighborhoods. It was happening very fast: dozens were confirmed dead already and many more missing.

On a clear day, the craggy peaks of the Serra dos Órgãos are visible from Rio. Their sawtooth outline rises just beyond the bay to more than seven thousand feet, topped with impossibly steep formations like the Dedo de Deus, the Finger of God, a slender column of granite that ensnares clouds drifting in from the ocean. These fluted spires gave the mountains their name; Serra dos

Órgãos means the Organ Range. The cool climate of the mountains has long drawn Cariocas looking for relief from the heat
of the flats. The royal family spent their summers in the Serra's
heights when Brazil was an empire in the nineteenth century; German and Swiss immigrants settled the lush valleys, leaving their
traces in steep-roofed cottages that seem forever in wait of snow.
Now Rio's well-off retreat to weekend homes there, and the gen-
tler climate supports farms that supply nearly all the vegetables
and fruit consumed in the city below.

The mountains are also an extreme manifestation of the state's
roller-coaster terrain and its characteristic inequalities. Cities there
have grown organically to a great degree, defying grids, squeezing
and curling around whatever nature threw in their path: skyscrap-
ers rise against mountains; roads hold lakes and hillocks in boa-
constrictor loops; concrete creeps onto marshy bogs. Settlements
grew over decades with little or no long-term planning, more
often than not without supporting infrastructure and with negli-
gible monitoring for safety or the environment. As a result, housing developments strangle riverbanks, cling to denuded hillsides,
spread into floodplains.

This is a landscape in which the man-made and natural have
struck a precarious balance. Add to it the relentless sunshine and
awesome downpours of the tropics and you've got a mixture that
is equal parts spectacular and lethal. During the summer months,
clouds can gather into great bruised hammerheads and flash-flood
streets in the time it takes to gulp down a *cafezinho* at a corner
bar. I've seen fifteen minutes of rain send so much water charging through the underground pluvial system that it gushed out of
manholes in powerful geysers that popped off the heavy metal lids
and kept them dancing more than a foot off the ground. Storms
like this could turn a trash-choked creek into a dam that broke
violently, and the exposed flanks of a mountain into avalanches of
mud. It happened nearly every summer.

In the previous year, 2010, torrential rain had plunged the state of Rio into chaos. Trees were knocked down, taking power lines with them; rivers overflowed their banks, ripped craters into the asphalt, and flooded Avenida Brazil in the middle of the rush hour, forcing drivers to abandon their cars. The fire department had to use rafts to pick up desperate commuters. Mudslides in the resort of Angra dos Reis, in Ilha Grande, and in the city of Niterói across Guanabara Bay added to that year's death toll of more than three hundred.

This was why downpours such as the one that lashed at my office window that January evening left Cariocas on edge. My parents had a home up in the mountains. I knew the area and I was all too familiar with the way houses grew more modest toward the outskirts of town, until they were just hand-laid brick walls that rested, without foundations, on granite bedrock or topsoil.

Outside my window, branching bolts of lightning coursed through the leaden underbellies of storm clouds like angry veins. The rain worsened. I turned up the TV so I could hear the news over the wind that whistled through the cracks and rattled the glass panes. In between phone calls in which I tried to confirm the extent of the damage, I filed a short piece to the wire. With each phone call, the news was grimmer. The death toll was climbing in leaps. I updated the article with new information as fast as I could get it. It seemed that whole mountains were starting to give way.

By 9 p.m., the news had tipped from tragic to catastrophic. A series of huge landslides had left nearly two hundred dead and hundreds more missing. I had to get up there, but by then it was too dark and dangerous to drive. I'd leave early the next morning.

I was on my way by 5 a.m. with the photographer Felipe and the AP's veteran cameraman Mário Lobão. Diarlei Rodrigues, a taxi driver who had become a part of the video crew, drove us. The rain fell in sheets that erased every sight and drowned every sound outside the car. Within an hour and a half of creeping along through an eerie, blank landscape, we reached Teresópolis, the city of Teresa, named after the wife of the Brazilian emperor. Petrópolis, named for the emperor himself, Dom Pedro, was also suffering heavy damage.

We parked as close as possible to the disintegrating slopes, then rushed toward them on foot, against the flow of families escaping with whatever belongings they could carry: sodden pillows, a stereo wrapped in plastic, supermarket bags lumpy with photo albums, clothes, shoes. The cobblestoned road that led past my family's home was washed out. There were deep muddy craters where the black stones had been. We worked as we walked, talking to survivors streaming downhill in the rain. It took us most of the morning to reach the foot of one of the avalanched mountains—a distance of no more than two miles.

At the fringes of town, whole slopes had crumbled, turning entire communities into sliding graveyards. The immense furrows left behind looked like open wounds that continued to disgorge a viscous red mud.

We decided to split up the team. Felipe and I wanted to go farther up to search for survivors who might be stranded and see what rescue efforts were under way, but the video camera made Mário far less mobile. He and Rodrigues would remain at the bottom of the slopes that day. Felipe and I picked one gouged mountainside and clambered as we could, clinging to trees and roots to follow the path of a blown-out creek that had swept away its bridge and scores of homes along its bank.

Flanking this trail of devastation there were cars and trucks flipped like toys, and several buildings ripped open by the force of the flash flood to reveal the strangely intact half of a living room or the remnants of a bathroom. Within the great churning trough, there were the remnants of entire homes and lives—PVC pipes, sheets, plastic buckets, bits of a dinner table, a mattress, a teddy bear, shattered bricks, broken glass, a family portrait in a plastic frame.

There were also bodies in the mud. Sometimes they were mangled into something shapeless, a torso stripped of clothing by the water, the bones inside smashed and breaking through the skin, sometimes distinctly human—a manicured hand sticking up through the sludge, or a man's face frozen in a moment of wide-eyed terror, his mouth and nose stuffed full of mud.

For hour upon hour we worked, trying to gauge the degree of destruction and interviewing survivors about the extent of their loss as warm rain continued to lash the saturated terrain. The sky was leaden and close, with a low, oppressive cloud ceiling. The dense greenery of the forest that bordered the mudslides heaved and pulsed under the storm's blows, giving the impression the land was gasping for breath.

Terrified families cowered in the houses that remained, unsure of what to do as an angry red river rushed a few feet away. The loose soil around the small brick homes melted away, the danger far from over. There was no visible government help at that point. It wouldn't come for days: the rain and fog obscured the jagged peaks, keeping away the helicopters. The government later justified their lack of action by saying that the terrain was too steep and rough for safe rescue operations.

In the absence of the state, people rescued themselves. Families dug up and carried their dead on makeshift gurneys as I watched. One father put his twelve-year-old son's body inside a refrigerator tossed up by the mud to protect his boy from the roaming dogs as he turned back to dig for three other children and his wife. He'd put their photos inside a plastic folder and showed them to whoever passed by; he'd ask if they'd seen his missing family, and clung to the hope one of them had escaped. One elderly man with rheumy blue eyes sat on a log, beyond concern for the rain spatter-ing his face, running through the stubble of his gray hair. His sod-den T-shirt hung from his wiry frame. He'd lost his entire family, the thirteen people who'd lived in three side-by-side homes, and would not leave the ground in which they lay. There was nothing else for him, he said, but to sit with them, his hands helpless on his knees, big farmer's hands, thick and knobby-jointed like uprooted trees, dark with mud.

When Felipe and I hiked back to town at the end of the after-noon, we walked past long lines of mud-covered wretches who were trudging back up, navigating the slippery muck in flip-flops, picking around sharp metal edges and tile shards, their hands wrapped around plastic supermarket bags bulging with food and water for survivors who were too old, too young, or too hurt to make the trek themselves.

After filing our stories and images from the car, we went look-ing for the local cemetery. Night was falling and it still rained when we found it. The rust-colored soil was churned and pitted with open graves. Those holes in the ground were terrible things: a hundred gaping maws in the earth, surrounded by a glutinous mud that sucked at our shoes when we walked.

Diggers wore masks to keep out the smell as they worked. The morgue overflowed in the first few hours, and bodies needed to be buried fast. The summer heat worked quickly on the drenched corpses. Families gathered around fresh mounds topped with simple crosses of unfinished pine.

One family was lowering a small casket under the rain into the wet hole in the ground. I approached them, looking for one more story that would help carry this tragedy to readers who'd never heard of Teresópolis. A man, the uncle of the child being buried, stood dry-eyed and silent. He showed me the photo of a little boy not yet three years old. A woman who might have been the child's mother, or an aunt, held a blue plastic truck with big black wheels.

Behind me, someone by another grave site was keening, screaming a name: "Maicon! Maicon!"

I started to feel physically sick. So far, I'd controlled my own feelings by focusing on the work: reporting, calling in information, going out for more. But after fourteen hours of this, I was beginning to crack. Leaving the family, I walked quickly past the wailing mother, who by now was trying to throw herself into her son's grave, still calling his name. I was running by the time I got to the edge of the cemetery and found Rodrigues's taxi. It was empty. I pulled open the door and took refuge in the back. The image of the three-year-old boy stayed with me; he was my nephew's age. These people spoke Portuguese, a language that for much of my life I had used only with family. Their pain felt close, personal. Alone for the first time that day, I cried hard, punching the seat in front of me. More than crying, it felt like vomiting. I could no longer hold the contents of the day.

When it became too dark to shoot, the crew returned to the car. The cameraman took in the scene with a glimmer of sarcasm in his eyes. He'd been doing this kind of work for nearly as long as I'd been alive, and he kept feelings at bay. As we drove off, he went on to mimic the scene from the cemetery, starting with his version of my dash to the car. From then on, any overt sign of emotion on my part drew sniggers from the guys and high-pitched cries of "Maicon! Maicon!"

I didn't cry again, but over the next six days, my frustration over the inefficiency of the rescue effort grew. The worst of the disaster happened on January 11 and 12. It wasn't until January 15 that I saw the first representative of the state, a national defense soldier, on the devastated bank of a river where houses had been razed days earlier. With a clean uniform and a rifle across his chest he stood out as an island of order and tranquility amid the chaos. I stopped.

"What are you doing here?" I asked.

"Our work here today is to prevent looting," he answered.

There was not an intact house left within view. Nearby, a line of men and women trudged uphill with their supplies in plastic sacks, heads bent earthward, without a glance for the soldier.

I hiked miles each day, hoping to understand the extent of the destruction, but had seen only a few dozen slides. At the end of the week, when the rain eased into occasional showers, the mist lifted, and rescue personnel showed up in greater numbers, I begged a ride on a helicopter. Only then I did I understand the immensity of what had happened. There were thousands of shredded mountainsides. Rivers had changed course. Roads were destroyed, bridges washed out. Many of these slides were in isolated areas where families remained for days, rationing their food and praying for help.

I probed those I interviewed for what I imagined was their shared indignation. Many of them had suffered losses I couldn't fathom—their entire family, their home, their neighborhoods were gone. What I heard was bewildering: "We're in the hands of God," they said, shrugging, wrapping the handles of their wet plastic bags once more around their hands. "Deus dará." God will provide.

They talked about their dead with feeling, but my questions about expectations of help from the government were met with blank stares. I looked for revolt and found a forbearance I took for passivity.

Only six months later, when I returned to the same neighborhoods and found everything virtually unchanged, the houses still ripped open, roads still obliterated, the mud now dried and cracking, and the mayors of the two most affected towns indicted for funneling away the recovery money, did I begin to grasp the reason for their equanimity.

The people there had expected nothing, anticipated no help, and so were not disappointed when it didn't come. They did what they could for their own and for their neighbors. Just as they'd res-

cued themselves, they now chipped away with pickaxes and shovels
at the mud that held fast like cement, unearthing what was left of
their homes one wheelbarrow at a time.

Two years later, I visited again. None of the five thousand
homes promised by the state's governor and financed with federal money had been built. This was bewildering to me, but the
residents shrugged it off. They had no time or energy to waste
clamoring for help that wouldn't come, at least not in this lifetime.
They saved themselves. What they couldn't do, "Deus dará."

I spent six days in Teresópolis during the rains. After the first
day and a half, Rodrigues, the cameraman, and the photographer
had taken off for the neighboring town, Nova Friburgo. Its downtown had been washed out. They'd left me with Bira, the driver
who'd helped me during the Alemão siege.

He was as broad and deep as a chest of drawers, raised in the
working-class suburbs of Rio, evangelical, married with children.
Their photos were framed next to the steering wheel. While I did
my work he sat in the car, smoking. We didn't talk about much
other than logistics. That's what we were doing late one evening at
our hotel when he asked, between bites of a soggy white bread
and ham sandwich, why I'd never married. I ignored the question and turned to the TV. I was too tired for a line of questioning
I'd heard too often since my return. He pressed on: Did I have a
boyfriend? Cleaned up, I'd look okay, he offered.

I nodded and took another swig of Johnnie Walker, the hotel
bar's only offering other than a fiery *cachaça*. I saw myself through
his eyes: disheveled, dirty, unmarried, so different from the women
he knew. He meant well, but the last few days, and for that matter, the months since I'd returned to Brazil, had been bewildering
enough without a reminder of how little I fit in. I knocked off the
whiskey and went to my room.

We left for Rio the following afternoon. The hour-and-a-half
ride back to my apartment was silent. As he dropped me off, he

looked for something to say: "Do something to your hair. You'll feel better."

I ran the two floors up to my apartment, still in the muddy jeans, socks, and shoes I'd worn all week. It all reeked of death. Each morning in the mountains I had pulled these things on and tried not to think of all that was embedded in that dirt. As soon as I walked through my door I tore these off, stuffed them in a plastic bag, and tossed them down the trash chute. I wanted to leave that behind, clean myself, scrub off the grit under my nails, and wash the stench that lingered in my nose and on my skin.

I put on a bathing suit and ran to the beach, looking for the Rio fix: the sun-flecked sea, warm breeze against the skin. But the hour-and-a-half ride had not put enough distance between what I'd seen in the mountains and the sparkle of Ipanema on a hot summer day. The beach was packed. The golden light, the free-floating libido of Rio in the months between New Year's and Carnaval, all those bodies so juicy with life—it all struck me as grotesque.

I headed back to my still-empty apartment. Curled up on the camping pad that served as my bed, I shut out the brightness of Rio's summer and let the events of the last few days swell and take over my thoughts. This was not my tragedy and the pain wasn't mine to feel, but some of that suffering had made its way in, like the mud that had become embedded in my clothes, my shoes, under my nails. I carried scraps of lives with me, bits that never made it into articles: there was the family that had saved for years to build a house and then had died in it; there was the mother mourning her little girl who had been so smart, so good in school, there was the nephew who took me along as he looked for the bodies of his aunt and uncle in the ravine below where their house had stood. For the next few hours, I gave myself over to grieving for these people, these names and faces that I knew only briefly but whose stories were now meshed with my own.

Felipe, the photographer, had stayed behind in the mountains,

working in the town of Nova Friburgo in increasingly appall-
ing conditions for nearly three weeks. Later he told me that he
couldn't wash the smell away. He took several showers, scrubbing
himself, but couldn't get rid of the stink of death. Eventually he
realized it had permeated the hair on his body. He had to shave
himself entirely to get rid of it.

"It was fucked-up, man. Fucked-up," he said, shaking his head.

In a bizarre coda to that week, Bira, the taxi driver, suffered a
freak accident after dropping me off. He'd stopped at a gas station
to refuel. His cab ran on natural gas, as many in Rio do. Something
went horribly wrong; the car exploded in flames. He'd been inside.
The cab's doors and windows locked automatically. Bira was strong
enough to break the window on his side and hoist much of his
torso out through it, but he was left with severe burns over much
of his body. I learned about it at the office on Monday. We took up
a collection to help his family.

I went home reeling from the news. I'd been in Brazil for two
months. It wasn't supposed to be like this. My daydreams of return
had been suffused with feelings of belonging, of being surrounded
by people who looked like me, who spoke the language of my
grandparents. I knew there would be surprises, but this homecom-
ing was tougher than I'd anticipated.

There was no welcoming glint of recognition in anyone's eye,
no identification of the latent Brazilian under the rather American
way I carried myself. I walked too fast and asked direct questions.
At parties, I found myself awkwardly inching back, trying to keep an
arm's length between myself and some Carioca who would inevitably step in to close the gap. Even the cadence of my speech alerted
others that there was something off. I wasn't from around these parts.

Instead of letting me feel finally at home, life in Rio was a series
of reminders of the strange, hybrid creature I'd become. I'd come
to expect that moment when whoever I was talking to looked at
me askance and asked, "Where are you really from?" Taxi drivers

who picked up on my foreignness ran me in loops around town; waiters added surcharges to the bill. I'd never felt so out of place as in those first few months back "home."

One of the aspects of Rio that I found most difficult was the violence that permeates life. This could be the violence inherent to very unequal societies, reflected in the neglect of people and the environment I'd seen in the mountains; or the overt aggression represented by the shoot-outs in the hills and the police patrol cars that rolled by, their windows spiked with nozzles of semi-automatics. Cariocas lived with this and carried on with a resilience and calm that eluded me.

Nearly one thousand people died in the mountains around Teresópolis; more than two hundred were never found. Over the next few years I returned dozens of times and would always look for scars in the mountains' great sloping shoulders. I'd fall into distraction and find my eyes combing the landscape for particularly steep gradients, clear-cut hillsides, or poorly anchored homes where the land would give if there were another sustained storm. I saw potential tragedy everywhere.

I wasn't entirely wrong. After the destruction, the media had pointed to existing surveys done in all three of the most heavily damaged towns that outlined the risks. The rainfall had been heavy and targeted: at the peak of the storm, as much water came down in one day as was expected in two weeks. But this is not unusual for a tropical summer. Massive storms do happen and could happen again. There were people living in danger all around the state. Everyone knew this.

Little has changed since then. Data from Rio's geological services released in September 2013 showed there were more than 207,000 people living in areas of risk in Rio de Janeiro State, nearly all of them in favelas. About 100,000 of them are in the capital, followed by the same outlying cities that were struck in 2011: Nova Friburgo, Teresópolis, and Petrópolis.

CHAPTER 9

BEAUTIFUL AND BROKEN

Rio is a stunner. Tom Jobim, the city's eternal poet, sang this beauty in his "Samba do Avião": Cristo's arms open wide over Guanabara Bay, sheer boulders dropping into the sea, Copacabana hemmed in white. "Este samba é só porque, Rio eu gosto de você . . ."

Cariocas are proud of their *cidade maravilhosa*. Beachgoers in Ipanema clap every summer afternoon as the sun sets behind the Dois Irmãos peaks, grateful for another day in their Marvelous City. The natural setting is also Rio's biggest selling point: the 2016 Olympic bid videos lingered on it, and the United Nations declared the city's landscape a World Heritage Site.

But the truth is that up close, Rio stinks.

Zoom in on the postcard and you will see trash clotting the waterfront and sewage percolating from broken pipes, blooming into fetid puddles on the sidewalks. Centuries of ill treatment have devastated much of this landscape: lakes curdle with dead fish when pollution brings down oxygen levels, and the waves that lap the shore are often too tainted with fecal bacteria for swimming. Stretches of marshland and Atlantic rain forest are being cleared for new development with little regard for ecosystems, and hours-long traffic jams cast an acrid haze over the horizon.

That week in the mountains confronted me with one of Rio de Janeiro's greatest paradoxes: the environment that made this city and this state exceptional has been abused to an extreme.

In the Serra dos Órgãos, I'd seen the horrific consequence of clear-cutting forest on slopes and riverbeds. In that case, the cost of environmental neglect was measured in lives. As a journalist, I went back to work after the mudslides with new questions. What were the effects of negligence in other areas? What were its costs, and who was made to bear them?

If there ever was a moment to turn this around, it was in these years before the Olympics. The city's bid had included promises to clean up the bay and plant 24 million trees. There were also new laws, such as a 2010 federal measure that required the elimination of unregulated dumps in four years.

I also hoped this moment would go beyond the old *para inglês ver*—efforts made for the sake of foreign eyes—and would awaken greater awareness among Cariocas of the long-term consequences of continuing to disregard their greatest gift. My concerns weren't only journalistic. I had come back to reclaim Rio and find my place in it. A year into my stay, I felt its crenellated mountains and scalloped beaches were as much a part of me as the sounds of Portuguese and the nationality named on my passport. They were my home and my heritage, too.

I started by looking at Rio's trash—my own trash.

Surveys told me that much of it, just like most of Brazil's garbage, ended up in unregulated, open-air dumps. This included my own waste, which wasn't separated out in recyclables and compost, as it had been in San Francisco, but all went into the same plastic bag and down my building's chute. That was the last I saw of it. So, I wondered, what happened to that bag?

It wasn't hard to trace. My waste and that of Greater Rio's 13 million people all went to one place: Gramacho, a mountain of garbage so vast it weighed over 60 million tons and covered an area the size of 262 football fields.

Its scale was overwhelming. I went with Rodrigues, the driver, and the AP video and photo crew. As we approached, the taxi joined a line of eighteen-wheelers that rumbled outside the front gates, waiting their turn. I watched as each truck was allowed in and started to climb a steep mountain. The flank that faced the entrance had been layered again and again with clay, creating a smooth dome zigzagged with roads. Underneath, there were decades' worth of trash. Crawling up its slope in single file, trucks that stood nearly thirteen feet tall looked like a parade of children's toys. This was where my garbage ended up—somewhere on this monumental mound.

The real work took place on the other side, where Gramacho faced Guanabara Bay. There the waste was uncovered and slouched in rolling heaps toward the water. I stepped outside the cab and tried to find my footing among the slippery, uneven jumble. The rancid smell clogged up my nose and mouth as if it were some thick, gummy substance that would choke me if I sucked in too much at once. Fat black flies dive-bombed like tiny twin-engine planes, the hum of their wings making my skin crawl even before I felt their touch.

Trucks climbed up and onto the piles, sending well-fed vultures hop-flying to safety, then poured out their loads. Men and women reached into the cascade and whisked away what they could, working fast, trying to beat the other hands grabbing into the same stream. Once the trucks backed away, the trash pickers bent over what remained, combing through it for any valuables they might have missed. The vultures circled, impatient, then swooped back in for the scraps of food.

Guanabara Bay spread from the foot of the mound like a dark, oily stain. Cristo, serene and blind, kept watch from across the water.

Gramacho was one of the continent's largest dumps, and jutted out of the western shore of the bay like a rotten tooth. The landfill had operated for much of my life, springing up on the marshy shore sometime in the late 1970s. For most of that time, it ran with little oversight, contaminating the air, ground, and water around it. At its busiest, it never closed; around 900 trucks disgorged 9,000 tons of trash onto it every day.

The toxic juice produced by its fermenting organic matter had flowed into the bay and seared all vegetation it touched, opening a ring of devastation. The methane gas it exuded had polluted the atmosphere and created the danger of occasional explosions. The heap even posed a risk for the airplanes heading to the international airport less than three miles away: the resident vultures collided with airplanes 286 times between 2008 and 2011.

The situation was no different for most cities in the state. In 2010, only 10 percent of the 20,000 or so daily tons of garbage produced by Rio state went to planned waste management sites. The rest went into open-air heaps. The 1 percent of refuse that was recycled was culled by *catadores*, the men and women who sifted through the waste in search of material to sell.

In Gramacho, they made up a ragged army of five thousand. On that February day in 2011, I found them in an uproar. After decades of anonymity, the *catadores* and the landfill itself had been propelled into something like fame.

It started when a Brazilian artist, Vik Muniz, visited back in 2007. Muniz worked with unusual materials like dust, diamonds, or sugar, and often wove social issues into the work. From his connection to the workers came a three-year project that incorporated their particular skills and the materials they rescued from Gramacho.

Muniz had photographed them in poses drawn from classic works of art: Jacques-Louis David's *The Death of Marat*, or Pablo Picasso's *Woman Ironing*. Then he'd blown up the image until it was large enough to fill the footprint of a warehouse nearby. Recyclables sorted into colors were used to fill in the image, composing a mosaic of what had once been trash. These monumental portraits were then photographed from above.

The work had changed Gramacho. Before this, some of the *catadores* had never seen a photo of themselves. Seeing their own image built out of the garbage that both stigmatized and fed their families was transformative. It also materially improved their circumstances. Money from the art sales had returned to the community, and they'd built a sorting center to make their jobs easier, with a kitchen and a place to rest.

A documentary, *Waste Land*, had recorded this process, and it was up for an Oscar. The award ceremony would happen the week after my visit; if the documentary won, the people of Gramacho might see their own faces flash on the television screen, bringing them into Hollywood's grandest party, even if remotely. Expectations in Gramacho had never been higher, and the life of the *catadores* had never been better.

Amid all this came other news: Gramacho would be closed down.

In spite of recent improvements, such as the clay layers that made the mound impermeable, and a system to capture the toxic liquid that had long leached into the bay, shutting down Gramacho was key because of what it represented, with its hordes of trash sorters, its size, and the degradation it wrought on its surroundings. A licensed landfill was already under construction in Seropédica, a town forty miles away.

Environmentally, it was the only way to go. The move was expected to reduce carbonic gas emissions by 1.9 million tons per year, according to the city government. As I picked my way through the waste, I looked for someone who could tell me what this would mean for the *catadores*.

One young woman stayed away from the scrum. She wore hot pink leggings under a mesh of torn fishnet tights, with short denim cutoff shorts on top and knee-high galoshes. Black tights covered her arms as protection from the waste and the sun; a T-shirt tied over her head draped down her back. She surveyed the scene with a keen eye, a hand on thrust-out hip, a heaping bag full of something by her side. Amid the ruin of Gramacho, she'd managed a postapocalyptic glamour, and her defiance in face of degradation around set her apart.

Twenty-one-year-old Sueleide da Silva had learned the trade from her mother, who worked the piles of refuse for twenty-five years until she lost her eyesight to an infection contracted from trash falling from a truck. Sueleide had her first child by the time she was fourteen; by fifteen she was pregnant again, working at the dump alongside three of her sisters. None of them attended school beyond the fourth grade, but together they supported their own children and their mother.

She had never known a life away from Gramacho. Her skills were honed to its particular demands. During the day, she explained, the *catadores* worked with their eyes, trained to spot the shine of glass and metals. But deliveries ramped up at night, so children learned from their parents how to differentiate materials by touch and sound, telling apart the fourteen types of recyclable plastic and the various grades of paper.

Most of the *catadores* lived in lean-tos of plywood, tin, and cardboard that had sprung up a short walk from the dump. They didn't earn much: cardboard went for 10 cents a kilo; printer paper for 13 cents if clean, 11 cents if dirty. Glass, heavy and hard to handle, fetched 14 cents. Sueleide's specialty was printer paper. The load was lighter, and on a good day she took home $40. It was a decent living; Brazilian minimum wage was less than $300 a month.

There had been talk of the dump's closure for years, but it was always just that—rumors. Back in 1996, there had been some big changes. Authorities put an end to child labor and registered the *catadores*. Rules restricted Gramacho to taking in only household trash; industrial and hospital waste were diverted to more appropriate sites.

Now the bosses said the closure was certain. Sueleide was skeptical. Improvements, sure, but to close Gramacho? It was a world unto itself and had offered up the soda bottles, cardboard boxes, and old magazines that, cleaned and categorized, had fed three generations of her family. She could not imagine a day when the teeming heap of possibility would no longer exist.

The people of Gramacho, *a gente de Gramacho*, were afraid, Sueleide said. The state-of-the-art landfill in Seropédica had no room for *catadores*.

There were provisions made for the workers. Wells were being drilled into the mound. Gases generated by decomposition were expected to generate energy and raise about $360 million over fifteen years. A portion of this would go to the workers, in addition to a lump-sum payment of $7,500. Job training was offered to the *catadores*. But Sueleide kept her expectations low, perhaps out of the abundance of hard knocks her short lifetime had delivered.

One single stroke of bad luck won't land someone in Gramacho. Motioning at the others, and perhaps thinking of her own family, she ticked off the problems: disease, domestic abuse, drug addiction, illiteracy, unplanned pregnancies . . . Her voice trailed off. Six months of job training won't solve any of these, she said.

"You don't end up in Gramacho because you have options," she said. "Most people here can't read properly, and every job out there, they want you to have high school, college. You have people here who don't know what to do with a pencil."

Places like Gramacho are reminders of the complex ways history, culture, and the economy have interacted with landscape to shape Rio. Closing down the landfill was essential to restore the marshes around it and clean up the bay, but the closure would bring difficulties far beyond replanting mangroves and restoring the crab count. I had gone hoping for a feel-good story about Rio on the mend, but left with Sueleide in mind.

The documentary about Gramacho and the artist didn't win the Oscar. There would be no clear-cut victories there, no neat, happy endings.

The landfill was shut down in June 2012, less than a year after my visit. The job training was a flop, as Sueleide had predicted: most of courses required high school degrees, and the average *catador* had four years of schooling. Nearly half of them couldn't read or write, as she had pointed out.

Then the state environment secretary signed a big contract to set up a recycling center. This could work, I thought; the people of Gramacho could put their knowledge to use. I went back to look for Sueleide and her kids in the shacks near the dump, to see how they were faring. She was gone. No one knew where she'd moved, what she was doing now. She'd disappeared into the city.

When I returned two years later to visit the recovering marshland around Gramacho, a biologist pointed out the hovering buzzards a stone's throw from the dusty main road.

"Another dump," he said, explaining that illegal trash deposits often spring up in a neighborhood after one is shut down. "You can always tell because of the vultures."

Even as patches went up in one spot, the problems reemerged elsewhere. Hard as it was to close the dump, it was harder to change attitudes.

• • •

How could a population of beachgoers who are so proud of their city coexist with the degradation of the very landscape that defined them? The answer lay, in part, in the Carioca approach to life, this elusive Rio Zen. They lived with an intense focus on the moment, on what was close by and immediate. They cared intensely about their homes, their friends and family, the good times to be had right here and now. But try to nail a Carioca down with plans for the weekend and you'd find the future is nebulous, whether it is tomorrow, next year, or the next generation.

The same nearsightedness applies to public spaces; they are too distant from the individual to register as worthy of concern or protection. What belongs to everyone belongs to no one, and so construction waste is dumped on the marshes, coconut husks are left on the sand when their sweet water is gone, and candy wrappers flutter from the hand to the street, into sewers and into the ocean . . . away.

Although there are laws that forbid littering, anyone who has ever spent New Year's Eve in Copacabana Beach and watched the sun rise over sand fouled with beer cans, sandwich wrappers, and empty wine bottles knows this is widely disregarded. Every January 1, a legion of sweepers in bright orange uniforms gathers up to four hundred tons of trash from Copacabana's sand.

It took an education campaign in 2013, enforced by inspectors with the power to impose hefty fines on the spot, to make a dent in the Carioca's littering habit. Under the new rules, flick a cigarette butt on the ground and it could cost you $75; toss a beer can and it could rack up a $200 fine. Throw an old couch or a useless TV into the bay and the fine would be over $400. This approach showed immediate results: within the first month, the waste management company reported downtown's streets were 50 percent cleaner. It seems the fine made littering an immediate, personal concern, bringing the consequences close enough to snap Cariocas to attention. Only time would tell whether this law would sink in and become a habit and a value.

I had moved to Rio knowing that litter and waste management were serious problems. But there was another environmental issue that caught me off guard: air pollution. During the still, dry days of winter when rain eluded the city, a brown sock of smog lay over the horizon, smudging the thin blue line between sky and ocean.

The recipe for Rio's pollution is particular to the place. The same topography that makes the city so pretty also makes it impossible to lay down a straight road. Traffic is forced to travel along winding ribbons of asphalt that loop around lakes and squeeze through tunnels. Add to this a car fleet that tripled in twenty years, with no significant investment in roadways, and you've got an idling, honking mess that pours its dirty fumes into the city daily. A survey by TomTom, the GPS manufacturer, found that Rio has the third-worst traffic in the world, behind only Moscow and Istanbul. Indeed, the state's environmental agency blames 77 percent of air pollution on cars and buses.

This also means the city lauded by the UN for the quality of its outdoor life has some of the worst air in Brazil. When a World Health Organization report compared local measures of airborne particulate matter in 2011 they found Rio's count was three times above recommended levels.

Rio's problem is also Brazil's problem. Traffic is a growing problem nationally, adding to the damage done by polluting industries such as steelworks.

The grime in the air became apparent once I had settled into my apartment. A day or two after I had mopped them, the wood floors were already covered in a slick black layer made up of the oily exhaust that wafted from buses mixed with marine spray from the ocean half a block away. Wiping this stuff up made me wonder about the inside of my lungs.

Indeed, over the next year I went from being a healthy, once-a-season-cold type to a chronic sniffler who suffered from sore throats, sinus infections, and other respiratory problems every other week. I imagined the balloonlike alveoli in my lungs as petri dishes at the hands of some mad scientist who mixed in rubber particles from tires, soot from burned oil, and fungal spores. By this time, my furniture and clothes had arrived, and had fallen prey to one of the huge drawbacks of tropical seaside living: humidity and mold. My leather shoes, belts, and purses were soon covered in a fuzzy white layer. Useless wool jackets developed fungal bloom patterns, rhizoids grew through the spices in their jars, and the tea clumped into toxic balls.

As the months wore on, I found myself defeated by the microscopic particles that embedded themselves in the fabric of my couch and in my lungs. I resisted leaving the apartment I'd struggled so hard to find; finding another would be hard, and there would be a hefty fine for breaking the mandatory thirty-month contract. But by the time I sneezed blood all over my computer while sitting at the front row of a press conference with the International Olympic Committee I decided it was time to leave my almost-on-the-beach place with its exorbitant rent, its mildew, and its bus fumes and find something easier on my lungs and my pocket.

I settled in Flamengo, a residential area facing Guanabara Bay. While Ipanema had represented a certain image of Rio that I'd craved, it was this neighborhood that had served as my parents' first foothold in the city. Its streets were lined with stately old trees and Art Deco buildings that offered soaring ceilings and a distant view of Cristo. The beach was too polluted for swimming, but that also meant cheaper rent. I fell for its muted rhythms and the elderly ladies in strings of pearls who walked their key-chain-sized dogs in the early morning.

Plus, my new apartment faced the Morro da Viúva, or Widow's Hill, a glorious granite dome that was enclosed by buildings on all sides but luxuriantly forested on top. Anywhere else, it would be crisscrossed with hiking trails, but in Rio it was little known outside the neighborhood and seemed diminutive compared to the twin humps of the Sugarloaf just across the bay. But thanks to its crown of trees, I finally had a picture window with a view onto swaying palms, the occasional troop of monkeys and chattering flocks of parrots.

A jog and swim at Ipanema Beach was no longer just steps away, but this neighborhood has its own waterfront park, the Aterro do Flamengo, a greenbelt that stretches from the downtown airport of Santos Dumont, along Flamengo Beach, to the small sheltered cove at Botafogo.[1]

The first time I ventured alone into the Aterro after my move, the syrupy musk of the cannonball tree's cream-and-crimson flowers brought back one of those dormant memories that lie buried for years. I remembered myself as a toddler under these same trees, contemplating the fleshy-petaled flower that filled my hands, and the moment when I dug into its stem-filled heart and tore it apart. The smell lingered on my fingertips, a reminder of the shame that had filled me after that first conscious act of destruction. Decades later, the honeyed scent under the trees brought back that afternoon, the pang of guilt. It also closed a loop—there was something of myself in this city after all.

---

1 The Aterro do Flamengo's origins were also wrapped in a great story. Its construction was coordinated by Lota de Macedo Soares, a daughter of the Brazilian elite and self-taught modernist who administered the park's development while carrying on a dramatic affair with the poet Elizabeth Bishop over sixteen years. Lota dreamed up much of what makes this park unique, such as the light posts that soar 150 feet high and cast a glow like moonlight.

My jogging route went into the park, past the cannonball trees with their extravagant flowers, to the bay's shore, where I'd stretch and look out at the granite monolith of the Sugarloaf rising across the water, just beyond Botafogo Bay with its little slip of beach and its scores of bobbing sailboats and fishing vessels. To the left was the long stretch of white that was Flamengo Beach. At my back, Cristo soared above the high-rises.

When traveling along South America's shore on board the *Beagle*, Charles Darwin stopped in Rio de Janeiro. It was late fall in 1832. The ship had turned into Guanabara, and anchored right there, within the shelter of Botafogo. Nearby he found "a most delightful house," and stayed for two months, walking the sand, collecting specimens, going for long horseback rides, and making notes that exclaimed on the exuberant fauna and flora.

It was after such a ride on June 1, 1832, that, particularly taken with what he saw, he wrote in the diary: "I do not know what epithet such scenery deserves: beautiful is too tame. Every form, every colour is such a complete exaggeration of what one has ever beheld before."

Reading this, I thought he might have stopped where I did during my run, and looked over the water to see the oblique afternoon sun striking gold out of the Sugarloaf's grayish pink rock, and felt lifted by the sight, much as I did.

And yet, it was at that point that the stench of sewage became overpowering. The water in Botafogo cove, where Darwin had collected coral, was now so contaminated it had not been deemed safe for bathing in decades. Give in to temptation on a hot day—a few brave souls did—and you'd risk fungal growth on your skin, a bout of hepatitis, or the stomach cramps and diarrhea that come with an *E. coli* infection. The state environmental agency found the water along Flamengo Beach too polluted for human contact in about four of five tests. The Carioca River, which empties into the bay right by Flamengo Beach, runs gray and dead with sewage.

For all of the environmental devastation I'd seen in Rio, no aspect seemed more incongruous than this rampant abuse of its waterways. That spot by the bay, with its quintessentially Carioca view and its stink, became a daily prompt: Rio, beautiful and rotten.

CHAPTER 10

THE FIRST CARIOCA

Rio was born by the water, and water shaped it from the start.

The city was founded on the narrow strip of sand between two granite peaks at the mouth of Guanabara Bay on March 1, 1565, part of a Portuguese effort to ward off the menacing French. Rio's port was a principal connection between Brazil and the world beyond through the twentieth century. Beach culture influenced some of the most quintessentially Carioca traits—their informality of dress and manner, their ease of movement, and their comfort with their bodies.

Natives of the state of Rio de Janeiro are known as *fluminense*, a word that comes to the Portuguese from the Latin *flumen*, for river. Those born in the city of Rio are called Carioca after the trickle of a river I ran by daily—though most would be surprised to learn this. Indeed, few know the Rio Carioca's name, or even think of it as a river at all.

Its banks have been cemented and, for much of its trajectory, its flow is shunted underground. By the time it reaches Flamengo Beach and empties into the bay its water is so foul that a sewage treatment plant was installed across its mouth in 2002. Anyone passing by could be forgiven for assuming that this gray, dead discharge is part of the wastewater treatment system, and not a stream born less than three miles away at the feet of Cristo, among granite boulders and lush forests.

The river wasn't always a foul conveyor of waste. There was a time when Rio depended entirely on the Carioca. It was the city's most important water source from the sixteenth century, when Portuguese sailors had relied on it to replenish their fresh water supplies, until the nineteenth century, when Rio's needs grew beyond what it could offer. Because of its unique relationship to the city, this river first sparked local environmental awareness by making clear that abuse of the natural surroundings—the degradation of the slopes through which the river ran—could have direct and dire consequences for the population.

Because it was Rio's principal source of drinking water, the river's course was legally protected through the seventeenth and much of the eighteenth century. Indeed, a notice concerning the Carioca issued on February 16, 1611, by the Câmara de Vereadores, the local council, may be among Brazil's first environmental regulations: "... water from the Carioca will be kept clean as is required, and there will be no planting of things such as bananas and vegetables. ... The margins along said river shall remain covered in virgin forest ... and when use is made of said river's water for drinking and washing clothes, this shall be done in the area set aside for it."

The Carioca fed Rio's first planned drinking water delivery system in the seventeenth century. A stone aqueduct replaced it in the mid-eighteenth century, guiding the Carioca's waters down the mountain and into the city.

Remnants of that water delivery system are still visible, including the tall stone fountain in Praça XV square, in the historic downtown, where the populace would gather to draw water, and the elegant white Arcos da Lapa, or Arches of Lapa. Originally part of the aqueduct, the Arches carried the river's water to the public fountains below from the eighteenth through the nineteenth century.[1]

When Charles Darwin climbed to the tip of Corcovado, then without its Cristo, his walk started along the Rio Carioca's aqueduct:

> *The path for the few first miles is the Aqueduct; the water rises at the base of the hill and is conducted along a sloping ridge to the city. At every corner alternate and most beautiful views were presented to us. At length we commenced ascending the steep sides, which are universally to the very summit clothed by a thick forest.*
>
> *. . . We soon gained the peak and beheld that view, which perhaps excepting those in Europe, is the most celebrated in the world. If we rank scenery according to the astonishment it produces, this most assuredly occupies the highest place. . . .*

In spite of legal protections, the trees that once covered the mountains of Rio had been largely cleared by the mid-nineteenth century to make way for coffee plantations or to be burned as fuel. When Darwin hiked along the river and up the Corcovado, the landscape that so moved him was already marred.

This led to erosion, and endangered the Carioca's source. That threat prompted Rio's first reforestation effort: under Emperor Dom Pedro II, land around the springs began to be expropriated in 1844, and an extensive replanting campaign took hold.[2]

Regardless of the regulations, residences encroached on its banks over the years. It was channeled and eventually had its lower

---

1 Once the Carioca aqueduct was abandoned in 1896, the Arcos da Lapa were put to use as support for the trolley tracks that connected downtown to the heights of Santa Teresa.

2 The project seeded tens of thousands of trees on the denuded slopes, and led to the creation of the Tijuca Forest and the Paineiras Forest in 1861. This was the core of what would later be the Tijuca National Park, smack in the middle of Rio and one of the world's largest urban forests.

half sealed into subterranean passages, only to reemerge as a rank canal by Flamengo Beach, where I first became acquainted with it.

Prompted by the Carioca, I began to dig up information about water pollution and learned the Carioca was a microcosm of what happens to waterways all over the state.

Rio treats only two-thirds of its waste. This means that one out of three times someone flushes a toilet, the contents stream, un-processed, into rivers, lakes, bays, and the ocean. This is no secret. The state environmental agency, INEA, warns residents to avoid the beach for twenty-four hours after a heavy rain, because down-pours rinse out the rivers and turn the ocean into a cesspool.

Nor is Rio's condition unusual. About 54 percent of Brazilians are not hooked up to pipes that divert sewage away from their homes. Even fewer are connected to a wastewater treatment sys-tem. This deficiency stands out when it is compared to other basic services: 98 percent of Brazilians have access to electricity, 81 per-cent have running water, and 91 percent have telephones. In 2013, 70 percent of Brazilians had cell phones—many more than had basic sanitation.

But Rio could do better. It was one of the first cities in the world, after London and Hamburg, to benefit from modern sewer-age infrastructure. Dom Pedro II, who was behind the reforesta-tion effort around the Carioca's headwaters, also ordered the city's first sewage pipes in the mid-nineteenth century.[3]

Rio's location in ocean-level alluvial plains at the foot of for-ested mountains made drainage a struggle from the start. A lack

---

3 Before Rio's first sewage system was installed, enslaved men carried barrels of excrement to the bay in the evenings. Historians say these porters were called *tigres*, or tigers, for the stripes left on their skin by the spills. The habit of throwing the contents of chamber pots out the window was also common, with results so disastrous that an 1831 municipal decree sought to regulate the activity. From then on, the waste could only be thrown into the street at night, and after three warnings of *Água vai!* or "Here goes the water!" Failure to obey led to fines and hefty compensation to the victims.

of basic sanitation added sewage to the marshy landscape. Plagues were so notorious that merchant ships avoided its port during the summer months. This was economically disastrous for a trading city. It was after a devastating yellow fever epidemic that lasted from 1849 to 1851 that the emperor granted the government powers to hire a sanitation and cleaning company. The job eventually fell to the British-financed Rio de Janeiro City Improvements Company, later known simply as City. Works began in earnest in 1862. By 1887, Rio had seven treatment stations.

In spite of Rio's early start, more than a century later, the state's streams and rivers delivered about 480 Olympic-size swimming pools' worth of raw sewage to the bay, every day. It made nearly all beaches along the bay too polluted to swim; its stench greeted me every morning when I ran past the mouth of the Carioca. Sewage burbled up from burst pipes and pooled along the curb of my street in Flamengo. Neon-green cyanobacteria, which feed on this organic matter, scummed up the lagoons out west.

How did this happen? Some of this waste flowed, raw, from favelas that had no sanitation. That was easy to see and smell. But that was also only part of the story.

At a conference on water quality, I learned about the invisible elements of Rio's failing sanitation system. Much of the pollution comes from the parts of town that officially benefit from a sewerage system. This happens, in part, in areas where the network is old and oversubscribed. Old pipes break, or back up and overflow into rainwater drainage systems, into subterranean rivers, or out of manholes.

But not all of this contamination is accidental. There are also illicit connections between homes, buildings, or entire shopping malls that feed sewage straight into rainwater pipes, or into rivers, lagoons, or the ocean.

I saw this when, in an attempt to clean up Rio's south-side beaches, the state's environmental department sent a tiny robot with a camera to inspect the underground plumbing in one of Rio's toniest zip codes, Leblon. The inspection found an expensive beachfront hotel, a mansion within a gated community, and a high-rent residential building all illegally pouring their waste into the water main, which empties—you guessed it—right into the Atlantic, at the beach frequented by the same people who produced the waste in the first place. Rio's sewage problem clearly goes beyond not having the means or resources to do the right thing.

Cariocas, as usual, have learned to manage. Before going to the beach, they check the newspaper's back pages. Next to the weather, there is a list of the stretches of coastline that are unsafe for bathing that day.[4]

The cost of environmental degradation, however, isn't measured only in hot days spent at the beach without a cooling dip in the ocean. The real toll is the population's health. A four-year study by the Instituto Trata Brasil, a water and sewage public interest organization, looked at the correlation between health and wastewater collection. In 2011, the latest year examined, Brazil's public health system had 396,048 patients hospitalized because of intestinal infections presumed to come from contact with sewage. More than one-third of those who got sick were children under five.

To learn how Rio got this way, I went to conferences and interviewed experts. But to grasp what it meant, to see how life is strangled out of a river, I turned to the Carioca—my Carioca. I decided to trace it as Darwin once had, up the mountains and back in history, from its mouth at the bay to its source, somewhere on ridge of the Serra da Carioca, the Carioca Range.

Standing on Flamengo beach where the stream flows into the bay, I turned my back to the water and looked up toward Cristo, hovering 2,300 feet above the city and three miles away. Between

---

4 Even the beach showers that run on generators plunked on the sand are not safe, as they tap into contaminated groundwater.

us lay a valley that encompassed the neighborhoods of Flamengo, Laranjeiras, and Cosme Velho, where visitors boarded the little train that took them to the statue's base. That was the course of the Carioca. The question was where to look for it, and how to recognize it in the congested urban landscape that lay ahead.

For help I called on Phellipe Nascimento Silva, a bald twenty-eight-year-old whose generous grin turned his eyes into bright half-moons above his round cheeks. He'd grown up within earshot of the Carioca in a favela called Guararapes, high up in the Carioca Range, and now he coordinated a group called Anfitriões do Cosme Velho, the Hosts of Cosme Velho. It trained teenage boys from Guararapes as tourist guides and taught them environmental responsibility. I learned about the group when it partnered with the national park employees for a daylong cleanup of the Carioca. This was the only public show of concern I'd seen for the river.

Phellipe's community had particularly strong ties to their plot of land in the mountains. A farm had once occupied those slopes, and Guararapes's first residents were farmworkers. In 1967, they pooled their savings and bought the eight acres of land on which they lived. Pride of ownership anchored Phellipe and the community to the land.

We had scheduled to meet at the little information stand Anfitriões had set up high up in Cosme Velho. To get there I jumped into a cab in Flamengo and headed up the valley, moving slowly through the congested traffic of a high-density canyonland of buildings.

When the road widened into a plaza and bus terminal, a placard caught my attention. I stepped out of the cab and into the swirling mist of the overcast afternoon. "Rio Carioca," it read, and gave the length of the river, 2.6 miles, and its destination, Flamengo Beach. It was the first sign of the stream since I'd left the flats, and I was glad for it—nothing else about this place hinted that a river ran through it.

Behind the graffiti-tagged sign was a cement wall, about waist high, enclosing an oblong opening. I peered into a shallow well. It was a window onto the subterranean river. We'd been driving right over it the whole time. Gray water rushed past the unbroken darker gray of its cement banks, filtering through shredded plastic bags, broken toys, and sun-bleached soda bottles. The cloying smell of pure sewage was familiar. We were some two miles from the beach and already the Carioca was no more than a conveyor of waste. Still, it was a glimpse of the river. I was on my way.

I was back in the cab for just few minutes when we passed a narrow entrance to a dead-end street. From the taxi I had seen quick flashes of color within—pastel yellow, robin's egg blue, pale pink, and minty green. I'd been on the lookout for this. It was the Largo do Boticário, a square named after a druggist who'd done very well for himself by bottling and selling the waters of the Carioca for their healthful qualities. He'd owned this land and in 1836, he broke it up into lots for sale. I asked the driver to pull over, and walked in along a narrow lane paved in wide flagstones to an intimate little plaza.

A hush closed in as I stepped into the square and away from the busy street. Facing me, silent and shuttered, were two- and three-storied neocolonials, dilapidated, with patches of crumbled plaster but still showing their bright colors. The forest rose behind them, filtering the watery light of the overcast afternoon into a dappled green. Hand-painted tiles with blue, white, or yellow geometric designs ran in decorative friezes around windows, doors, and benches.

The drizzle thickened into a soft rain, heightening the colors and bringing a chill to the air. In the middle of the square was a small pillar that read, in Portuguese, "You who live in this nook, blessed by water and silence, remember that the enchantment of this place depends on you."

Indeed, the corner felt ethereal, set apart from the frenzy of the metropolis. I heard the three-toned call of the flycatcher, the coo of a dove, the drip of water from the eaves onto the stone below and, under these layers, a whisper—the sound of a rushing stream. I turned around. I'd walked right over the river. The flagstone walkway was a tiny bridge over the Carioca.

Kneeling on a cement bench bordered with tiles that had spiderwebbed with cracks, I looked down. The river was walled in, with ancient stone steps leading down to the water, but here it gurgled along on a natural riverbed, through moss and clumps of grass, under fiddleheads of ferns that nodded and dripped in the rain. The fresh scent of wet vegetation was still tainted with sewage, and the water had a whitish hue, but it was distinctly cleaner. Much of the pollution poured into the river below this point, as it ran under and through densely populated middle-class neighborhoods, including my own, Flamengo.

Minutes later, I found Phellipe huddled under a white tarp with his teenage charges. The boys were surly; it was wet and downright cold. They didn't expect many tourists. Phellipe was free; from that point on, I'd go with him, to see the Rio Carioca he knew.

In his car now, we turned up the mountain. Soon the pavement went from asphalt to well-worn black cobblestones. Houses gave way to trees on a road carved into the mountain. He pulled over. A deep valley ran parallel with the road. On the opposite slope, the modest brick homes of Guararapes clung to the steep terrain. This was where he lived, he said, pointing at a well-built plastered home near the top. To the right and above the community, a wall of greenery rippled in the rain, dotted with the mango-yellow and fuchsia copses of the first blooming trumpet trees. The Tijuca National Park surrounded Phellipe's stretch of the community.

And then I saw it: a steam ran at the very bottom of the crevasse. It was the Carioca. We picked our way down to the path by the water. Here was something that looked and smelled like a mountain creek as it meandered past smooth boulders and bamboo thickets. A mutt, unused to strangers, growled at us. Phellipe shushed it. We walked along the dense vegetation by the water's edge: strangler figs, towering jackfruit trees with their lumpy, rough-skinned fruit, and a tangle of vines that draped to the ground. Raindrops tapped on the broad leaves of banana trees.

Here and there, tubes of PVC tubing snaked down the hillsides, each contributing one home's worth of waste to the stream. This was where the problem started. There were no other homes above. It was no different than what happened farther down the line, except in Guararapes it was aboveground, visible.

Knowing pollution of this sort happened elsewhere, everywhere, was no help to Phellipe. The fact that his own community contributed to the slow death of the creek he'd bathed in as a child upset him. He dropped his cheery veneer and began to talk, his right hand making hard chopping motions as he listed his efforts with Anfitriões: they'd helped organize trash pickup along the river to prevent flooding when it rained, and set up a community recycling program. The money they raised was used to buy bags of rice and beans for the poorest in Guararapes.

"We work with the national park, do our part with the kids, teach them something about this place," he said as we turned and hiked back out of the valley. "It belongs to us. But we have no resources to deal with this," he said, pointing at the pipes dipping into the river.

Back in the car, Phellipe released his pent-up frustration. The only faces of government the residents of Guararapes, and the nearby favelas of Cerro Corá and Vila Cândido, saw regularly were the police officers who started patrolling once a UPP was inaugurated in mid-2013. Otherwise, these favelas went without basic services, whether it was sanitation or the shoring up of the precarious slopes that sometimes crumbled in the rain, as they had in 2010, taking down a house with three little girls who'd been asleep inside. Phellipe was among those who dug until daybreak looking for them, only to find they'd been crushed under a water tank.

It was getting dark, and we were drenched. But Phellipe had one more thing to show me: the Mãe d'Água, a name that means Mother of the Water. I'd never heard of it, but I was curious. We headed up the mountain again. The road turned and doubled back as it led us higher. On the left plunged a ravine; on the right rose the mountain, dense with greenery. We were deep in the forest, the only ones out there in the gloom and the rain. He pulled over at a tight bend in the road. Outside, the air was rich with the decay of leaves, wet earth, and the flowering of something intensely sweet. Birds trilled in the heavy tree cover. Walking across the street, I looked down at the ravine and saw the tops of the redbrick houses. We were above Guararapes. A trickle of the river spewed from a pipe that ran under the road, cascaded down, and collected in a pool below.

Phellipe led me back across the street, to a small flat-roofed structure of granite blocks with a broken-down doorway nearly hidden under a shaggy canopy of vines and encroaching vegetation. Graffiti tags in red and black covered the outside. This, Phellipe told me, was the Mãe d'Água, where the Carioca was first gathered and channeled into the aqueduct for delivery in the city below. I'd wanted to see the river's origin, and this was it, he told me.

I'd biked past it before and never gave it a second look. Now I saw that on the side facing the street there was a stone plaque with deeply etched writing. It was so covered in graffiti I had to trace the sharp angled letters with my finger to understand: "During the reign of Dom João V . . ." This was the name of the Portuguese king under whom it had been built, and at the very bottom, the year: 1744.

Just above us, beyond a broken-down iron fence, were the

reservoirs where the water was collected before flowing into the aqueduct. A waist-high gate was shut with twine. All of it was abandoned. Phellipe was clearly ready to leave, but I couldn't just yet.

In his *History of Portuguese America*, published in 1730, the historian Sebastião da Rocha Pita described a "copious river called Carioca, of pure and crystalline waters." Locals believed its waters "made gentle the voices of musicians and beautiful the faces of women," he wrote. That was the river I wanted to see.

Phellipe shrugged his shoulders. I could do what I liked; he was done being wet and would wait in the car.

I vaulted the arrow-tipped spikes of the fence and lowered myself down on the other side. Mangoes and overripe jackfruit littered the ground; the humidity intensified their sweet-sour scent. A banana tree held out its little hands of ripening fruit. No one had bothered to harvest any of it; the place felt truly abandoned. Straight ahead was a stone wall mottled orange and green with lichen and moss. A stairway led up its side.

At the top were the old reservoirs, three huge stone basins where much of Rio's water was once held. They now had saplings sprouting out of cracks in the sturdy masonry, their roots slowly prying apart blocks of granite. Toward the back there was a smaller reservoir, and above it what looked like a control room. I climbed farther, stepped in. Broken glass crunched under my heels, and what was left of wooden windowsills and doorjambs lay soft and rotting underfoot.

The mountain loomed behind the reservoir, enshrouded in vegetation that swayed with the rain. Dusk deepened the shadows, but I could hear the rush and gurgle of running water.

I stepped gingerly over the thick stone wall that circled the back of the reservoir and onto the mountain's variegated granite. There the river ran clear and cold. It spouted out of a thicket above, then coursed along a sharp fault line in the rock. Below my feet it dove down and around the reservoir, into a diversion that would send it pouring above Guararapes.

I sat with it for a moment, feeling the bare rock beneath me, fingers in the water, drenched by the rain. The darkness brought the forest close, and the air was soft, deep, lanced with sounds of life heard but not seen. I felt if I cupped the stream in my hands I should see reflected in it the Carioca, the mountain, the landscape that unfolded around as it once was, as Darwin had seen it, too beautiful for words; as the historian Rocha Pita had seen it a hundred years before Darwin; and as the indigenous Tupi had seen it before the Portuguese ever set foot on this mountain.

The city I loved, with its arresting combination of rock and water, white sand and emerald forest, was a mutilated poem, missing some of its grandest passages: the whales that had once migrated past Ipanema, their passage now recorded in the name of that rocky outcropping, Arpoador; the dolphins that are part of the city's shield, now seen far more often emblazoned on the sides of municipal buses than in the polluted bay; and the Carioca itself.

I had gone looking for a physical river but also for the story that it told about the city. The two have been closely twined for centuries; the Carioca had shaped life in Rio, and Rio in turn had transformed the river. It was now a turbid reflection of the metropolis and its perverse relationship with its privileged natural setting.

I got up, cold and dispirited, and walked down to the car where Phellipe waited. As he drove me back down we chatted about his work, and what he hoped to see for his community, the teenagers he worked with, the river.

What would it take for the Carioca to run clean all the way to the ocean? Money, tremendous political will, and cooperation from the population. It would also take coordination between the city of Rio, responsible for the welfare of its rivers, and the state of Rio, in charge of Guanabara Bay, the ocean, and the beaches.

None of this was forthcoming.

If one looked beyond the river to Guanabara Bay, the outlook was a little more promising. Cleaning it up was one of Rio's Olympic bid promises. The bay would host the sailing competition; floating trash could ensnarl a boat and cost an athlete a medal. This created a firm deadline and directed funds to the issue.

Carlos Minc, the environmental secretary for the state of Rio, had assured me that Rio would be ready in time. He had launched a series of programs that, if successful, could go far toward cleaning Guanabara Bay and bringing basic sanitation to the population around it.

Some of the plans, such as the closure of dumps like Gramacho and the use of the minirobots within Rio's existing plumbing to root out illegal wastewater connections, were already under way. Others were just beginning. They included hooking bayside towns to a sewerage system, increasing the capacity and number of sewage treatment plants, and installing floating fences called eco-barriers across the mouths of rivers to keep out the trash that floated down.

Another plan was to build treatment units like the one at the Carioca's delta across the mouths of the five most polluted rivers draining into the bay. Of course, this would help clean up the bay, but would do nothing to improve conditions in the rivers. It simply recognized the waterways had become conveyors of wastewater, and treated them as such.

But even under the Olympic time pressure and with funding available, many of these projects were running late; several had not started at all. After the Olympics, there would be no drive to do it. Like most Cariocas, I was skeptical of how much would really be accomplished.

This wasn't the first time Cariocas had heard promises like this. In 1992, after the first UN environmental conference in Rio, authorities announced a large effort to build waste treatment plants with money from international bank loans and the state. More than twenty years and $760 million later, of the four plants built and inaugurated with due pageantry, one plant treated a trickle of sewage; the other three had never treated a drop. Why? No one ever built the connections between the plants and a sewerage system, or set up the pumping stations to feed them. Then, too, there had been money and political will, but not enough to stop the whole project from falling to mismanagement and corruption.

Axel Grael took a longer view of the issue. He was the former head of the state environmental agency and president of Projeto Grael, an environmental cleanup and education nonprofit that focused on the bay.

The Grael family has a keen interest in seeing conditions improve. They also know Guanabara Bay far better than most; it is their backyard. Axel's brothers, Lars and Torben, are Olympic medalist sailors who refined their skills in its waters. Torben's daughter, the twenty-two-year-old Martine Grael, also grew up sailing in the bay and hoped to qualify in the Rio Olympics.

When Rio hosted the World Military Games in 2011, Grael's nonprofit was hired for an emergency cleanup of the sailing lanes. Using specially outfitted boats with nets, they hauled half a ton of trash out of the water just ahead of the race. This kind of Band-Aid approach wouldn't do for the Olympics, he said. This work took years, decades, to carry out well. He was not optimistic.

Rio had been born by the bay, by the mouth of the Carioca. A walk from its delta to its source took me back in time and revealed much about the past, and how the city's waterways became so polluted. But to see where the city was headed, I needed to leave the old city behind and go out west, to the suburbs of Barra da Tijuca and beyond. They were Rio's urban frontier. A drive out there was a glimpse of Rio's future.

CHAPTER 11

LONG LIVE CONSTRUCTION

Pushing through undergrowth in galoshes and a raincoat, picking off the gnats that stuck to my face, I wondered for the third or fourth time that morning whether this outing was a good idea.

The ankle-deep mud threatened to suck my boots off my feet and I was having trouble sticking close to the man in front of me, a biologist in a chewed-up canvas hat and those funny-looking FiveFingers shoes. Plus, we were looking for *jacarés-do-papo-amarelo*, or broad-snouted caimans, and I wasn't quite sure how I'd feel when we found one. These South American cousins of the alligator are extremely territorial and grow to between six and eight feet long. Older males in the wild can reach eleven feet of tough leather, teeth, and muscle, with a bite that could easily crack a turtle shell. Or a shinbone.

This bushwhacking was part of a class given by the biologist Ricardo Freitas. He's a caiman expert and offered the only hands-on classes on crocodilian handling in the country. Twenty-five academics and wildlife veterinarians had flown from central and northern Brazil to Rio for the chance to learn Ricardo's techniques. By the end of the weekend, we'd know how to capture, measure, tag, and then safely release the pissed-off, manhandled creatures.

Western Rio was the place to find them. This stretch of the city stood at the foot of a mountain range that included metropolitan Rio's tallest peak, the Pedra Branca, and was enshrouded in a 31,000-acre forest, the Pedra Branca State Park. Runoff coursed from its heights into the flatlands, where mangrove forests and interconnected lagoons sheltered more than five thousand creamy-bellied *Caiman latirostris.*

Ricardo was optimistic. It was just a matter of time, he whispered over his shoulder. They loved this narrow, leafy channel that formed a natural bridge between two brackish lagoons. This marshy landscape had always been their home, he said. Jacarepaguá, the neighborhood I'd driven through to meet him, had an indigenous name that meant "place of *jacarés.*"

But more than that—they had nowhere else to go. Running alongside the walled-in banks of this little canal were residential streets with gated buildings where penthouse apartments sold for a million dollars.

Women wrapped in neon spandex leaned over the railing to watch Ricardo muck around as they headed for their constitutional along the beach less than two blocks away. An elderly couple walking their poodle stopped to ask: was it true the beasts could snack on pets?

The contrast was surreal, but the home of jacarés—the region that included Barra da Tijuca, Recreio dos Bandeirantes, Jacarepaguá, and others—was also the fastest-growing part of the city. Nowhere was Rio's physical transformation more visible than in its western suburbs.

As fast as change had come over the past few years, this process would only continue to accelerate until 2016. This ecologically fragile part of Rio would host the greatest number of Olympic venues. According to Rio's bid, the sporting event would highlight the city's natural assets and provide leverage to remedy existing damage. These promises had been an essential aspect of selling Rio as a candidate city. A discourse analysis of the Olympic bid showed that "environment" or its variation, "environmental," was the second most used word after "security."

How did the fast-paced development of the west side, and the impending Olympic project, fit into this picture?

The answer started with the crocs. They'd been there first. They were also tougher than other species, built to adapt and withstand conditions that could wipe out other critters. They would be my gauge.

To Cariocas living in a city squeezed by natural features, where buildings rise shoulder to shoulder, blocking views and airflow, the western suburbs offered space. Relatively undeveloped until the 1980s, the region had absorbed most of Rio's residential expansion since then. I knew the area well. My parents had moved into one of its first gated communities when they relocated to Rio from abroad; decades later, my brother followed after his second child was born.

Going to see my family meant an hour's drive from Flamengo. The route itself reveals Barra's appeal. It starts within the perennially jammed streets of Botafogo, once an elite bedroom community, now a throughway in which streets are lined with a jumble of residential buildings, shops, schools, and government buildings and the roads are thick with buses, motorcycles, cars. Pedestrians spill off its narrow sidewalks and cyclists weave through traffic, each adding to the confusion. The drive continues through the clogged streets of other packed neighborhoods—Humaitá, Jardim Botânico—before diving into the tunnels that lead out west.

To enter Barra da Tijuca, the first of the western neighborhoods, after all that chaos and congestion is like coming up for air.

Drivers emerging from the last tunnel have the ocean on the left and a lagoon backed by luxuriantly green mountains to the right. A sign says "Welcome to Barra."

Gone are the pedestrians, the diesel belches, the visual clutter. The west is sleek, with sixteen-lane highways, luxury malls, and gated communities. This is a landscape designed for cars, not pedestrians. Residential life is contained within condomínios, guarded and enclosed collections of buildings and houses that promise to deliver everything that was lost as Rio grew: tranquility, fresh air, safety. Some of these condomínios hark back to that paradise lost with names such as Nova Ipanema, or New Ipanema, where my parents lived, or Novo Leblon. Others have even more nakedly aspirational names that suggest, in English or a suitable European language, a privileged life: Les Résidences de Monaco, Riveira dei Fiori, Barra Golden Green. The rarefied airs are partly justified: if considered separately from the rest of Rio, the region has a Human Development Index score on par with Norway and New Zealand.

Maintaining this segregated lifestyle in an unequal society has a cost that goes beyond condo fees and gasoline bills; it is essentially a life behind gilded bars. Going to see my parents means driving up to gates flanked by armed guards, then waiting as one security officer, protected by a cabin, calls their apartment. Permission to enter granted, the gate opens and I pull into an idyllic once-upon-a-time land where children still play in the streets and where there are extensive landscaped gardens for running and hiding as well as playgrounds, sports fields, swimming pools, a restaurant, and a bar. One's entire life, or at least a certain kind of life, could be completely contained within the community's tree-lined streets: there is a hair salon, a massage studio, waxing and manicure facilities, a bakery, a convenience store, and a private school.

The Barra way of life has a lot of takers—including the Olympic Games. There will be competitions in the south, along Ipanema,

Copacabana, and Flamengo; in the center-north, home of the Maracanã and Engenhão stadiums; and in Deodoro, in the northwest. But the west side will host the main Olympic sports cluster, with fifteen venues housing competitions from boxing and table tennis to swimming and gymnastics.

As the Rio 2016 Organizing Committee put it, the region provides a "truly beautiful setting . . . surrounded by lagoons, mountains and parks." They forgot to mention the beaches—more than sixteen miles of dazzling white sand facing the Atlantic. The potential was evident, and most everyone wanted a piece.

This meant the place was a construction zone. On each visit, I watched construction crews birth high-rises of 10, 15, 20 stories out of earthen craters. While the population of Rio had grown about 8 percent between 2000 and 2010, Barra's population grew by 47 percent, according to the census. But that's practically sluggish compared to stretches even farther west—Jacarepaguá, Recreio dos Bandeirantes, and other neighborhoods—where the buildings popped up like mushrooms after the rain to house a population that had expanded by up to 150 percent. Altogether, Barra and the eight surrounding neighborhoods had added an astounding 278,000 new residents during those ten years. Traffic thickened and slowed to a crawl even on the sleek new highways.

This mad race showed no signs of stopping. Hotel chains were busy adding nearly 4,000 rooms in the area in anticipation of the Olympics. Between 2010 and the Games, Barra was expected to gain another 65,000 residents or so, and Jacarepaguá, another 53,000, according to the Instituto Pereira Passos, an urban planning organization connected to the city government.

Even the transportation projects that were promised as one of the most useful Olympic legacies in this gridlocked city—an extension of the subway and nearly one hundred miles of exclusive bus lanes, part of a Bus Rapid Transit (BRT) system—all fed the west side. The Transcarioca BRT linked it to the international airport;

the Transolímpica BRT, to working-class neighborhoods to the north. The Transoeste BRT, the first one completed, plowed over virgin marshland as it reached from the center of Barra to the city's far western border. New gated communities sprouted in its wake.

All this, remember, in the "place of jacarés."

No one knew Rio's caimans like Ricardo, the biologist who'd founded the Instituto Jacaré. Since 2000, when he established the research center, he'd caught, tagged and cataloged nearly five hundred of them. But on the wet, early spring day when I joined him on the banks of that muddy creek, a southwest wind streaked with rain lowered temperatures. Leaden clouds smudged out the sun. It wasn't good caiman-catching weather. The cold-blooded animals found it warmer in the water.

After a few hours of tramping around, we'd seen dozens of eyeballs and nostrils prick the creek's surface, but few caimans loitering on the banks. Those we did see slid with surprising speed through the brush and swam away as we approached, shying away from the bits of fish tied to a rope that we dragged through the water as bait. Although Ricardo said the caimans generally posed no threat to people—or poodles, for that matter—we were not ready to wrestle a healthy, unwilling croc out of the water. We decided to break for lunch and try later. If the caimans weren't out in the cold, there was no reason why we should be.

I went with Ricardo, his intern Camila, and a handful of graduate students to a beachfront barbecue joint. Almost on cue, the clouds broke and let through a watery sunshine. We huddled around an outdoor table and ordered a bucket of beers. Even in informal Rio, we drew stares: after a morning of sloshing around canals, we were covered in mud. With the dirt, our bush-beating outfits, and green-eyed Ricardo's five-day beard and beaten-up hat, we could have been extras in an Indiana Jones movie.

The conversation turned to the flurry of development that was burying these wetlands in concrete slabs. Much of this new construction, from the Olympic sites to the mega-highways to the private housing, was being done by draining or filling the marshy land. This was anathema to the croc lovers gathered there.

Ricardo reached into the ice bucket for a beer. The Pan-American Games should have been a lesson, he said.

"We're still cleaning up and paying for that mess," he said.

The 2007 competition was seen as a trial run for the 2016 Olympics. But as Ricardo pointed out, it could also serve as a warning. Operationally, the games were a success, but their price tag was a shocker. The competition that had been billed at $250 million cost public coffers at least $1.15 billion, according to the Tribunal de Contas da União, or TCU, a federal auditing body. It may be more; at the time of the report's writing the government had not fully accounted for all expenses. Even without knowing the total cost, the 2007 Pan-American Games was the most expensive in the history of the event, and fifteen times more expensive than the previous edition in Santo Domingo in 2003.

Beyond being grossly over budget, the Pan-American Games also left behind structures that were underused and expensive to maintain. Some were passed on to private initiatives and closed to public use. Others were just plain shoddy, including the Pan's most visible and most expensive venue, the Estádio Olímpico João Havelange, also known as the Engenhão. At $192 million, it was six times over budget. It was also passed on to the private sector—in this case, a soccer team—for a modest rent of $15,000 a month plus maintenance expenses.

The stadium turned out to have such serious structural defects that it was forced shut in March 2013, less than six years after its inauguration. The absurdity of it was on everyone's mind: Rio's mayor had admitted in a press conference that "depending on wind velocity and temperature," the roof could collapse or blow off.

The Engenhão had never been a popular arena, but with the Maracanã closed for Olympic reforms, it was the only one Rio's teams had at the moment. Shutting it down left soccer-mad Cariocas without a stadium—for how long, no one knew. Officials estimated it would be back up in 2015, after yet more money was spent expanding its seating capacity from 45,000 to 60,000 for the Olympics, when it is slated to host the track and field events.

Most of the Pan's venues had been built out in the west, establishing the model that would be followed with the Olympics. One in particular became a symbol of the poor planning, the expense, and the questionable motives that marred many of these works: the Vila Pan-Americana, or Vila do Pan. This condomínio of seventeen buildings was raised on a forested strip of land between a creek and the Camorin lagoon through a public-private partnership, a collaboration between local government and a construction firm. It was meant to house the athletes and later be sold as residential units.

The project raised questions from the start. Yes, the state had a desperate need for housing—in 2007 it was 338,068 units short. But most of the demand was among families earning less than eight thousand dollars a year, according to the Brazilian Institute of Geography and Statistics. Why were Rio authorities creating incentives for private enterprise to build yet another upper-middle-class development?[1]

The Vila do Pan was also a very expensive option for housing the athletes. Each day they spent there cost taxpayers $568.50—nearly double the $300 daily rate charged by premium hotels in the area.

But the Vila's biggest flaw was only revealed once the athletes

---

[1] In addition to not helping remedy Rio's low-income housing deficit, building the Vila do Pan required the removal of about one hundred favela houses. The reason given was that these houses were an environmental threat.

were gone. Its pastel-colored towers had been laid over unstable clay. In the years that followed, the ground shifted and subsided, sending long, jagged cracks down the condomínio's streets, exposing water and gas pipes, tilting electrical posts, and bending the metal gates.

Even as the city started building its Olympic sites, it was still throwing fistfuls of cash at the Vila do Pan to fix the disaster. Initially estimated to cost about $2 million to correct, the sinking grounds had swallowed more than $15 million by 2012. All this for apartments no one could love: in spite of the land grab out west, the Vila do Pan has never been more than two-thirds occupied. At night, when Barra's towers light up, its buildings are pocked with darkened windows.

The TCU concluded its report on the Pan-American Games by mentioning that they had provided a chance for this naturally exuberant city to set right its serious environmental problems. This opportunity had been wasted, the report said; efforts made were "timid, insufficient."

Now the Olympic preparations presented the city with a new chance. But from the perspective of the ecologists, biologists, and zoologists at the table, the Olympics were doing more harm than good. The new bus thoroughfares, the rush to build bigger, better, faster, funneling ever more residents into an area unprepared for the onslaught . . . Ricardo exhaled in frustration, took another swig, shook his head, and unleashed a stream of invective.

"The reality is fuck the animals, fuck biodiversity, fuck the laws, and long live construction," he said. "All of this is being done because some people will make a lot of money, and it's being done with no monitoring, no support, no rescue of species."

This was often how construction was done in Rio, he said. Out west there was simply more of it, happening faster than anywhere else in the city, with very little being done to mitigate the deforestation, loss of wetlands, and habitat disruption that it caused. Regulations governing construction on beachfronts and wetlands were being plowed under, he said, along with the flora and fauna. The laws that required a study of environmental impact before building were just not taken seriously.

"It's all just eyeball. You take a look around, see if you can spot animals. That's your environmental impact report," he said.

At that point, waiters interrupted us with great, bloody platters piled high with steak, grilled chicken, and sausage. Ricardo served himself a heaping plateful of beef and before tucking in, threw out a rhetorical question. "Really, what is the law when it stands in the way of what the government wants to do?"

That was the crux. Instead of providing oversight, Rio officials were actively shoving aside regulations to speed up the construction process. The most egregious example of this circumvention was the golf course being built for the Summer Games. I'd been following the story, as golf would be included in the Olympics for the first time in over a century.

From the start, negotiations surrounding its location were fraught. According to Rio's Olympic bid, the golf competition would be held at the private Itanhangá club. But in June 2011, Mayor Eduardo Paes announced to visiting members of the International Olympic Committee that there had been a change in plans.[2] Instead of refurbishing the private club, the city would build a brand-new course on a gorgeous stretch of white sand and coastal marsh bordering the Marapendi lagoon and facing the ocean. Best of all, he pointed out, this would come at no cost to the

---

2 Later in 2012, an investigation by city council members found that Itanhangá, the golf club named in the bid, was never approached about hosting the golf tournament. A letter released to the press by the club's president confirmed this; it also said he believed the club could have met Olympic requirements.

public; the developer would be paid with the right to build around the course.

The first hurdles were environmental. The plot, although degraded in parts by illicit removal of its white sand, was a legally protected area and home to a number of jacarés and other critters, among them two threatened species found only in Brazil—Lutz's tree iguana and the Fluminense swallowtail butterfly. But those were just the first concerns. Others would emerge as the project was pushed forward in 2012.

In March, the name of the course designer was announced by the local organizing committee with due pomp—after all, it would be a state-of-the-art three-hundred-acre course. A developer was chosen to lead the $30 million job. The cost would be borne by the construction company, as the mayor had said. As compensation, the firm earned the right to build twenty-two new high-rises right behind the course, facing the landscaped grounds, the lagoon, and the cool blue Atlantic beyond.

Official go-ahead came during an extraordinary session of the Rio de Janeiro City Council called for the afternoon of December 20. Most Cariocas were well into their summer vacations by then. In the meeting, council members approved one measure with several astonishing provisions. First, it green-lighted construction on the protected area. It also sliced an additional fourteen acres of forested grounds from a neighboring natural park—also habitat for the threatened butterfly and iguana—and added it to the course. Finally, it increased the height limit of the buildings that would be raised by the course developer from six to twenty-two stories.

The price tag on one penthouse apartment in the super-deluxe condomínio next door was $6 million. That's just the value of one penthouse.

The whole thing was authorized by the mayor in January 2013, still during the summer holidays, and rubber-stamped by the city's environmental department in April. There was no environmental impact report; the project was never put to public debate. Work began immediately.[3]

I raised the issue with Ricardo. As a biologist working in the area, he had been watching this unfold and, I hoped, could offer some insight on what a three-hundred-acre pesticide- and herbicide-fed lawn would mean for the region's ecology. This was marshy land, and the water table was high. Chemicals that leached into the groundwater would necessarily spread to the lagoon nearby.

But this was a charged topic for the croc expert. When the area was first mentioned as the site of the Olympic golf tournament, he'd sent an email to the local organizing committee warning that if they built a golf course out west, they'd have unexpected guests. He got no answer. But once work began and the jacarés started to show up, the company managing the site for Rio 2016 hired Ricardo to manage the animals.

"It's not that all of a sudden they're genuinely concerned with what happens to the jacarés," he said. "It's just that, because of the Olympic Games, they're a problem, and they need to be dealt with."

We wrapped up the lunch. The sun was burning off the puddles. Ricardo took deep drags on his cigarette as we talked and made our way back to the creek.

Ricardo fundamentally disagreed with the construction of the golf course, but figured the crocs would be better with him than without him. Part of what motivated these weekend courses was seeing the damage done when the crocs got in the way of construction or showed up in someone's swimming pool. They could end

---

3 Later, the head of the city's environmental department explained that the purpose of the environmental impact report is to investigate alternatives. As the city council and the mayor had already determined the golf course location, there was no need for a study.

up shot or injured—often with broken necks after being lassoed and yanked around.

Then there was the money. He earned twenty dollars an hour teaching ten hours of classes a week at a private university. The rest of his time went to the institute. He had to take consulting jobs to supplement his salary—things like pulling caimans out of condomínio fountains. Protecting jacarés on the site of the 2016 golf course was a good gig.

"I love my job, I love the animals, but there is no return in it, no money, no time to publish," he said, stubbing out his cigarette on the side of his pants and putting an end to the conversation. "So. Let's catch come crocs."

The afternoon was warm now, the air thick and moist; good weather for jacarés. Their eyes and nostrils cut through the creek's nearly stagnant surface. Several were sunning themselves by the water. We spread out along the banks. I stayed with the intern, Camila, who was standing on a narrow footbridge spanning the creek and tying squishy fish parts to the end of a rope. Once she had her line baited, she threw it into the water and gave it a couple of tugs so that it slapped the water like a flailing fish. This awakened immediate interest: a couple of crocs turned in our direction. A few more slaps of the rope and two pairs of protruding eyes began gliding our way. Their wakes spread, overlapped, and seemed to stir up interest in the other caimans. We had an audience.

One middle-aged woman in sarong and bikini top stopped on her way to the beach to berate Camila for fouling the wooden bridge with the fishy stench. It was true the bag reeked. So did Camila, who was elbow-deep in blood and guts. Face smeared with fishy goo from pushing up her glasses with dirty hands, Camila glared at the beachgoer's fleshy, receding back.

"And they complain the jacarés are aggressive," she said under her breath. "She sniffs her own shit all day and she's complaining about fish?"

That was also true. Although the creek linked two lagoons in protected park areas, the smell was unmistakable: human feces. This creek was foul with sewage. It had the stink of the Carioca River and the same whitish scum frothing the banks. The wastewater poured out under the bridge from one of several cement tubes that opened over the stream. As I watched, a condom slid out and plopped into the water, its latex body undulating gently like some unknown invertebrate.

These western suburbs were sold with the promise that they offered Rio as it used to be—safe, calm, clean—but they were quickly catching up with the worst aspects of the old city. The mad dash to develop meant construction had far outpaced infrastructure; most buildings in Barra, Recreio, and Jacarepaguá had been thrown up before the region had a supporting sewerage system. This meant they either built their own treatment plants, as the law required, or they dumped their sewage fresh out of the toilet into the streams and lagoons via the rainwater mains. With little monitoring, entire gated communities, malls, and office parks did the latter.

According to the state secretary for the environment, Carlos Minc, nearly $35 million were being invested in new pipes and pumping stations in the region to improve the situation. The new infrastructure would run through what was being called the "Olympic Axis," and included the future Olympic Park, several centers, hotels, office parks, and condomínios. During a visit to the construction site in September 2013, he'd said projects costing $350 million had already brought significant improvements over the previous six years. During that time, sanitation in the region had gone from zero to 60 percent. This was indeed real progress. With the new lines in the ground, any new construction would have a formal system available to which it could connect.

The problem, as Camila pointed out in a huff, was what we

could see and smell in the canal. The vast majority of houses, high-rises, and stores erected before the infrastructure was in place had been blithely pouring their untreated waste into nature for decades. Once sewage pipes were installed in the area, they were expected to follow the law and connect to the formal system within sixty days—at their own expense. Whether this happened or not, the water and sewerage company began charging them for the service, the street was checked off the dirty list, and the percentage of the region considered to have basic sanitation treatment grew.

This was why the canal that opened onto the beginning of Barra beach rendered that stretch of ocean unfit for bathing, although official statistics showed 85 percent of the neighborhood was reputedly connected to sanitation treatment. That canal was the end point of the western lagoon complex and its direct connection to the ocean. It was so foul with sewage that one biologist referred to it as Barra's rectum. From that opening, a brown stain fanned out over the ocean.

The state environmental department did spot compliance checks, fining some of the larger violators. This included several large condomínios that were found pouring their wastewater into lagoons and creeks that, as Camila had noted, were within reach of their residents' noses as they enjoyed their spacious porches.

Minc, the state environmental official, had taken to physically stoppering pipes carrying sewage from the most egregious repeat offenders. He called this simple but effective strategy an "ecological cork." But there was not enough manpower to check each building, each mall and office park; there was also no treatment available to the favelas that had sprung up to house the army of service workers who staffed the west's housing complexes. And so the creeks filled with sewage, turning neon green when the summer sun fed the photosynthesizing cyanobacteria that thrived in them.

Untrammeled development without adequate planning, together with Rio's habitual environmental neglect, resulted in what we could see in the canal that day: shit flowing, unchecked, even along Rio's urban frontier.

"The biggest danger to us in this work isn't really the jacaré, it's the water," Ricardo said, explaining the risks start with exposure to hepatitis A and go from there. "That's the reality we work with as urban biologists."

As we continued the conversation, four crocs had surrounded Camila's slapping fish. They hung back, cautious. Then in one furious whip of the tail, one of them lunged for the fish and snapped its jaws around it. The rope with the bait was tied so that it looped around his upper jaw. As the animal thrashed, this closed around its bony upper mandible although the tether stayed loose.

"Hold steady!" Ricardo yelled as he ran off the bridge and down to the banks of the creek. He waded in, stirring up bubbles of sulfurous gases and cursing the filth he was sinking into. "Shit, shit, shit, fuck this fucking shit!"

As the caiman calmed down, Camila slowly walked toward the bank, gently pulling the ensnared croc through the water. The animal shook its massive head every once in a while in annoyance, but otherwise allowed its body to glide toward Ricardo.

Once near the muddy shore, Ricardo took the rope and tugged it toward land, where we waited. As he pulled, the professor explained that this process of capture and measurement doesn't hurt the animals. Inexperienced handlers often use a tool that looks like a stick with a metal loop at the end to lasso the animal. The length of the stick keeps the crocs away and makes the handler feel safer, but it isn't flexible and can dislocate or break the animal's vertebrae, he said. The method he was showing us required some training but was safe for the caimans.

It took some tugging to land the croc, but once there, it stood absolutely still, as if wondering what to make of all this. Its mouth, which turns up at the corners, giving it a wicked grin, was agape and showed jagged, yellowed teeth; its golden eyes, divided by a narrow black slit, were on us. Ours never left it. We had all seen how fast these creatures could move.

Ricardo approached, tapping the animal on the nose a few times. Its mouth opened wide. Ricardo held his canvas hat in his hand, then thrust its brim toward the croc. The great maw snapped shut; the ecologist immediately reached underneath its chin with one finger and tilted its head all the way up. He then pinched the jaws shut between his forefinger and thumb.

So that was why Ricardo's hat looked so chewed up. This time the caiman missed it, but sometimes it was faster.

"You've got to work with its anatomical limitations," he said, still holding the jaw shut with one hand.

Although the jacaré's jaw is powerfully muscled, nearly all that strength is used to cinch its viselike bite, he said. Once the mouth is closed, the musculature to open it is weak—so weak the jaws can be held together with two fingers. Ricardo swung his leg around the croc, crouched over it, and taped the mandible shut. Once the feet were also bound, the animal could be measured and studied. This one was six feet long and sixty-four pounds. Figuring out the gender required Ricardo to stick a finger in the animal's cloaca, an all-purpose excretory and reproductive opening, to search for a curved, retractable penis. The croc submitted with resignation. No penis was found—it was a rare female.

The less experienced members of the institute got a chance to handle the next bit of work: give the croc a microchip tag between its clawed fingers and slice off a designated sequence of scales on its tail. This combination gave the animal a unique marking and gave the researchers blood and bits of osteoderm—thick, hard jacaré skin—to test for heavy metal exposure. As they worked, Ricardo took a moment to answer some of my questions about what all the west-side development meant from a croc's perspective.

Ricardo was thrilled that this animal was female. That's because 85 percent of the nearly 500 jacarés captured so far in their survey are male. They're not sure exactly why this is yet; more study is needed. But they have a theory. The abundance of organic matter—the fermenting shit that burped up gases when Ricardo walked into the creek—makes the muck along the banks where the animals build their nests warmer. Since gender is determined by temperature, an imbalance there could lead to a preponderance of males. The long-term effect of this skewed ratio was obvious.

There were myriad other problems. Their food options were growing more limited: a look at the content of dead animals' stomachs found they were living largely off insects and food people threw at them—things like crackers, sometimes still in their packaging. The crustaceans, fish, frogs, birds, and small mammals the jacaré usually relies on were rare treats. As creek banks were cemented and condomínios loomed alongside lagoons, the crocs had difficulty finding room for their leafy, muddy nests. Ricardo had even found them nesting inside the big cement tubes that carried sewage. The scarcity of food, the close quarters, and their territorial nature made for an unhealthy combination that led to fights. Even their genetic diversity was threatened. The built urban environment made it increasingly hard for animals to travel to other ponds to crossbreed.

The sun was starting to set. Our croc had long stopped struggling and had given herself up to being probed, handled, and photographed. There would be a lot of caiman-themed Facebook uploads that day. Our work done, we untied the creature and watched as she slid back into the water and became another pair of golden-yellow eyes pricking the murky green surface.

The crew was packing up and preparing for the nighttime part of the course. This involved capturing jacarés in the water while balancing in a little rowboat, then hoisting the thrashing animals on board for measuring and tagging. I'd seen the boat. It was strapped to the roof of a car, and was about as long as some of the crocs out there. I'd had enough. I left them to it and headed to my parents' house for dinner. Within fifteen minutes the guards of Nova Ipanema were raising the security gate for me.

Six months later, I thought of Ricardo and his crew again. The Sunday paper carried a full-page advertisement for Riserva Golf, the condomínio that would rise by the Rio 2016 golf course. The super-deluxe marble-and-glass-skinned high-rises had apartments that were "suspended mansions," the ad said, costing between $2.3 million and $23 million each; even before the towers were erected, 60 percent of the units were reserved for prospective buyers. I'd clearly underestimated how much was to be made from this transaction.

The copy sang the new venture's pedigree, calling attention to such details as the filigreed glass entrance inspired by the Louis Vuitton store in Singapore. But the real attraction was the astounding natural surroundings: "the Marapendi lagoon, the vegetation of the Marapendi reserve, the blue ocean, and the future Olympic golf course." There was no mention of the crocs.

CHAPTER 12

THE BUSINESS OF SEX

It was midafternoon on Tuesday, the last full day of official Carnaval festivities, and the euphoria that builds during the five-day holiday was reaching its boiling point. A mass of revelers waited for the Banda de Ipanema, one of Rio's most beloved *blocos*, or roaming bands, under a furious afternoon sun. I stood on the beach, my back to the ocean, my arms wrapped around a palm tree, and wondered how long I'd last.

The permissiveness of Carnaval, the heady sensuality of Cariocas, and the ubiquitous beer sellers with their Styrofoam coolers conspired to turn the barely clad crowd surging past into an eroticized tangle of slick, tanned limbs that shimmied to the beat of the approaching band and threatened to dislodge me from my perch. This was the live-and-let-live Rio de Janeiro of stereotypes at a fever pitch, and the tableaus unfolding suggested that the city's reputation for openness and a fluid view of sex was at least partly deserved. In the thick of the crowd, eyes met, hands groped, and legs entwined as strangers of similar or opposite genders locked lips and bodies together with a hunger that was as intense as it was brief; seconds later they parted, carried by the throng into the arms of other anonymous revelers.

I was an island of fully clad sobriety in this surging erogenous sea, and worse, I was working, or trying to work; my reporter's notebook was tucked into the waistband of my shorts to keep from getting lost. I could feel its metal coil digging into my belly and its hard cover softening with perspiration.

I was attempting to report about an ongoing anti-homophobia campaign and the growth of gay tourism, particularly during Carnaval. More than a quarter of the three million or so tourists who flood Rio every summer are gay, lesbian, bisexual, or transgender. I intended to interview a few, which was why I had parked myself near the Rua Farme de Amoedo, a notorious open-air cruising ground, right when the most gay-friendly Carnaval *bloco* made its final and most disputed sally.

Not only was I getting smeared with other people's sunblock and sweat and drenched with sprays of the sweet sparkling cider that is a favorite with festive drag queens, but I was stuck, trapped by the humanity that surrounded me, and no one, gay or straight, could be bothered to stop for a chat. There is no sin south of the equator, songwriter Chico Buarque wrote; he could have been standing where I was that day when the words came to him.

It wasn't until the band had squeezed loudly, gleefully past that I let go of my tree and waded against the human tide toward Farme de Amoedo proper, looking for friends who'd said they could help. As I got closer to Farme's epicenter, there were fewer women, and for that matter, fewer men wearing anything beyond a *sunga*, the narrow band of spandex that Carioca men wrap around their midsection as beachwear. On occasion the *sungas* were accompanied by a Zorro mask, a pirate eye patch, or spray of jewel-hued feathers. But there was no mistaking it: the business on Farme that day was sex.

Eventually I found my friends, an engineer and a university professor as lithe and fit and attractive as the rest, but fully clad. We headed to the sand to sit and talk for a bit. With them was a young Frenchman on his fourth visit to Rio's Carnaval. Three out of four of Rio's LGBT tourists fit roughly into the same category as my new acquaintance: between twenty and thirty-five years old, in the city for about five days and ready to live it up.

These young men loved Rio and Rio loved them right back: LGBT visitors dropped upward of two hundred dollars a day, nearly triple what heterosexual tourists spent. This explained in part Rio's outreach and advertising campaigns. Certainly, the city cultivated a relaxed, accepting image, as the secretary of tourism had said: "The city of Rio is welcoming in its essence, and Carnaval is when it shows that most clearly." But there was also a lot of money to be made by packaging and selling this hospitality.

We spread sarongs on the sand, grabbed a round of beers, and I asked the young Frenchman what kept him coming back. He smiled. Not far from us was one of the outdoor showers Cariocas used to wash off the salt water after a dip in the ocean; our eyes followed a swarthy young man as he sauntered over for an open-air rinsing-off ritual that was as much a bath as a calculated display of body parts toned to perfection.

"There is so much seduction everywhere," said the Frenchman, sitting cross-legged by my side, his fingers fluttering generally in the direction of the showers, the sidewalk beyond, and the bars whose tables spilled out onto the street. "You are in overdrive, all the time."

Even after repeated returns, he was still a little shy of diving into the muscle-bound throng and hadn't mastered the Carioca confidence required to approach a stranger and extract a kiss. But he had also never paid for his liaisons, although such exchanges weren't uncommon among foreigners in town for a quick dip into Rio's good times, he said. This too I had gathered from the mismatched couples, gay or straight, canoodling on the beach. He found his partners online, at bars, on the beach and was never short of desirable company.

Rio certainly had its appeal—it had been elected the "Sexiest Place on the Earth" by the LGBT travel site TripOut, and with good reason—but it wasn't without a dangerous undercurrent.

Just days before, a taxi driver outside the international airport had attacked a gay couple from northern Brazil with homophobic slurs, then punches. The assault wasn't as serious as other cases of violence against the LGBT population that I'd written about since arriving; the men recovered and the driver was arrested. But it was also a sobering reminder of the social tensions coursing through Carioca culture.

I understood Rio's appeal to someone like my French interviewee. The shameless sexy on display had long been one of the city's more enticing aspects to visitors. This was a place where the heat and humidity encouraged a certain indolence, a sway and drag of step, and discouraged a whole lot of clothing. Men sauntered about shirtless and women reveled in their curves no matter their years and fitness level. This meant you could be engaging in some innocent or decidedly dull endeavor—bagging your purchases at a pharmacy or riding the elevator to the office—and suddenly get an eyeful of some deep cleavage or a clearly outlined rear end. This seemed to keep the collective libido stoked.

To me, this comfort with flaunting the flesh was refreshing after long seasons in countries where any display of the body was either forbidden or a pleasure permitted only to the thin, the young, and the perfectly fit. The Cariocas' apparent freedom, their exuberant public displays of affection, and their libidinous street parties often led foreigners to see Rio as a great free-for-all, a sexually fluid place that harbored few inhibitions.

Even while living abroad, I knew the reality wasn't that simple. True, sex seemed to be everywhere: in by-the-hour motels that did a banging business during lunch and after work; in the prime-time soaps churned out by the Rio studios of *Globo*, with their juicy close-ups of in-depth kissing; and in the explicit photos advertis-

ing the services of prostitutes—male, female, or transgender—that
turned downtown phone booths into cornucopias of sex to satisfy
any appetite. And yet, there were cases like that of the visitors
beaten before they even left the airport, and the more serious attacks that killed more than three hundred LGBT people a year in
Brazil.

"It's a city of extremes, Rio," the Frenchman granted, saying he
had heard the occasional homophobic comment. He'd never been
assaulted, but the worry hovered in the background. "Sometimes
I worry a little bit, I'm not sure how far I can go. Maybe I look at
the wrong guy in the eyes a little too long, maybe they're not gay."

Sorry I'd forced the conversation into such a gloomy turn, I let
my friends go back to the fun and elbowed my way to the subway.
Street parades had been going on for weeks. They start well before Carnaval's official opening day, and linger for days past their
traditional ending at noon on Ash Wednesday. I was beginning
to cave under the relentlessness of this inescapable party. Youngsters belted out Carnaval *marchinhas* inside the metro station, the
acoustics making their bass drum reverberate like peels of thunder;
sequined dancers on their way to the official Sambódromo parade
stuffed themselves and their great plumed shoulder harnesses into
the train and made the carriage pulse as they samba-stepped along
to some impromptu singing; by the time I got off at Flamengo Station, the pervasive tah-cah-TAH tah-cah-TAH tah-cah-TAH that
had once left me so nostalgic for Rio rung like a jackhammer inside my skull. I shut myself in my room, turned the air conditioner
way up, and churned out the article I'd been reporting.

That evening, disinclined to face the frenzy again, I curled
up on my couch to mull over the multi-hued hedonism outside.
At first glance, Brazil gave the impression of being a progressive
place: it had the world's largest gay pride parade, although in São
Paulo, not Rio; the prostitutes who traipsed up and down Copacabana's sidewalks had their profession codified by the Ministry of

Labor; the president, Dilma Rousseff, was a no-nonsense former guerrilla who took her oath of office accompanied not by a husband, as she was long divorced, but by her daughter.

Yet places of prostitution were being shuttered as the city gentrified, and reports of violence against women and the LGBT population were on the rise. Increased awareness of rights was a big part of this, certainly, but it didn't explain the numbers entirely. I turned these thoughts over in my mind that night and in years that followed as I tried to come to terms with another of Brazil's idiosyncrasies, brought to its zenith in Rio: the vibrant openness around issues of sex, sexuality, and gender relations that seemed to flourish alongside, and in spite of, deep pockets of machismo, homophobia, and a potential for violence. Now these areas were also undergoing a rapid succession of legal, social, and structural changes. What did this transformation mean for those whose lives were entangled in it?

The business of sex has been a notorious part of this port city since its earliest years. In 1820, French traveler Jacques Arago reported prostitutes to be "as numerous as at Paris," present "in every quarter and in every street." A journalist who wrote vivid memoirs of fin-de-siècle Rio, Vivaldo Coaracy, found the city replete with painted ladies who called from windows, bars, and brothels, part of echelons of depravity "that started with cachaça in São Jorge Street and ended up with the obligatory champagne of the chic pensions in Catete."

Convivência—the live-and-let-live art of coexistence—has always been a guiding principle in Rio. The city is dense, with deeply etched hierarchies of class, race, origin, and occupation. It is only through skilled maneuvering and obeisance to a shared code of conduct that distinctions can be maintained in such close quarters. Foreigners are often oblivious to the terms that regulate these interactions, and mistake Rio for a liberal paradise where blacks and whites, rich and poor, migrants and locals, prostitutes and ladies who lunch can mingle easily and without prejudice. Nothing could be further from the truth.

There have always been rigid, if unspoken, rules about sharing space. Vivaldo Coaracy, the journalist who wrote about Rio at the end of the nineteenth century, gave an insightful description of this balancing act in his account of the Confeitaria Colombo, a café that still serves full afternoon tea under gilded mirrors more than one hundred years later. Earlier in the day, well-to-do ladies would cluster around the little tables, gossiping and eating cake. Around 4 p.m., they cleared out en masse, leaving only the languid gentlemen of the literary set, still nursing their sherry. By 5 p.m., the place filled up again, this time with madams and prostitutes, some of them minor celebrities who would then hold court among the crystal and the marble.

I'd seen the same complicated ballet on the sidewalks of Copacabana: traditional restaurants with bow-tied waiters spread their tables onto the black-and-white mosaic walkway where prostitutes also cruised for clients, families took the evening air, street vendors hawked miniature Cristo statues to tourists, doormen kept watch, and beggars beseeched them all for change—each highly conscious of his place and his relationship to others, careful not to overstep his bounds and create unwelcome interactions.

As Rio de Janeiro began to polish its image, however, the balance created by this carefully orchestrated *convivência* was upset. The city's bordellos could be described as blight or as beloved institutions, depending on who's being asked, but while Brazilians largely shrugged their shoulders at what they saw as an entrenched aspect of urban life, blatant prostitution wouldn't do when the city was under the international spotlight. With the World Cup and the Olympics looming, the brothels, saunas, and clubs where the trade was plied began to suffer the biggest crackdown in decades.

The first to go had been the infamous Help!, a colossal disco-thèque whose neon lights had throbbed in the heart of Copacabana for twenty-five years, offering johns—most of them gringos, as it was a tourist favorite—their choice from among the two thousand prostitutes who rotated through during the week. It was closed down in January 2010 to make way for a music museum designed by the same firm that gave New York's Lincoln Center a facelift.

Another of the city's storied bordellos, the 1902 neoclassical Hotel Paris, was shuttered in 2011. It had anchored the lower-tier sex trade in Tiradentes square for decades. With its closure, Rio's respected prostitution rights organization, Davida, lost its home and dozens of prostitutes lost their place of work. The French brothers who bought it planned to turn it into a boutique hotel, Le Paris, with a rooftop pool and a daily rate of six hundred dollars.

The scrub-up extended to the square itself, which had been one of Rio's oldest cruising parks, surrounded by bars, theaters, musi-cal revues, and entertainment to suit all tastes. Its shrubbery had provided cover for prostitution and same-sex encounters since the days when Brazil was a monarchy. Now sex workers were being shooed from the ancient *sobrados* that surrounded it as the two- and three-story town houses were being converted into cultural cen-ters, art galleries, and office spaces.

This kind of turnover was happening all over the neighbor-hoods that would be most visible during the sporting events—downtown, the touristy south-side, and the port area, said anthropologists Thaddeus Blanchette and Ana Paula da Silva.

The couple have been studying Rio's sex industry since 2004. She's a Carioca of many generations, petite and very sharp; he's a native of Oshkosh, Wisconsin, with wire-rimmed glasses, a shaggy lefty-professor beard, and a disarming manner. Together they maintain a database of more than 50,000 reports about the places where people pay for sex in Rio, and draw from it a sprawling map of the industry with its 600 or so brothels. These range from a single tumble-down *sobrado* where sex can be had for a dollar a minute, to industrial-scaled Uruguaiana 24, a nondescript office building with four stories dedicated to the sex trade, to the exclusive Centauro, a three-story venue on a leafy Ipanema street that charges clients $60 just to step in the door. Centauro is a *termas*, or sauna, where clients relax in robes at the whiskey bar or take a steam bath before picking services from a menu that starts at $200.

The image-cleansing campaign of Rio's mayor was nothing new, Thad and Ana Paula told me over dinner one evening. The city has a history of pushing prostitutes out of the way: there have been eight government-led removals, cover-ups, or attempts to quash red-light districts over the past century. The most recent was in 1996, when a *zona* was cleared out to make way for the city's new administrative center. Carioca sense of humor being what it is, the imposing new structure was promptly nicknamed the *Piranhão*, or big piranha—slang for a sexually voracious woman.

A look at the times when the city turned against its prostitutes revealed primarily three motives, they said. The first were moments of international visibility, when officials wanted the city to look good to foreign eyes—the traditional *para inglês ver*. This was the case in 1920, when King Albert of Belgium came to town and police swept through, arresting lower-class prostitutes. It happened again in 1968, when police boarded up the main red-light district to conceal it from view during a visit by Queen Elizabeth II.

Another force had been urban renewal. This was behind the clearing out of the *zona* that had stood where the municipal administrative offices now rises, and more recently behind the closure of Help! and the Hotel Paris.

The last factor was the zeal of a powerful individual, such as a police chief or high city official who, seized with concern for the city's moral or physical health, had clamped down on the sex trade. This had happened during a vast sanitizing campaign in the first decade of the twentieth century and again under a particularly righteous police captain after World War II.

I'd landed in Rio at an extraordinary moment when all these factors seemed to be bearing down at once. Beyond brand-names like Help!, dozens of smaller, lower-end brothels were being shut down every year. What I didn't understand was the legal justification for all this. After all, prostitution has been listed under the Ministry of Labor's Classification of Occupations since 2002. The ministry describes sex professionals as men or women who "seek sexual programs; attend and accompany clients; participate in educational activities in the field of sexuality." This listing allowed them to take advantage of retirement and social security benefits, along with sick leave and other labor rights. I'd assumed this kind of official recognition guaranteed them a certain degree of protection.

This was why I'd invited the anthropologists over for dinner. Technically, prostitution is legal, but when officialdom deemed it necessary to go after prostitutes, it wasn't hard to find ways, Thad said. Although selling sex is a legally protected activity, profiting from it or inducing someone to do it is illegal, and the laws are vaguely worded. Profit can be interpreted as anything from exploitative pimping to running a brothel to renting an apartment, he said.

"You could sell a prostitute this piece of bread, and if someone wanted to go after you for it, they could," he said, holding up a chunk of the home-baked loaf he'd brought.

That meant sex establishments were always vulnerable to raids and remained open at the whimsy of the municipal or state administration or the local precinct chief. Plus, prostitutes were just as vulnerable to the forces of urban renewal and gentrification that were shifting thousands of lower-income residents in the city through eminent domain, increased rents, the sudden enforcement of long-neglected building codes, or demands for payment of old debts.

To understand what it would mean for the women (although there were plenty of men in the business, the majority of Rio's prostitutes were women) I spent some time at the next potential target: Vila Mimosa, a chaotic jumble of modest storefronts that make up Rio's biggest red-light district.

To the nearly two thousand women who rotate through this working-class *zona*, prostitution provides full-time work or a way to supplement incomes earned as cashiers, maids, or manicurists. To clients, Vila Mimosa offers quick, easy sex and a cold beer in a convenient location. It is just one subway stop from downtown and a five-minute walk from a station serving dozens of major bus lines. Highways connecting the heart of the city to far-flung suburbs crisscross nearby.

The Vila occupies an unattractive geographic space, sandwiched between highways, rail lines, and warehouses. But in this changing city, what had been undesirable was suddenly prime real estate. The area was right on a proposed route for the planned bullet train that would connect Rio to São Paulo—one of the projects aimed at revamping Brazil's decrepit transportation infrastructure. Before the government opened bidding to prospective builders, I stopped by.

I got there just after 5 p.m., when offices downtown disgorged hordes of workers and Vila Mimosa's business picked up. Bass-heavy funk rattled metal tables set out on the sidewalk and shirtless men fired up makeshift grills next to coolers of beer. Women in thong bikinis or Day-Glo lingerie that popped against their dark skin lounged about in plastic chairs, swinging their heels, or leaned against doorways, smoking, waiting. They were young and old, fresh-faced and worn, brunettes and bottle blondes. I saw bellies scarred by C-sections, crisscrossed with stretch marks, rippling with rolls of fat squeezed by too-tight elastic bands. I also saw lithe, flawless, taut young bodies and faces as mainstream pretty as any picture in a magazine. They represented a cross section of Rio's working-class women, much as you'd find in an express bus headed for the northern suburbs at the end of a long day.

Although the bullet train was still in the planning stage, the women were worried. Cris, a curvaceous black woman who was getting ready for rush hour by applying bright pink lipstick to match her vivid spandex top, agreed to talk over a beer.

She was frank. There's nothing appealing about Vila Mimosa. The bottom floor of most houses had been converted to basic bars—chipped Formica counters, plastic stools—or nightclubs blaring distorted music out of insufficient speakers so dancers could gyrate under a lone disco ball. The sex took place on the second floor, where small, windowless cubicles branched off a narrow central corridor. For as little as eighteen dollars, a customer got twenty minutes on a plastic-covered foam pad atop a cement bunk. These curtained-off spaces offered little privacy. The sound of flesh slapping against flesh resounded in the hallway. The briny smell of fresh semen and sweat came in waves over the searing chemical scent of disinfectant. Cleanup was a bucket of water and roll of toilet paper.

But the money she made there was at least double, on a good day triple, what she could make elsewhere, she said; it had helped raise her children, buy a small house, and furnish it. She was now forty-eight years old and saving for retirement. Demolishing the Vila would push her out at a time when starting over elsewhere or in a new job would be unbearable.

"My clients come here, they know me," she said. "And it's safe. I know all these girls. When we leave at night, there's transportation here, and there's always someone keeping an eye on you."

I'd hear many variations on that story. Some, like Cleide de Almeida, remembered what removal was like. She grew up in the red-light district's old downtown location, one of ten children of a woman who cooked for the prostitutes there. Now she headed the Vila Mimosa residents and business association.

"The women were forced into the street," she said. "They worked out of cars, wherever they could, until we were able to buy up property here. It was a terrible time. We tried to move, but word got out and residents there waited for us and fought us off when we got there with our trucks."

While the women in Vila Mimosa waited to learn their fate, the crusade on visible prostitution continued. In March 2012 the federal government asked more than two thousand websites that promoted Brazil as a sex tourism destination to take down explicit content. In June, as thousands of foreign dignitaries and environmental activists boarded flights for Rio+20, the United Nations Conference on Sustainable Development, a hundred officers swarmed Centaurus in Ipanema and eleven other well-known brothels in Copacabana. All were on the short list of venues that cater mostly to foreigners. The official warrants for the raid listed corruption—police often take a cut of these large establishment's profits—but also money laundering, drug trafficking, and sexual exploitation, among others. Three people were arrested, including Centaurus's manager, and the women working there disbanded.

The manager was released a week later. By August, the international media attention had died down, the environmentalists had gone home, and Centaurus was up and running again. In early September, a judge dismissed charges against the two other men who had been arrested, arguing that none of the prostitutes had complained of being exploited and that "adult women cannot be treated as if they were invisible, without agency and ability to make rational choices."

The judge went on to conclude that the raid had been motivated by a "repressive political climate generated by sanitizing measures intended to prepare the city of Rio de Janeiro for the sporting mega-events of 2014 and 2016."

I believed he was right. So when Thad told me in early 2014 that he was going to do a recount of establishments to see how many remained open, I joined in. With only a few months to go before the World Cup, I wanted to get a better sense of how much had changed.

We hopped on our bikes in midmorning, armed with Thad's map and a plan to tackle downtown. Our goal was to visit thirty-two establishments that day. That sounded like a lot, but I soon realized it was only a fraction of the sex businesses in the area. There was barely a block that didn't have a brothel or *termas* of some sort. We hit them, one by one, tallying the number of patrons, the number of women, the number of shuttered façades.

Most were threadbare old *sobrados* with boarded-shut windows, dark and airless even in the middle of a sunny summer day. It was January, when most Brazilians take their month of vacation. Many of the joints had only two or three visible customers; a handful had more. Women in bikinis or underwear would perk up when we walked in, but their smiles drooped once they realized we just wanted some bottled water and a quick chat with the manager.

There were attempts at décor: Christmas lights wrapped around the bar, bits of tired tinsel hanging from the ceiling, or balloons that danced to the back-and-forth sweep of a tabletop fan. One had a jukebox, but it only worked when a client bothered to feed it money. Song over, the silence closed in again. These details were meant to liven up the atmosphere, but instead they created a sad, expectant air, like at a birthday party where the guests had failed to show.

At a place called Vanessa's Bar, the prices were posted on the wall, starting at $15 for 15 minutes of straight-up oral or vaginal sex with protection. Of that, $1 was for the condom and $6 to the house. The prostitute took home $8. A beer was $3. This represented the going rate in these spots, which served the downtown crowd—not the businessmen, but the office boys, the drivers, the delivery guys. The higher-end *termas* aimed at the men with suits charged entrance fees of $22 or $45 and did not allow women to enter, unless they were prostitutes. Thad would visit them without me.

We took a lunch break at the Beco das Sardinhas, a pedestrian passage taken over by greasy spoons all specializing in fried sardines. Over an oily pile of deep-fried goodness, we discussed the morning's work.

Yes, the hypocrisy of shutting down a brothel around a big international event made me cringe, as did the inherent injustice of shoving aside prostitutes or anyone else to make way for a tapas bar or a cultural center where they'd never feel welcome. At the same time, the working conditions in these places were abysmal; many of these *sobrados* weren't just eyesores, they were also unsafe. At one place, the aging floorboards were worn so thin I could see the room below through the cracks.

None of this was new to Thad. Since Davida, the prostitutes' rights organization, had been kicked out of the old Hotel Paris, its founder, a former prostitute called Gabriela Leite, had died of cancer. She'd been a charismatic woman who'd worked for recognition of the field she'd chosen and professed to love. Without her, the organization was leaderless and without a home. This left Thad and Ana Paula as the most prominent prostitutes rights activists in Rio. While we visited the brothels, Thad took notes, but he also passed on a card with a phone number where they could report abuses and problems. This number was his cell phone.

"Listen," he said, gesturing with half a sardine. "I'm not like Gabriela. I think that in the majority of cases, prostitution is not cool. There are women who like it, but often it's just . . . what other options do they have? People say prostitution isn't dignified. Is it dignified to wash someone else's bathroom for a minimum wage that won't allow you to feed your kids, or to depend on a man? What dignity is there in these other options? That's the problem."

After lunch, we made a few more visits. As the afternoon wore on, there were more clients. One of the last brothels we visited, around the 5 p.m. rush hour, had a steady stream of customers—I counted ten men climbing its steep stairs in five minutes. This one wouldn't let me in, either. Sometimes wives come, the bouncer at the door explained. They cause a scene.

That was fine. What I'd seen that day would linger with me for a long time: the women, their exposed bodies and the effort in their smiles; the stuffy rooms with their red walls, pink balloons, and plastic flowers. We'd also answered my question about what was happening to Rio's brothels: of the 32 places we'd visited that day, 11 had closed down since the last time Thad checked. Several had received warnings from the city about the physical conditions of the building.

In the months before the World Cup, I looked up the projects and improvements for which places of prostitution had ostensibly been removed or threatened with removal over the last few years. None of them were in place.

Vila Mimosa was still operating, as the government had tried and failed three times to attract bids for the bullet train. The Museum of Image and Sound, which was to take the place of Help!, was still a construction site, and the boutique Le Paris hotel remained a paper dream, stymied by the owners of a mattress store who operated on the ground level and refused to budge.

Thad was right. This crackdown was largely another case of *para inglês ver*, bolstered by gentrification and moralistic zeal, and motivated more by a concern with appearances than with making Rio better for its residents. The welfare of the women involved was last on the list of priorities.

• • •

The shuttering of brothels was part of the physical transformation of the city, and easy to measure: Thad and Ana Paula were taking care of that. But there were other social, cultural, and legal shifts that were reshaping the murky arena of sex and sexuality in ways that were less tangible but would have lasting repercussions.

One arena that was undergoing significant change was the position of women at home and at work, and with it, the relationship between genders. Some of these changes could be explained easily through numbers: women now made up about 60 percent of college graduates; the wage gap between women and men shrank every year; nearly 40 percent of women in the last census had said they were the head of household, with another 30 percent saying they shared the responsibility with their partner.

Underlying this was a very rapid demographic shift. I had to look no further than my own family to see a great arc from mothers who had a soccer-team roster of children to the current generation, in which the adults outnumbered the doted-upon babies. My grandmothers, who'd grown up with eight and eleven siblings, had borne six and seven children each. My parents in turn had three kids. My sister, brother, and I had three, two, and zero children, respectively. This averaged out to 1.6 children each—just under the national average of 1.9 per mother recorded in the 2010 census.[1]

Plot those numbers and you have an astonishing slide, particularly for a Roman Catholic country where abortion remains illegal and where there was never any official incentive toward birth control. Somewhere along the line, women across social and edu-

---

1 The 2010 census was also first to record a fertility rate that was lower than 2.1 children per woman, the number necessary for the population to replace itself. This trend was expected to continue, with the federal bureau of statistics projecting the fertility rate would drop to 1.6 by 2020 and 1.5 by 2030.

cational strata had seized control of their bodies. This precipitous drop took developed nations a century or more, but happened in half that time in Brazil.

The federal government was one unexpected agent in this transformation. When President Lula launched the conditional cash transfer program Bolsa Família in 2003, the money went to women in 93 percent of cases. This began to work a rearrangement of power within families. The money boosted women's status within the family; anecdotal evidence showed it helped them break out of bad marriages and take charge of household purchases. The biggest difference, according to studies, was in their ability to make birth control decisions. This was momentous, as by 2014 the program reached one-fourth of the population.

In other countries, a host of adaptations had followed the switch to smaller families. Most had a direct impact on male-female relations: postponed weddings, delayed motherhood, a greater number of couples living together without marrying, and higher divorce rates. As with the drop in the number of children, this was also happening in Brazil, but it was taking place very quickly indeed.

The consequences of this upheaval were still rippling outward, further complicating Brazil's already complex gender picture. Even during Carnaval, those days of permissiveness when men wore skirts and many of the usual rules were subverted, machismo still thrived. The groping and kissing in the streets was very often consensual, but not always. During my first Carnaval I'd almost deployed an elbow-to-the-nose move on a drunken lug who tried to force an interaction, and I'd heard from countless women who were groped or kissed against their will, or who faced a barrage of insults when they turned down a man's advances.

Beyond the anecdotes, there was hard evidence that traditional, male-dominant gender roles and violence against women remained a real and often unacknowledged problem.

Take one extreme measure: rape statistics. The number of cases had jumped in 2009, when a new law broadened the definition to include sex acts beyond copulation, but had continued to increase nationally and locally, going up around 50 percent in the state of Rio over the three years that followed.

The increase was due in part to more reporting. Campaigns and hotlines encouraged victims to notify police; a new law protected victims of domestic violence, and specialized, women-only police stations took their complaints. But regardless of the numbers, many of the attitudes remained unchanged, and women still shouldered the blame for attacks they suffered. A 2014 survey showed 65 percent of Brazilians agreed with the statement that if a woman is abused and remains in a relationship, it's because she "likes being beaten"; 58.5 percent concurred there would be fewer rapes if women "knew how to behave"; and 26 percent agreed that "women who wear revealing clothing deserve to be attacked."

These beliefs were so pervasive they extended even to PUC, Rio's elite private university, which gave its female foreign exchange students a pink pamphlet informing them that "the policy 'no means no' does not apply to all circumstances here (in Brazil). If a girl places herself in a situation where the guy understands that she agreed with having sex . . . he will do all he can to make her cope. And this will hardly be sexual assault, much less rape." This is an astounding position for a major university to take; it also reveals something deeper.

The position of women in Brazil might be shifting, but this would not be a simple, linear progression so much as a period of turbulence with great gains in some areas and ugly pushback in others.

CHAPTER 13

LOVE IS ESSENTIAL

The temperature was rising within the auditorium of Rio's Justice Tribunal. Brides and grooms in full wedding regalia took up all the seats and the rows brimmed over with veils, ballooning skirts, top hats. The aisles were dense with friends and relatives. They had come from all parts of the state; many of the men and women about to married had woken up before dawn to take full advantage of the free makeup, hair, and photo services offered by the state of Rio before the ceremony started at 3 p.m. With just a few minutes to go, emotion was running high. From my perch by the stage, I could see hands shaking as they pinned on a last-minute veil, clipped on a bow tie, or blotted out the sweat pearling on powdered brows. Bride and bride held hands; grooms checked each other's hair one last time.

Rio was about to celebrate the world's largest gay wedding, bringing together 130 gay and lesbian couples. Its size underscored the ceremony's bold message: same-sex marriage was not only legal but encouraged by the state of Rio de Janeiro, which advertised, organized, and paid for the whole bash with public resources.

Every detail was deliberate, meant to bolster the political significance of the day. The building was part of the justice system's infrastructure. The state courts' choir would sing, along with transvestite Jane di Castro, who would perform the national anthem.

How had Brazil become such a bastion of gay rights? Watching the nervous couples settle and the ceremony's officiants gather on the stage, I tried to reconcile this reality with one I'd known as a teenager.

Homosexuality had not been a crime in Brazil since 1830, when Emperor Dom Pedro I instituted the country's first penal code and eliminated references to sodomy, but discrimination and violence against homosexuals was rampant in the 1980s. News reports described that terrifying new disease, AIDS, as a "gay plague," and the archbishop of Rio, Dom Eugênio Sales, published an op-ed calling the virus "nature's reaction to sexual perversion."

Homophobic slurs were common currency among kids at my school, and soccer stadiums echoed with chants of *viado*, faggot. In the newspapers, I read reports of death squads targeting gays and of the impunity that followed. There were approximately 1,200 gays, lesbians, and transvestites murdered between the mid-1980s and the mid-1990s, according to the Grupo Gay da Bahia, one Brazil's oldest and most respected LGBT organizations.[1]

Twenty-one years later, I returned to find a place that, at least on the surface, seemed its mirror opposite. The defense of rights

---

1 The broad picture was grim, but the rights movement also scored some early victories: in 1985, the Grupo Gay da Bahia pushed the National Health Counsel to remove homosexuality from the roster of sexual deviations. During the elaboration of Brazil's new Constitution in 1987 and 1988, a Rio-based LGBT group lobbied hard to include sexual orientation in the section that forbade discrimination on the basis of "origin, race, sex, color, and age." It was not included, but the discussion raised awareness; protection from discrimination was written into several state Constitutions, and later became law in over one hundred cities, including Rio.

was no longer dependent on nonprofit organizations with uncertain funding. The state and municipal governments had picked up the rainbow flag. The city had a sexual diversity department; the Carnaval Without Prejudice campaign that had initially drawn me to write about the issue was their initiative. On the state level, Governor Cabral established a department that fostered gay rights. Public service announcements denounced homophobia and everyone, gay, straight, and in between, partied together in the streets.

In San Francisco, one of the global epicenters of the gay rights movement, I'd covered the battles for equal marriage rights as they played out in courts, voting booths, and the streets. Same-sex couples won the right to wed, lost it, only to regain it in 2013. Even then, fewer than half of American states legally recognized same-sex relationships.

But it was back home, in the world's largest Catholic country and one with a growing number of conservative evangelical Protestants in the legislature, that I would first see the LGBT community enjoy the full panoply of rights, marriage among them. I had not expected this.

A whole infrastructure had been established to ensure that these rights would be respected. The new state agency had set up reference centers around the state and staffed them with social workers, therapists, and lawyers equipped to handle anything from a workplace discrimination claim to an emergency request for housing for a gay teenager kicked out of her house. Working closely with state police, the department had trained 7,200 police officers in LGBT rights and pushed law enforcement to include in their reports whether homophobia was a factor in a crime—an essential step to improve data collection.

But not all was bridal veils and roses. Tension between entrenched cultural norms and new social mores often exploded in violence. In fact, the number of LGBT murders in Brazil had continued to climb year after year, reaching 338 in 2012.[2] The state of Rio ranked fourth on the list.

To understand this contradiction, I went to Claudio Nascimento, a militant with deep roots in Rio's gay community. He led the state superintendence for LGBT rights; his own experiences followed the path of Rio's, and Brazil's, gay movement. He could help me fill in the gaps.

We met in his office. It was somber, with dark wood paneling and heavy, serviceable furniture clearly inherited from a previous occupant. Claudio himself burst into the room an hour late and in candy-cane splendor: a button-down shirt in red and white stripes, a red tie, and a white jacket. He had a broad, earnest face, with high cheekbones and almond-shaped eyes, and an open manner uncommon in a political figure. We talked for hours over the next couple of days.

His story began like that of so many of Rio's poor: in the northeast. Claudio was born one of fourteen children of a sprawling and destitute family from Bahia. One of his first memories was the bone-jarring bus ride that took them south in search of work. Five-year-old Claudio's immediate family took up half the bus.

They came with scant resources. His mother never learned to read; his father deciphered words using bits of newspaper in his spare time. Claudio had a drive that set him apart from his siblings. He made it to college, but left it before completing his degree. The political whirlwind that coursed through Brazil in the mid-1980s claimed him, first as a neighborhood activist, then as a student leader, then, at fifteen, as a member of the nascent Partido dos Tra-

---

2 The rise in LGBT murders was broken in 2013, when there were 312 murders, or one every 28 hours, according to the Grupo Gay da Bahia. The hint of improvement suggested by that dip was dispelled in the first, violent month of 2014, when there were 42 murders, or one every 18 hours.

balhadores, the Workers' Party, which would eventually carry Lula and Dilma into power.

It was at a leadership conference that another young activist turned to him and teased: "You're not as revolutionary as you say you are." Then he leaned in, and they kissed. Claudio lost focus, walked out of the meeting, and took the bus home. With a single kiss, that boy had moved him in a way no girl ever had. As the familiar outskirts of Rio scrolled by—the brick homes with their barred windows, the tangled wires that loop like tropical vines from post to post, the kids perennially chasing a ball—he realized nothing would be the same. He had come out to himself. Coming out to his family, his friends, his community would be much harder.

"My family was conservative, poor, and very religious," he said. "I had a deep connection to them, to my neighborhood. I was afraid of how they'd react and of being cut off from them."

Desperate about his quandary, he threw himself in front of the commuter train two weeks later. Police officers pulled him out of the way in time. That brush with death changed his mind. He would live. Where and how, he didn't know. There was no plan. He walked home, came out to his family, threw clothes into a backpack, and left. He was eighteen years old.

For the next eight months he slept on couches when he found homes open to him, in parks and on public benches when he didn't. It was in one of these public squares that someone handed him a mimeographed flyer: "Come join this struggle. If you're gay or lesbian, come participate." He went.

This was 1989. That year, the Brazilian Health Ministry recorded 8,993 cases of AIDS, but there was no articulated government response to the disease. The still-incipient gay rights movement narrowed its focus to fighting the epidemic and supporting the sick, but the virus seemed unstoppable. The number of people infected more than doubled in the next four years. Among them was a young activist, Adauto Belarmino Alves—Claudio's partner.

Those were grim days of watching friends die with little support and suffering from great stigma. They pushed Claudio to do something bold, outrageous even: he and Adauto starred in Brazil's first public gay union celebration. It was April 1994. He was twenty-three and Adauto twenty-nine. The ceremony was a personal choice, not a publicity stunt, but it also came at a moment when visibility was key, Claudio said.

The celebration was heavily symbolic, held in Rio's health and social welfare workers' union and officiated by a former Catholic seminary student. It included many of the trappings of a traditional wedding: the two drew up a contract establishing their commitment and registered it with a notary public; they signed up for linen, silverware, blenders, and all the rest at a big department store; and they walked in wearing matching orange blossom tiaras. Afterward, in interviews, Adauto spoke openly about his HIV status. The press was aflutter. Their union heartened the LGBT movement, but it also touched many who'd had no personal connection to the struggle for equal rights.

The next year, 1995, Rio hosted its first international LGBT conference and held Brazil's first gay pride parade. The number of AIDS cases continued to rise.

That was when Brazil took an unprecedented step that landed it on the front lines of the global fight against the epidemic. The public health system began to distribute the expensive antiretroviral drugs free of charge to all who needed them. It was a constitutional requirement: Article 196 declared, "Health is a right of all and a duty of the state."

Because government officials had little experience in the field, they leaned on the activists and nongovernmental organizations that had been directly involved with HIV/AIDS work, bringing them and their ideas into the public health system.

In short order, this collaboration turned the country into a model in the treatment of HIV/AIDS. Brazil drove a hard bargain over prices and patents of antiretroviral drugs with foreign pharmaceutical companies, created conditions for producing the medication domestically, and organized aggressive prevention campaigns.

At first, the number of new infections continued to climb, reaching 23,546 in 1997, the year Claudio lost Adauto. By 1999, Brazil registered the first slowdown in the rate of new infections. The joint efforts of government and civil society were beginning to bear fruit. Brazil had turned the corner.

The long struggle and the collaboration with the government left LGBT and AIDS organizations stronger, with infrastructure, leadership, funding, and connections. As the 1990s drew to a close, activists found they had solid platforms from which to articulate demands that went beyond public health. Broader issues of safety, justice, and equality were back on the table not only in Rio, but nationwide.

Change accrued within all three levels of government, and across the three branches. Soon a patchwork of laws, court rulings, and new interpretations of existing regulations began to come together and create a substantial set of rights.

By the time gay marriage was declared legal throughout the country in 2013, there had been so many gradual changes that little commemoration or outrage greeted the decision. It wasn't until it was celebrated Claudio-style —with the world's largest collective gay wedding—that it reached a wider public.

Nearly twenty years had passed since Claudio's own commitment ceremony, but aspects of that first celebration marked the mass wedding in the Justice Tribunal's auditorium that day. It was all very moving, the gathered families, the nervous fiancés, the historic significance of the moment, but no opportunity was lost to make a point.

About a dozen judges, government officials, and sundry legal authorities crowded the stage, each ready with a speech about the momentous occasion. As they droned on for the next two hours, the brides and grooms began to fidget. It wasn't until Claudio stood to recite a poem by the Portuguese writer Fernando Pessoa—"Love is essential; sex, a mere accident. Can be equal. Or different"—that the gathering shifted from stiff political rally to poignant wedding extravaganza.

When the two presiding judges finally told the couples to stand and face each other, a murmur moved through the crowd. Some, like Marcos Carvalho and Celso da Silva, a balding couple in matching black leather jackets, had waited thirty-four years for this.

Once they'd exchanged rings, all semblance of formality was swept away as women fell sobbing in each other's arms, bouquets flew up in the air, men whooped and swirled suit jackets above their heads. Next to me, Marcos and Celso fell into a long hug: this was about love, but it was also the end of a very long fight.

"I'm from the time when homosexuals had to run from the police," Celso told me. "I've waited a lifetime for this moment."

By this point, the happy din echoing within the hall made conversation impossible. Marco and Celso invited me to continue our chat at the reception, a cocktails and hors d'oeuvres affair also sponsored by the state and held on a downtown rooftop.

I found them outdoors, taking in the view of the bay. Between one croquette and another, they told me their story. They met, they fell in love; they faced some hardship, they overcame it; they built a house and raised a child. It was as unique and as ordinary a story as that of any couple. Now it had the name it had earned over thirty-four years: a marriage.

Marco and Celso also told me more about the changes of the last four decades. Rio had become more progressive, they said, but there were sectors of society that found this new visibility threatening. Not long ago gay life was largely clustered around a few nightclubs in Copacabana; transvestites had to wash off their makeup before stepping into the street. Now they were claiming space not only in clubs and bars and sidewalks, but also in Rio's courts, beaches, schoolrooms, and restaurants—everywhere.

"This provokes some anxieties," Celso said mildly.

When this tension explodes, the most frequent victims are those on the fringes of Brazil's unequal society: those who are poor, who are black or mixed race, who live in suburbs far from the glitz of Ipanema's Rua Farme de Amoedo. They are more vulnerable, he said.

Travestis were frequently a target, Celso said, using a word that applied interchangeably to drag queens, cross-dressers, and transsexuals. I should talk to the ones who worked as prostitutes in Rio's Lapa district. He knew just the person to help: Luana Muniz. He pulled over my notebook, wrote down her number. Go find her, he said. She's been around.

I had heard of Luana Muniz—tall, blond, and tough, a sort of transgender fairy godmother of Lapa.[3] A TV show had gone undercover years ago and caught Luana in a dress that was more straps than fabric, slapping around a prospective customer who, in her estimation, had wasted her time.

There were a few travestis making a splash in high fashion, a rarefied world far more accepting of gender ambivalence. Lea T,

---

3 Rio's demimonde had these antiheroes, among them Madame Satã. Born João Francisco dos Santos in Pernambuco, where his destitute parents reputedly tried to trade him for a mare when he was a boy, he'd found a home in Lapa in the 1930s and earned his nickname from a winning Carnaval costume. He was unabashed about his homosexuality, a friend of samba composers, and an ace with the knife, which he used against police and tough guys in defense of the neighborhood's transgender people and prostitutes.

a stunner with plush lips and marked cheekbones, had been the first, joining the ranks of Paris couture label Givenchy in 2010. But I wasn't interested in the Gisele Bündchens of the transgender world. I wanted to know to what degree these contradictory aspects of Rio were reflected in the lives of travestis not protected by fame, class, or money.

I gave Luana a call. She agreed to see me, but she warned: "I don't do boring and I hate dumb questions."

It was easy to pick out Luana's *sobrado:* it was the hot pink heart of Lapa, a gaudy bauble among pastel neocolonials. Some of them still had the chipped, weathered fronts they'd worn for decades, but many had been completely redone and housed the bars, nightclubs, and restaurants that drew thousands to the neighborhood every night.

The metal gate in front was graced with a larger-than-life portrait of the diva herself in a black dominatrix getup, breasts ballooning above a corset that highlighted her waspish waist. The graffiti artist rendered her in bright red lipstick, lounging on a plush red throne with a tiny crown sitting at a jaunty angle on her head. Her eyes, narrowed and looking askance at the viewer, conveyed the same message I'd picked up during our short phone conversation: She's the queen of queens. Step gingerly when you walk into her realm.

I rang. A buzzer clicked and a door swung open, revealing a narrow, dark hallway. The stairs leading to the second floor were so steep I couldn't see the landing above. Only when I reached the top and turned left, toward the living room at the core of the century-old house, did I see Luana and the others. Reclined on couches, sitting on the dining room chairs, balanced on the edge of the table itself were most of her tenants, the twenty travestis who lived in the rambling townhouse's eighteen rooms, plus the caretaker who doubled as a bouncer—a large lesbian with a crew cut who came and went with a silent nod.

Luana rose to greet me. I recognized her from the graffiti: the same piercing eyes, now in sapphire contacts, the thin, disdainful eyebrows and the commanding height. Her hourglass silhouette was wrapped in a floor-length purple sheath with a deep décolletage. She flung her tresses around to the side in a practiced whiplash move, tilted her head, and extended a hand: "Welcome to my office, *querida.*"

Office wasn't the first word that sprang to mind. The space felt like a cross between a college dorm and a cabaret dressing room. The walls were covered with a profusion of posters of actresses, models and singers—Marilyn Monroe, Audrey Hepburn, the samba star Alcione, and the Rio drag queen Lorna Washington— all orbiting a large photo of Luana herself in full stage getup, all feathers and glitter.

At 5 p.m., the house was just starting to stir. One tranny sipped her coffee slouched over the table; a half dozen piled on the larger couch like puppies. Others traipsed back and forth, hair mussed, sleepy-eyed, in tank tops or slips. Luana introduced me. There were Cariocas in the bunch, but many more were immigrants from other states or other countries trying their luck in the big city. All worked as prostitutes and paid for a room in the big house.

Luana made that clear: they paid rent and no more. "I'm a landlady, not a pimp," she explained as we settled down to talk.

From our couch she kept an eye on all that went on, scolding like a den mother when the chatter opposite got too loud. "Is your little conversation more important than ours?" she fired at the youngsters. They shut up, doe-eyed. "Não, madrinha."

Madrinha, godmother. It was clear the fifty-four-year-old Luana was much more than a landlady. I would see over the course of the evening how she could be mother, father, nurse, role model, and therapist. The young ones got advice and limits; some of the older ones, with varicose veins and lopsided, out-of-date boob jobs, got discounts on the rent. It was also clear she ran a tight ship: when she spoke, they listened; when her coffee wasn't hot or sweet enough, someone popped out of their chair to fix it.

Order restored, coffee just right, I asked my question again: what did all the new safeguards and laws mean to her and her tenants? She relaxed out of the straight-backed, on-the-offensive pose she'd taken so far, leaned back, and ignored my question. She'd start where she wanted to start: at the beginning.

She grew up knowing she wanted to be something else, something other than a boy. At first, she thought she wanted to be a woman. Her idols were Hollywood actresses; her daydreams were about men. Later, she learned that wasn't it, either. Over the years she molded herself into the person she wanted to be, "the best and the worst of all genders."

"People say we lead a *vida fácil*, an easy life. Easy life, hard life, I don't know. But I chose it. Look what a wonderful thing: I am Luana Muniz. God gave me the sensibility of a woman, the dick between my legs, and a brain. I made myself into this amazing person you see here today. I'm fifty-four years old, forty-three of them [spent] working as a prostitute. Can't deny there were some very hard times. But I don't regret it.

"These girls, on the other hand," she said, flinging a bunched-up napkin toward the gigglers, "they don't know hard. Their life is *mamão com açucar*." Papaya with sugar.

Luana was raised in a traditional, middle-class home. Her mother, a public servant and her father, a lieutenant in the army, had adopted her as a boy hoping she'd grow up to be a doctor.

"They ended up with yours truly," she said. "Poor things."

By the time she was eleven, she ran away from home and began trading sex for cash. There weren't many other jobs for the likes of her, then or now, she said. Her parents went out to find her the first two times she ran. By the third escape they let her be.

She started turning tricks at Praça Tiradentes, four blocks away from the hot-pink house she now kept.

"Lapa was the crib of the Brazilian travesti," she said. "Those who were here then are all gone, but I can speak for them. It was hard. They had to be aggressive, carry knives, fight. Men would come here to beat us up, for fun."

The military dictatorship years were the hardest, she said. Police would slap them around or throw them in jail, where they could be forced to clean up the place or to have sex with officers. Luana herself was once handcuffed to a lamppost on that very street and left there to be pelted with refuse, spat on, and called names by those passing by.

"It was painful back then. Really painful. It makes me sad to think about it. Now I am not afraid of men with guns anymore. Rats, elevators, and airplanes, yes. But not of any man," she said. "A travesti has to know how to defend herself."

She grabbed her purse and pulled out a short, black club with a wrist strap.

"This is Cristal. I carry her wherever I go. And then there's this," she said, reaching between her breasts to fish out a thin tube of pepper spray—illegal for civilian use in Brazil. She raised her eyebrows, tucked the tube back in.

"We couldn't go out during the day, we couldn't show our faces. Now I know what we do is not against the law," she said. "Back then, we just took it."

The violence in the streets played an important role in the exodus of Brazilian travestis to European capitals. Thousands left dreaming of acceptance, money, and fame—Luana among them. She went to Paris in 1980 and became "a moneymaking machine," servicing up to sixty men in an evening, between customers and voyeurs, and always charging in advance.

She was back to Rio a year later, "victorious and tacky as any-thing," carrying a Louis Vuitton bag full of dollars, with her first pair of breasts filling out a modest C-cup bra. She's now on her fourteenth pair, and they're big enough to overflow two DDD+ cups—if she wore a bra.

Over the next two decades she traveled back and forth as Brazil weathered its dark years and Lapa continued to crumble. She watched gay rights organizations gain their footing, even worked in one for a few years. But the trannies she knew, the sex workers who came from God-knows-where to make a living on Rio's sidewalks, they were still outcasts, she said.

"On Farme, the gays are rich, they're engineers, they take vacations," she said. "We could get sick and no one cared."

The whispering of the young travestis on the couch opposite had gone up a couple of notches, and now they were laughing hard enough to miss the narrowing of Luana's eyes. A fraction of a second later—thwack!—they jumped back. A ring with some two dozen keys attached had smacked the wall between their heads.

They looked up, startled into silence. Luana reached out her hand, purple porcelain nails extended in their direction.

"Here, here. Give them back to me. I warned you: have some fucking respect!"

Turning back to me, she continued: "We needed our own organization. So I created one."

Through the Association of Transgender Sex Professionals, which she made official in 2006, Luana connects travesti sex workers with welfare workers and health care providers, helps them plan for retirement, and provides funerals that families can't, or won't, cover. There were three that year, she said.

This is not to say things haven't improved, she said. They have. The relationship with the police is entirely different: they no longer persecute trannies and they don't demand kickbacks "because they know they're not getting any," she said. She has a strong enough relationship with law enforcement that during a recent crime wave in Lapa, Luana led a petition of business owners and residents asking for an emergency safety plan, and they got one.

As she talked, a young travesti tried to slink out the door. She was a wisp of a person, thin as a boy, nineteen years old, with a cloud of chestnut curls. Luana grabbed her by the hand as she passed, exhaling her impatience audibly.

"You're going where? To the market?" Luana gestured with disgust at the strips of spandex she wore as a skirt and a bustier over her budding breasts, then sent her back to change.

"These girls go out half naked. . . . They take it all for granted," she said, shaking her head. The neighborhood was changing fast; there were a lot of new people around, serious businesses like banks, not just the old bohemian crowd. It was best to be careful.

By this time, there was a steady parade through the living room to the shower as the girls got ready for the evening. It was time for me to go. I walked out with Luana, who needed to get medication for a sick tenant and resolve a territorial dispute between two trannies.

It was dark out; Lapa's lights were on, music and laughter poured out of bars and clubs, rhythms mixing promiscuously in the crowded cobblestoned streets. Once Rio's underbelly and the hangout of the marginalized, Lapa was now riding a wave of gentrification. I brushed past college girls, happy-hour office workers, and gaggles of tourists looking for refurbished samba joints that now charged twenty-dollar entrance fees. The travestis were there, too.

They were already striking poses on the corners, these über-women with their dramatic eyes, silicone breasts, and hard bodies. I thought about the other prostitutes I'd met and the forces pushing them aside, and wondered how long these travestis would hold on to their turf.

With Luana gone—and she would tire of being on the front

lines eventually—what chance did they have of defending their stretch of sidewalk? I drove away and watched them diminish in the rearview mirror, tall in their platform shoes, still and statuesque in the swirling crowd, silent flesh-and-blood icons of this marvelous city.

CHAPTER 14

DIGNIFIED LIVING CONDITIONS

The favela of Metrô is long and slender, squeezed into the narrow strip of land between the six-lane Radial Oeste highway and the tracks that serve the subway and railroad. The first residents were workers who came to build the tracks in the 1970s and stayed; over time, their conglomeration of houses became a part of the urban landscape, much like the railroad tracks they built. Most Cariocas zoom by without a second glance. If they notice the community at all, it's for the auto mechanic shops that line its outward face. It's a cheap place to get an oil change. But that's not what drew me there.

The favela is also within view of the Maracanã, so close its residents can follow soccer matches just by listening to the cheers that rise from the great concrete bowl. The stadium would host the final game of the World Cup and two years later, the opening and closing ceremonies of the Olympics. The city had plans for the neighborhood: a $63.2 million overhaul that included new access ramps into the arena, parking lots, a bike lane. A PowerPoint presentation by the public works department laid out details in January 2012.

Favela do Metrô was not in the picture.

As I approached the community, I stopped by a larger-than-life graffiti mural on one of the outer walls. It showed a boy wearing a Brazilian soccer jersey and crying. Next to him was a soccer ball whose black-and-white pentagons blurred and morphed into the cavities of a skull. In case the message wasn't clear, a banner above spelled it out in elaborate cursive script: *Destruirão minha comunidade por conta da Copa*—"My community will be destroyed because of the Cup."

I stepped into one of the residential lanes, trading the whoosh of high-speed traffic for the cacophony of children playing and television chatter. The houses were modest but solid, made of brick, some plastered and painted, some bare, all of them narrow, tightly packed, two or three stories tall. A gaggle of kids chased after a ball in a small, open area that doubled as their playground and public square. From open doors and windows came the smell of frying garlic. It was lunchtime.

In spite of the life in its streets, every alley bore signs that the destruction predicted on the graffiti outside was already under way. Metrô looked like it had been bombed. Some homes stood intact while the houses next door or opposite had been reduced to piles of brick and cement mixed with rusting rebar and broken glass, coils of severed wires and crumbled plaster. Sometimes a second story was smashed to bits, but the bottom floor was untouched.

The houses that still stood all had a number and the initials *SMH*, for Secretaria Municipal de Habitação, or Municipal Housing Department, spray-painted on their outside wall, along with a number. They were next.

The World Cup and, in particular, the Olympics, were billed as transformative forces that could revamp the city's infrastructure and provide the impetus and the funding to remedy old deficiencies. After a couple of years back home, I realized their impact was uneven and not always positive. In the high-rises in Ipanema, it helped fuel the ongoing real estate speculation, even as it drew more tourists; among the *sobrados* of Lapa and the port region, it brought urban renewal but also a wave of gentrification that was changing the character of the bohemian neighborhoods. The condomínios of Barra were experiencing a construction boom that was already proving unsustainable.

Rio's favelas were also undergoing tremendous change. Even during the recent economic bonanza, their population had grown faster than the city's as a whole, according to the 2010 census. They were home to one in five Cariocas, and there were more than one thousand favelas in the city.

After decades of minimal attention from authorities, these communities were the focus of several highly visible public policies. I wanted to see up close how these unfolded; what happened in communities like Metrô, how it happened, and how residents were treated throughout would give real insight into the city's broader transformation.

Rio's biggest handicap had always been inequality. This was manifested not only in income gaps, but also through vastly unequal access to public services and resources, even to basic civil and human rights. The treatment of rich and poor, even by state agents and institutions such as the police force, the legal system, and elected officials, had throughout history been grotesquely imbalanced.

Favelas are a physical manifestation of this chasm. They concentrated Rio's, and Brazil's, poorest and most disenfranchised citizens. I looked to these communities for an answer to one of my most fundamental questions: was the ongoing transformation going down to the bones, altering the structures that funneled resources, rights, and opportunities to some and not others, or was it a facelift that wouldn't affect the scaffolding underneath?

City government had announced two directives touching on

favelas in the euphoric months that followed Rio's Olympic bid victory. Together, they could have a dramatic impact on the face of the city and on the lives of favela residents; over time, they would provide my answer.

One was a bold urbanization program announced in July 2010. Morar Carioca, or Carioca Living, was a $4 billion program that promised to bring running water, sewerage systems, paving, and public lighting to all of Rio's favelas by 2020. This made it the most comprehensive and well-funded favela-upgrading program in the city's history. It also had a unique participatory element: in addition to urban planners, architects, and engineers, it included sociologists and anthropologists who led consultations with residents. The mayor declared it would be the Olympics' showcase social legacy.

Accolades poured in from abroad; Morar Carioca could be a global model for integrating shantytowns into the formal city. The Inter-American Development Bank called it "ambitious," and extended a $150 million loan; later, it won Rio a Sustainable Communities award from the climate change group C40 Cities.

The other policy was the flip side of Morar Carioca. It was the largest favela removal program Rio had seen in decades. I'd seen it at work in Metrô.

According to the mayor, this was a necessary evil. There were communities that encroached on environmentally protected land, were in the way of planned highways, or stood too close to future Olympic venues. Many of them "could not be urbanized," he said, explaining they were in areas that were too steep or swampy. But most of them had to be removed for the residents' own safety, because they lived in areas deemed unstable, prone to flooding or mudslide, he explained.

"It's a decision made based on geotechnical studies," he said. "We're not joking around. I'm not going to be responsible for people dying. It's for their own good."

The first concrete details of this great upheaval came a mere two months after the Olympic announcement, in January 2010. It was an initial list of 119 communities to be removed. Metrô was on that list.

I found the head of Metrô's resident association, Francicleide Souza, or Franci, as she is known, still simmering the day's pot of black beans. Her dark hair was pulled into a bun, and, although she was only forty-four, there were deep furrows between her brows. After turning down the flame, she stepped out of the heat of her small kitchen and into the alley so we could talk.

The news that they had to leave left the residents in despair. Favela dweller's homes are often their most valuable possession by far; most have no bank accounts, no savings, no pension fund, no plan B. The house represents a life's worth of scrimping for improvements and additions; it is the roof that will be over their head once they can no longer work and the inheritance they will leave to their children. Losing a home can ruin a family.

Metrô's residents were offered compensation, a slot at a homeless shelter or government-built housing in Cosmos, a working-class suburb in the far northwest. Neither option was feasible, said Franci. The average government compensation was $16,000, a sum that couldn't buy a home anywhere in a city where the square foot was going for an average of $400. As for Cosmos, it is forty-five miles away but it might as well have been on the moon. Traveling there from Metrô by a combination of buses and the train takes nearly four hours—one way. Moving would mean losing jobs, their network of friends, nearly all connection to the city.

No one wanted to go, but there was a lot of pressure to accept the deal.

"We were told we didn't have a right to anything, that we didn't even own the walls of our own homes," she said.

I knew that was not true; Brazil's constitution guarantees that anyone living on unused land for more than five years has a legal claim to it, although enforcing that right took the kind of money, legal know-how, and time that few favela residents had. Given Brazil's lethargic judiciary, the process of getting the title could take twenty years even for those who had legal help.

Afraid they'd lose what they had, about one hundred families caved under pressure and accepted the government's offer of housing in Cosmos, Franci said. The rest held on. Then the demolitions started: wrecking crews would come and tear down the emptied homes. Because favela apartments have shared walls, this began to compromise the safety of the houses that still stood. Franci's house sprang a leak in the roof; others said the demolitions weakened their houses so much they could collapse in a heavy rain.

The fear of having the single thing that stands between them and the street taken away—in exchange for what? where? when?—was paralyzing to some. Others, like Franci, put all they had into the fight to stay.

She'd arrived in Rio alone, another frightened nineteen-year-old migrant from the northeast looking for work. Twenty-five years later, she had a job, a home she'd built alongside her husband, and a family that she raised within Metrô. When her resolve faltered, she stepped outside her home and looked at the spray-painted initials—SMH—and the number that reminded her she could be next.

Over time, the strain on residents mounted. The rubble of the demolished homes was not removed, so the community began to look like a dump. Crack users moved into the crumbling shells; they smoked, slept, had sex, and defecated within yards of where families like Franci's lived. The remnants of gutted homes were littered with the plastic and foil *mate* cups they fashioned into improvised pipes. Rats made their nests in the garbage. This began to sap the willpower of the 267 families that remained.

When government officials returned to Metrô with an improved offer of units in a housing complex nearby, another hundred or so families took it, even though the apartments wouldn't be ready for months. It was a blind gamble, leaving what they had for a promise, but life had become miserable, Franci said.

"We're afraid all the time, unsure," Franci said. "It wears you down."

The selective destruction continued, undermining the integrity of the community and the resistance of those who remained.

When I approached the International Olympic Committee and Rio 2016, the local organizing committee, with questions about Metrô, they repeated the official city line. "No families are leaving their homes without an agreement signed with the city or compensation and a move-out deadline established according to the law," they said in an official statement.

Their response didn't reflect what I'd seen. Regulations forbade pushing people into distant housing complexes, destroying their homes before alternative housing was ready, and paying inadequate compensation, all of which I'd seen during my visits. But the shell game of responsibility allowed them to pass this burden back to local authorities.

Within the city, there was a specific agency behind the removals. The initials spray-painted on homes slated for destruction made that clear: SMH, the municipal housing authority. There, the man to talk to was Jorge Bittar. I was full of unanswered questions—How many people would be moved? Why were they being rushed out even before there were concrete plans for the region, or a place for them to go?

In addition to Metrô, more than one hundred communities had been targeted for demolition all at once. More than fifteen thousand people had been removed over three years, and many more were in line. Did the city's housing authority have the in-house expertise and the manpower to study each case in such a short period of time, and make adequate provisions? If so, where were those reports?

After weeks of calls and stopping by unannounced, I got an audience at the very end of the business day on a Friday.

In his glass-walled office, Bittar unfolded an architectural rendering of the area around the Maracanã. There were long, smooth ramps leading into the great oval. Over by Metrô, the ramshackle auto mechanic shops had been trimmed into an orderly row and warehouses had been converted to workshops. The houses were gone, just as they had been on the PowerPoint presentation I'd originally seen.

"We're giving these people dignified living conditions," he said, repeating the mantra I'd heard from the Olympic authorities and the mayor.

The quick visit was enough to gather quotes for a news article, but not to answer my broader questions. Facing the Friday night traffic on my way back to the office, I thought back to Franci cooking her family's lunch, to the children playing in the alley outside, and to the rubble that pocked the favela. There was more to this story.

There was reason for the lack of trust people like Franci placed in official assertions of goodwill. Campaigns to uproot favelas were old tropes in Rio, as much a part of the city as the communities themselves.

The state had never adequately invested in homes for lower-income workers or the poor, so they built their own on unused private or public land. Between 1870 and 1890 the city's population grew 120 percent, but the number of houses went up only 74 percent. From then until 1906, the city boomed with recently emancipated blacks and European immigrants; the number of new residents outpaced available rooms nearly three-to-one. By 1920 the first recognized favela, Providência, showed up in census records with 839 homes and six businesses.

Even as they expanded, favelas' existence relied on a tenuous balance of interests. On one hand, these communities allowed Rio's poor to live close to the wealthier neighborhoods where jobs were concentrated. The government largely turned a blind eye to these settlements, which provided a pool of cheap, readily accessible labor and required no investment of public money. On the other hand, the vast majority of residents had no land titles and occupied their plots at the will of authorities. A political or economic change could throw tens of thousands out of their homes.

This happened in the first few years of the twentieth century, when about 20,000 of Rio's poor were forced out of downtown tenements during an urban renewal program, and again in the 1960s, following a decade of rapid industrialization that fueled migrations from the country's interior to Rio and nearly doubled the number of favela residents from around 170,000 to 335,000.

This increase alarmed those who saw these communities as a problem, among them the right-wing governor Carlos Lacerda. He instituted the most radical favela eradication program the state had ever seen, clearing out more than forty-two thousand people between 1960 and 1965. Brazil's military rulers added federal muscle to this effort by creating in 1968 an agency known by its acronym, CHISAM. Its goal was the total eradication of Rio's favelas by 1976.

The particular sorrow of packing your things and stepping outside to watch the house you raised be torn down was inscribed in the landscape and in songs like Adoniran Barbosa's "Saudosa Maloca": "Se o senhor não tá lembrado, dá licença de contar . . . Que aqui onde agora está esse edifício alto, era uma casa velha. . . ."

"If you don't remember, sir, allow me to tell you, that here where there's this tall building, there was an old house. . . ."[1]

The communities carried a heavy stigma. Policy makers and much of the population spoke of favelas as urban pathologies that marred the elegant profile of the *cidade maravilhosa*. CHISAM's first coordinator, Gilberto Coufal, used this language of disease and infection to explain why simply giving favelas infrastructure wouldn't do: "Favelados will continue to think, act and live as favelados," he told the *Jornal do Brasil* in 1971. "The son of that man who lived in the favela will grow up, mentally, a favelado."

CHISAM's plan was to send the displaced population to housing projects. Many families went willingly at first, believing the promise of a safer, healthier environment for their children and eager for a home that came with a property title. Only once they stepped off the backs of open-bed trucks that carried them and their belongings did they realize they'd been pushed literally to the margins. These projects were in the far outskirts of the city, in remote areas without transportation, jobs, or the most basic infrastructure.

As the word spread of what awaited them, *favelados* resisted. Newspaper reports from this period tell stories of people who were shot, beaten, arrested, or disappeared for refusing to leave. The Praia do Pinto favela, which used to occupy prime land in Leblon, burned down in the middle of the night on May 11, 1969, while its residents slept. Their shacks were, back then, made largely of wood. News articles say five thousand *favelados* were left homeless, and thirty-two were injured; although residents said in interviews that some of their neighbors perished in the fire, the number of dead was never quantified.

The residents of the Catacumba favela, which overlooked the

---

1 Adoniran Barbosa happens to be from São Paulo, but Rio *sambistas* also spoke of this phenomenon.

Lagoa and Ipanema, countered the government's proposal with their own community improvement plan. It was published in the September 15, 1969, edition of *O Dia* newspaper.

"This favela can be sanitized and urbanized," they wrote. "We do not want alms, charities or handouts. With the approval of public powers, we will construct and pay for our own houses."

Their proposal was disregarded. The community's 2,158 homes were destroyed and the families dispersed among several housing projects. The official reason given was "instability of the soil and pollution of the nearby Rodrigo de Freitas lagoon," according to a 1972 report by the state's planning department. These justifications for removal—the safety of residents and the environment—would resurface decades later.

Until its closure in 1973, CHISAM tore down sixty-two favelas. Praia do Pinto and Catacumba were typical. Like them, about 60 percent of the communities removed had stood on valuable land in the south side and were resettled in the far western and northwestern suburbs. One of these housing developments, the Cidade de Deus, or City of God, took in the broken-up population of sixty-three different favelas. Its story—the abandonment by public officials, the hardship faced by the first families, its slide into the hands of drug traffickers, and the escalation of violence that followed—was typical, and was told decades later in a book and a blockbuster movie by the same name.

As the 1970s drew to a close, the military eased its grip; the country opened up and the specter of mass relocations dissipated. For much of the 1980s and 1990s, the word "removal" was largely retired from public discourse except in specific instances. In 1992, a city planning document proposed for the first time "integrating favelas into the formal city," and "preserving their local character." An urbanization program, the Favela-Bairro, or Favela to Neighborhood, began paving streets and installing public lights in 1994. It seemed to signal a change in attitude toward favelas.

Now the city was preening for World Cup and the Olympics, and that word, *remoção*, removal, was back in the headlines. Favela residents clearly remembered enough of the city's history to be wary of government officials who promised them "a dignified life."

How much had changed since Rio's last wave of removals?

I was still nursing my morning coffee one Saturday in January 2013 when I was jolted fully awake by a phone call: armed police in riot gear had surrounded a settlement and were preparing to invade. I grabbed my notebook and sped over.

The man on the other end of the line was Carlos Tukano, an indigenous native Brazilian of the Tukano tribe. Originally from an area of the Amazon that straddles northwestern Brazil and Colombia, he was the informal leader of a group of indigenous people of more than a dozen ethnicities including Guarani, Pataxó, Kaingangue, and Guajajara. They had come to Rio to work, to get medical care, to study, or to sell crafts in the streets. Without connections or a safe place to live, they had moved onto the grounds of an abandoned nineteenth-century mansion that stood right next to the Maracanã stadium.

Most of the roof had collapsed; vines crept up the walls. What had once been decorative trees in a planned garden had grown tall and wild, obscuring the ruins and draping them in shadow. It was within the garden walls, unnoticed by the drivers who sped along the highway nearby and the fans who streamed into the Maracanã, that Carlos and the others had built a clutch of modest houses out of brick and thatch. They'd named their colony the Aldeia Maracanã, or Maracanã Village.

As the community became more established, they began to host cultural events: storytelling for children, workshops on indigenous crafts, ceremonies. We met when an AP photographer did a photo essay on them, and I went along to write the copy.

Carlos was thoughtful and patient, with broad, high cheekbones and eyes that turned down at the corners, following the downward cast of his mouth. This mournful appearance hid a sharp wit.

"Want me to wear the headdress?" he asked during our first interview. "You know, so I can look like a real Indian." He grinned, gently mocking us and himself at once.

We had exchanged phone numbers and stayed in touch. It was during one of my visits that Tukano explained what bound the indigenous to this crumbling old mansion. I later confirmed the details in a 2011 report done by a historian and an architect for the city's commission on cultural patrimony.

The building and its grounds had been donated to the nation in 1865 by Ludwig August de Saxe-Coburgo-Gotha, the Duque of Saxe, husband of Princess Leopoldina, second daughter of Emperor Dom Pedro II. It came with one condition: that it serve as an institute of Brazilian indigenous cultures.

This request was honored for decades. The building housed the Service for the Protection of Indians until 1962, when the institution was transferred to the new capital, Brasília. The mansion was then converted into an Indian Museum. That operated until 1977, when the collection was moved to the museum's current location in Botafogo. The mansion was then abandoned until the indigenous began to reclaim the space in 2006.

In spite of this history, Governor Cabral announced in October 2012 that the building would be razed. Plans for the stadium's surroundings had no more room for Carlos and the Aldeia than they did for the Metrô favela.

Residents of Aldeia Maracanã learned of this through the news; no one bothered to explain the terms of their departure or the date. It wasn't clear why they had to go, or what was planned for the spot. Tukano tried to puzzle out what was in store from scraps of information he found in newspapers. He would spread his clippings on an outdoor table during visits and ask if I had anything new to share. Now months of guessing had come to an end. There was panic in Carlos's voice on the phone that morning.

By the time I arrived, the standoff between police and the indigenous had grown tense. Officers in black, Kevlar-encrusted riot uniforms and yard-long weapons formed a shoulder-to-shoulder barricade in front of the compound. The main gates were locked; through gaps in the rusty metal I could see the liquid gleam of eyes. From within came birdsong, singing, and the sound of a flute. Some of the indigenous sat astride the wall holding ceremonial bows and arrows decorated with feathers. Many had donned headdresses and painted themselves in black and red geometric designs.

A police commander told me they were just waiting for orders to enter; until then, they would secure the perimeter. Chanting rose from within the compound. I approached the wall and told one of the men perched above that I knew Carlos. A minute later, they lowered a wooden ladder. From the top, I surveyed the surreal scene: on one side, riot police dressed for urban counterinsurgency; on the other, bare-chested men in feathered crowns sang and shook rattles while women and children milled around and peered through the gate.

Carlos and the others had called to their side everyone they could; within the compound were at least two hundred activists, students, and journalists. There were men with faces covered by balaclavas or tied T-shirts observing the standoff from a tower that rose above the second floor. Their bows and arrows were not the wood-and-feather contraptions of the indigenous below, but professional archery equipment.

Carlos was among the hundred or so supporters gathered out back, where the residents' thatch-roofed houses stood. He was trying to speak over an agitated crowd that included many of the indigenous, an assortment of activists, an opposition politician, and two public defenders. It was chaotic; voices rose at once, opinions crisscrossed, unheard.

No one knew why the police had come without a judicial order to enter, but without one, they couldn't evacuate the residents, said one of the public defenders.

"This is absolutely arbitrary," he said. "It could be a bloodbath."

No one knew whether an order was really on its way or how far police were willing to go to enforce it if it came. The strain made the crowd restive. This situation didn't feel safe. There were too many angry people, few substantial conversations, and a lot of armed men beyond the gates—plus the guys in the balaclavas above. Carlos was calling for calm, but his voice didn't carry far.

"We cannot fight them with bows and arrows," he said. "They are going to come in. We have to stay firm, without aggression."

He was a leader for quieter times, not the type to take a platform and rally a crowd. I had a feeling that the Aldeia Maracanã might be the worse for it.

The police blockade lasted through the afternoon; at the end of the day, still without an order to enter, the officers disbanded. I went home as confused as I when I arrived. Was it possible this was all an intimidation stunt? If so, it worked. By the time I left the Aldeia Maracanã, tempers were frayed and heated voices whipped up arguments for and against various courses of action—leaving, staying, resisting, compromising, fighting.

The tension continued to build over months, with legal parrying in the courts, visits by attorneys, and ostensive police presence around the settlement. I was traveling when Governor Cabral sent in the shock troops, but I didn't need to be there to know what happened. It was all over the national and international news: officers in their *RoboCop* gear striding through clouds of tear gas and pepper spray as they handcuffed and dragged scores of indigenous and other protesters out of the compound by the arms or legs. Carlos was there, bare-chested, in a yellow-feathered headband, arguing with police in bulletproof vests.

The indigenous were resettled in metal containers furnished

with bunk beds in western Rio, next to a leper colony. The containers were plunked on a cement platform and covered by a tarp. They flooded with the first rain.

Following the events in communities like Metrô, Aldeia Maracanã, and dozens of others, I began to notice parallels between the removal program in pre-Olympic Rio and the one carried out under the military dictatorship during the 1960s and 1970s.

The settlements singled out then and now shared one very significant characteristic: they were on land that had soared in value. Removing favelas was often the last step toward unlocking a region's full real estate potential.

Decades ago, most demolished communities were in the south side. Now, nearly half of the targeted communities were in the west, Rio's booming real estate frontier and home to most Olympic venues. The second significant cluster was still in the sought-after south-central zone.

And where were these families being resettled? Two-thirds were destined for housing developments in the far northwest, beyond the mountains that loomed over Barra and Jacarepaguá. This area was getting 80 percent of the housing intended for the poorest *favelados*, the families subsisting on under $11,000 a year.

The far northwest is the cheapest real estate in town. It is also the region with the fewest jobs—only 8 percent, compared to 60 percent in the center-south—and the most deprived of essentials such as public lighting, sewerage, transportation, schools, and hospitals. Much like in the 1960s, the residents with the fewest resources were being relocated to areas with the least infrastructure and that were farthest from sources of work.

There was, however, one very revealing difference between these two waves of removals: the reaction of the targeted favelas. While in the past there had been some resistance, such as in Catacumba, where residents drew up their own urbanization plan, residents were far more organized now.

Some of the advances that had raised Brazil to prominence and brought it the World Cup and the Olympics, such as the economic stability, the decrease in inequality, and the expansion of its middle class, had also raised the population's expectations and made it harder to push through projects that they did not perceive to be in their interests.

This new awareness was also manifest in Rio's favelas. Residents were reclaiming stigmatized words like *favela* and *favelado*, or using the less loaded term, *comunidade*, community. Leaders like Franci held that favelas were not a problem but a solution, albeit an imperfect one, to the city's insufficient housing and mass transportation. Integrating these communities into the urban fabric by providing the amenities they lacked was simpler, cheaper, and better city planning than destroying and relocating them, they said, and they were ready to confront their elected officials to defend this position.

All this meant that resistance to removals was widespread and substantial in some cases—and that expectations were high for the Morar Carioca program, which had promised to upgrade all remaining favelas by 2020. According to its official guidelines, Morar Carioca would further "socio-spatial inclusion and the expansion of the right to the city," goals that touched the core of this *cidade partida*, this split city.

Soon after Morar Carioca's announcement, the city's housing authority hired a nonprofit organization to survey the communities, and the Institute of Brazilian Architects held an international competition for favela urbanization proposals, selecting forty firms.

The mayor touted the program often during his reelection campaign in 2012; when he won, its aims were incorporated into his second-term inaugural speech in January 2013: "To Cariocas, we will leave a legacy that will improve life in Rio, particularly among the poorest, with interventions in infrastructure, mobility, and a strategic vision for development."

And so, when Morar Carioca unraveled, the disappointment was sharp—for favela residents, who had answered questions about improvement they'd like to see; for the professionals who had developed plans that would never leave the drawing board; but also for those like myself who believed this was Rio's moment to address its greatest imbalance.

There was no official announcement of the program's dismantling, no explanation to the public, to the communities, or to the architects and engineers. Funding simply failed to materialize. The organization hired to poll favela residents had its contract severed immediately after the mayor's second-term inauguration. By mid-2014, four years after the program was announced, construction had started in only two of the forty projects.[2] The removals continued apace.

Sometimes this dizzying policy about-face could be seen within a single community. Residents in the Vila União de Curicica favela, for example, went from listing their priorities for Morar Carioca improvements to being slated for removal in less than two years.

I brought this up with Pedro da Luz, president of the Rio chapter of the Institute of Brazilian Architects. The organization is venerable, nearly a century old, and often called upon as the arbiter of planning debates, including those involving Rio's Olympic projects.

Pedro is a man of complete sentences and thoughtful pauses, but the unexplained demise of Morar Carioca broke his loping

---

2 What Rio's favelas did get were highly visible projects that opened them up to tourism and often required the removal of hundreds of families. A $20 million steel and glass elevator built in Cantagalo, which leads to a lookout over Ipanema, pushed out 300 families; another 2,100 families were resettled to make way for a $105 million gondola system in Alemão. Another gondola system installed in Providência for $37 million also pushed out hundreds of homes.

conversational stride and sent his fingers raking through his unruly gray mane.

"Public policy like this presupposes planning, commitment, follow-through," he said. "But this . . ." He held his hands open and empty before him and shook his head, as if to show there were no words that captured his frustration.

The institute doesn't get into public spats. But it had partnered with the city and lent the program its name and prestige, only to watch Morar Carioca be trotted out for political use and then gutted. Pedro was left holding the carcass of its good intentions, and was grasping for a way to be civil about the mess in his hands.

By abandoning the urbanization program and accelerating mass removals, Rio went from having a favela integration program to actively promoting spatial segregation of the poor; it also went from investing in the city's core to encouraging the expansion of its urban footprint.

This was in keeping with other decisions, such as building new western-centered transportation routes (the Transolímpica, Trans-carioca, and TransOeste), extending the subway to Barra, and placing most of the Olympic venues there. The fact that this region was car-dependent, still lacking in appropriate infrastructure, and built on a model of exclusive gated communities meant Rio was taking a path that was environmentally unwise, expensive to maintain, and a traffic nightmare in the making. This course would also heighten the city's historic social and economic imbalances, and inscribe them into the landscape.

"The city is physical, concrete," Pedro said. "When we make a mistake, it is a mistake that will last for forty, fifty years. That's a problem."

All of these changes were wrapped around the need to prepare for the World Cup and the Olympics. From the moment the city was chosen as a host, authorities began regularly invoking deadlines and creating emergency measures to meet them. This state of exception applied to refurbishing stadiums and building venues, but it also lent urgency and freed from regulatory trammels projects that were only indirectly associated with the sporting events. After three years in Rio, I began to understand how this state of exception was being used to reshape the city; Cariocas would live with its legacy for many decades, as Pedro da Luz had pointed out. This brought me back to my original questions: what city was being created here? Who stood to gain from it, and who would lose? How were the World Cup and the Olympics being used in this context?

These are not easy questions to answer. There are powerful political, economic, and social actors involved, but their interests and allegiances are not always explicit or easy to untangle. One of the places where these forces clashed prominently, revealing something of their inner workings, was in a small, west-side favela of about three thousand residents called Vila Autódromo.

CHAPTER 15

WE BUILT THIS CITY

Altair Guimarães knows about removals. He can tick off on his fingers the times he's seen his house torn down. The first was in 1967, when he was fourteen. The family home in Lagoa was demolished to make way for high-rises, and they were resettled in the Cidade de Deus housing complex. The second came when he was thirty-five, married, and a father of two girls. Their house was torn down to make way for a highway. They gathered their belongings and moved to Vila Autódromo, a small west-side favela ensconced between two highways, the Jacarepaguá lagoon, and what used to be Rio's Formula 1 racetrack.

He was fifty-eight when we met at Vila Autódromo's neighborhood association, a tall man with rough-hewn features and powerful hands that testify to the decades he spent working construction. He was facing the loss of his home for the third time.

Rio's Olympic candidature dossier called the city's west side "the heart of the Games"; it would be the site of the main Olympic sports cluster. As it happened, Vila Autódromo sat right in the middle of that cluster. According to the bid book, the Olympic Village, the Media Village, the main press center, and the international broadcast center would all be within a three-mile radius of the community. The Olympic Park would be right next to it, where the old Formula 1 track had stood.

Vila Autódromo's real estate had been rising in value for decades. The Olympics sent it soaring. Without delay, the city put into motion plans to clear out the community. Residents learned of this along with everyone else—through the news.

Altair spoke with an anger built over decades.

"You work your whole life and never have anything to show for it," he said. "They can't move us like we're trash, from one place to another."

Vila Autódromo started as a fishing village on the margins of the Jacarepaguá lagoon in the 1960s. It grew as Cariocas moved westward, taking in construction workers like Altair, who raised the region's first condomínios and then built their own homes nearby. They were soon followed by the vast array of service workers demanded by gated communities and shopping malls: maids, nannies, gardeners, janitors, security guards, doormen, mechanics, plumbers, waiters.

By the 1990s, developers had realized the west was where the city had room to grow. Vila Autódromo faced its first threats in 1993 and in 1996, when the city charged them in court with causing "damage to the urban environment, damage to the natural environment, and aesthetic, landscape and touristic damage," and requested "measures for the removal of people and things." Leading the effort was twenty-three-year-old Eduardo Paes, then in his first political position as deputy mayor of the west side.

The city lost its case, and the community secured several safeguards: more than one hundred families got titles to their land in 1997; in 1998, those who lived by the lagoon got a concession of use that allowed them to stay for ninety-nine years. In 2005, the City Council recognized them as an "Area of Special Social Interest," which meant they were apt for integration into the city. Construction boomed all around.

Then came the 2007 Pan-American Games. Many of its venues were in the neighborhood; this intensified development in the region and bolstered real estate prices. The threat against Vila Autódromo was renewed. Demolition crews came close enough to spray-paint the SMH tag on a few homes before the plan was overturned.

Still, this was nothing compared to the pressure that came bearing down on them once the IOC chose Rio as host of the 2016 Olympics. From that moment on, Rio authorities became intent on clearing out the community, and resorted to a wide range of tactics to achieve this.

The official reason for the removal shifted over time. The initial justification was that the city needed to expand two highways that met at its borders. Between 2009 and 2010, the mayor or his representatives offered up at least three more explanations: the area was too difficult to urbanize; it would be the site of the Olympic Media Center; it infringed upon a security zone around the future Olympic Park.

Residents fought off each allegation, with the help of activists and academics who had joined in a technical support team, but as the arguments against them morphed, their status remained unclear.

Then, in August 2011, the press gathered for the announcement of the winning design of Rio's Olympic Park. The contest included sixty proposals from firms in eighteen countries and was presided over by the IAB, Pedro da Luz's organization. There was much expectation surrounding this, not least from the residents of Vila Autódromo. What was in store for their sliver of land?

The winner was the British firm Aecom, an engineering and architecture company that had designed London's 2012 Olympic Park. Their plan came with a surprise: they made room for Vila Autódromo. There it was, right on the map presented by the firm, labeled and represented as a little cluster of homes tucked between two parking lots and a back entrance to the Olympic Park.

Did this mean the tiny favela would be able to stay, in full view of international news cameras during the competition and, perhaps more significantly, within sight of the high-end condomínios sprouting nearby? If not, why?

The answers came in fragments, and revealed much about the forces fueling Rio's transformation.

In October 2011 the city announced that it was taking bids from developers for participation in the public-private partnership that would build the Olympic Park. This was the same sort of deal behind the disastrous Vila do Pan and the Olympic golf course. The total cost of the 290-acre project was about $700 million. The federal government would pay for the sports arenas; the city would come in with $250 million. For their contribution, the developer would get the right to raise condomínios and hotels on 75 percent of the Olympic Park's grounds after the Games—a transfer of 217 acres of prime, publicly owned land to private hands.

The destruction of Vila Autódromo was built into the proposal; *simples assim*, as Brazilians say; as simple as that. The residents would be resettled in a housing project also built by the winning developer with federal funds on city-owned land.

Two days after the proposal's unveiling, the *Estado de S. Paulo* newspaper scrutinized what seemed a minor part of the deal: the city's purchase of the future housing project's plot. Expenditures that high had to be published in the municipal register. This one had something funny about it: the cost had initially been published as $1 million. The figure had been corrected and republished three times. Each time, the price had gone up until it reached $10 million.

The article revealed the plot's owners were two real estate development companies that had donated substantially to the mayor, to his chief of staff, and to three department heads directly involved in the removal of Vila Autódromo. Among them was Jorge Bittar, the head of the housing authority.

The two developers who owned the land purchased by the city were also responsible for three condomínios within a mile of Vila Autódromo. These units would rise in value once the favela was no longer visible from their balconies.

And there was more: according to a report by the city's geotechnical experts, about 70 percent of the plot purchased by the city was considered an "área de risco." It stood just under the mountains of Pedra Branca State Park, in a "medium risk" zone between the high-risk areas among the peaks and the low-risk flatlands.

Brought together, these bits of information allowed a peek into the black box of municipal decision-making. They also explained why most residents in the community were reluctant to leave. They understood what was happening. Many of them, like Altair, had seen it all before.

The growing number of reasons offered for their removal also fed their mistrust. There were at least two new ones in 2012: the first, explained in a city-produced video, had a feeder road of the Transcarioca passing right over Vila Autódromo. Another, offered by the mayor in an interview, held that "two-thirds of the community was in an environmental preservation area."

So was their eradication necessary because they stood in the way of a stretch of highway or because they occupied a protected area? Or by one of the handful of alternatives offered in years past? It didn't matter. Each new plan only emphasized the sense among residents that whatever the latest excuse, the real goal was their removal. There was a lot of money to be made and they were in the way.

• • •

As part of their effort to stay, Vila Autódromo did what the residents of another lagoon-side community, Catacumba, had done decades ago: they drew up their own urbanization plans. With technical help from a group of academics, they produced a study of what it would take to meet environmental regulations and bring services to their homes. The Plano Popular da Vila Autódromo, handed to the mayor in August 2012, was viable and economical. Their whole project cost less than that of the land purchased for their resettlement.[1]

But the city's plans went on unaltered. By early 2013, construction began on the housing complex to which residents would be moved even as most of the community remained steadfast in its refusal to leave.

There had been so many reasons offered for the removal of Vila Autódromo that I'd begun to collect them, like stamps or trading cards. A new chief of the housing authority gave me another: Vila Autódromo's land would be turned into a public park.

The situation was at a standstill when the mayor suddenly reversed course and agreed to meet with the residents in August 2013. He admitted he'd made a mistake and agreed to everything: to Vila Autódromo's permanence, to its urbanization, and to the resettlement within the community of any residents who had to be moved for environmental reasons. Those who wanted to leave would get market-rate compensation or an apartment in the housing project. All negotiations would include the residents' association and the technical advisors.

It was a startling victory. Vila Autódromo had been able to fight

---

1 This plan would later win the Urban Age Award, granted by the Deutsche Bank and by LSE Cities, a research center at the London School of Economics, in recognition of the effort made by the community to improve its environment.

off its demolition entirely. When the community announced this to the public, they signed the note with "Viva a Vila Autódromo! A Vila Autódromo Vive!"

Long live Vila Autódromo. It was a storybook ending.

But the story wasn't over and it wasn't simple. These stories seldom are.

In the months that followed the mayor's apparent capitulation, the city presented residents with yet another plan. This one would preserve the center of the community but would clear out the homes along its borders—nearly half of its houses—to create elevated access ramps into the Olympic Park. These ramps, raised six feet off the ground, would enclose the remaining homes in a belt of pavement and traffic.

The mayor offered to discuss this and answer questions in person but only with those who got an invitation in the mail. This led to even more anxiety and uncertainty. It wasn't clear why some were included and not others. What did it mean if you were chosen? Would the mayor be making new offers? Was this just another ploy to divide them?

This meeting was called for a Sunday in October 2013. The Wednesday before, about 150 people crowded into the favela's St. Joseph the Worker church to discuss what to do. Men and women lined up and took the microphone, though there nothing new in their recitations. They'd been in this together for years; they knew each other's stories and feelings. They weren't sharing information so much as reaffirming their convictions. If the city was trying to pull them apart, their words were a reminder of what bound them together:

"... We built this place; we built this city. We have a right to it," said Altair.

"... on Sunday, we'll only need to get one word in to tell the mayor what we think: no," said Inalva, a retired public school teacher.

Hovering in the back was Maria da Penha Macena. I knew Penha, as she was called, from other meetings like this; she kept busy plying everyone with coffee and cookies and seldom sat down.

She didn't go to the microphone, but I knew her story; it was the story of many of those present. Penha had cleaned other people's homes and cooked their food for decades to build her family's three-story home. They had saved for each load of bricks and bucket of paint; together they carried the cement, laid the tiles, and hung the doors. The building was their home: subdivided into apartments, it housed Penha, her husband, her daughter, her mother, her mother-in-law, and her mother-in-law's other children, Penha's brothers- and sisters-in-law, and their families. But it was also a repository of their memories, their effort, and their plans for the future.

By the time the meeting ended at around 11 p.m., the decision was made: they'd all go meet the mayor, invitation or no invitation. On Sunday morning, they gathered and walked over to the convention center, where Mayor Eduardo Paes was waiting in a conference hall auditorium, behind a moat and three levels of locked doors guarded by security guards. I went along. The residents chanted, they waded across the moat, they argued with the gatekeepers, waved their invitations around—and they eventually got in. All of them. They saw the mayor and heard his proposal.

It felt, briefly, like success; they'd achieved something that had been denied them. But what was won? It had been a long day. Much effort, planning, and energy had gone into preparing for it, and yet, as I drove away, I realized they were no closer to a resolution.

For years the city had waged a long and wearying war of attrition against this community. With its exclusive invitations and selective release of information, the meeting that Sunday had not been a real attempt to reach a settlement, just another step on the treadmill of proposals and counterproposals, concessions and reversals that spun on and on, with no conclusion and no rest. Residents there had lived with this for two decades, but the buildup to the Olympics was making it unbearable. They were exhausted.

The last time I went to Vila Autódromo was on a Saturday in March 2014. I was on my way to a family lunch and stopped to check on Penha and the others. An injunction blocking demolitions in the favela had been overturned days before, and already there were gaping holes where the first few houses had been punched out. The dust and noise of twenty-four-hour construction at the Olympic Park next door permeated the community.

At the residents' association, Penha and others were wrapping up a meeting with activists and academics. They had spent the morning polling neighbors about this latest defeat and drawing up new plans. After the meeting, I walked with Penha to her house. The sun was vicious; along the way, we passed the sad voids where homes had stood.

None of this seemed to weigh her down. Penha is tiny, no more than five feet tall, with small bones and a bright energy that got me thinking of hummingbirds. On our way to her house, she made quick stops to inquire after someone's sick baby, to kiss a friend hello, and to touch the forehead of a goddaughter who called out for a blessing:

"A bênção, madrinha!"

"Deus te abençoe e te dê felicidade," she answered. God bless you and give you happiness.

It was well past lunchtime when we got to her home; her family was waiting for her to eat and so was mine, but we stole just a few more minutes to climb up to the rooftop and look over at the future Olympic Park.

From the very top of the building, we could see the Jacarepaguá lagoon and the glare of glass-fronted high-rises on the other side. The Olympic Park was a pit of red mud. A welcome gust of air came over the water.

The mayor's first attempt to demolish this community had been in 1993—more than twenty years ago. What made him so relentless?

"They want to turn us into the Lagoa," she said, nodding in the direction of the lagoon. That made sense: Lagoa, the lagoon that stretches from the Botanical Gardens to Ipanema. After favelas were removed from its surroundings in the 1960s it became one of the most desirable addresses in town.

The story of Vila Autódromo is complicated, full of dead ends, reversals, surprises. But as Penha put it, it was also simple. It had happened before. If Barra was to be Rio's new south side, an enclave of privilege and exclusivity, Vila Autódromo had to go. *Simples assim.* None of this was new; it had always been this way.

Timbered mountains rose beyond the placid waters. This was one of the places were Rio's physical beauty asserted itself and demanded attention. What seemed remarkable was not what city authorities and their backers wanted to do, but the fact that they had been prevented from doing it—so far.

I had returned to Brazil counting on the economy and politicians, the World Cup and the Olympics as catalysts for change. Indeed, they were transforming the face of the city, for better or for worse. But I'd also found that ordinary people like Penha were driving a profound change by simply demanding their basic rights, including the right to be heard by their elected officials and to be treated lawfully.

Standing next to me on her rooftop in her cutoff shorts and flip-flops, Penha smiled and flapped her pink, "Jesus loves me" T-shirt in and out to catch the breeze. Whether she'd be standing there by the time the Olympics started in 2016 was anyone's guess. But that she was still there, enjoying the breeze, calm and unwavering, was extraordinary. This did feel like a victory—incomplete and temporary, perhaps, but hard-won and unprecedented, a bright kernel I could take with me as I drove away.

CHAPTER 16

THE WORLD BELONGS TO THE DARING

I was on vacation, hiking among glaciers and sheep in the mountains of eastern Turkey and disconnected for the first time in years from Brazil and the news, when I checked my email and found it full of puzzling messages. The connection was slow, so I stared in confusion at those subject headings—"Hope you're safe," "Are you OK?"—for a few seconds before the rest of the messages loaded.

Safe? I had no idea what they were talking about.

As their messages and Brazilian news websites appeared on the screen, my heart sank. What had prompted them to write was news, big news, big enough to show up in American papers.

Demonstrations were blanketing downtown Rio, São Paulo, and other state capitals; police were cracking down on protesters with batons, firing tear gas, pepper spray, and rubber bullets at close range. Images of bloodied protesters were all over my social media feeds. I saw the reason behind the worry piling up in my inbox. Journalists were particularly targeted. One photographer was hit in the eye with a rubber bullet; a handful of others were hit in the face. In photo after photo, the strikes looked deliberate.

The Brazilian Association of Investigative Journalism tallied fifteen journalists hurt in one day of protest coverage in São Paulo.

All of it seemed surreal, an anachronism reminiscent of the aggression unleashed by the military regime on pro-democracy protesters a generation ago.

What happened to the new Brazil, this up-and-coming country with solid institutions, a breath of equality, freedom of speech? The president and her two predecessors, the worker and the intellectual, had all fought in their very different ways for a government that represented its people, for democracy. Now marchers and reporters were once again being bloodied on public streets by police untrained or uninterested in peaceful crowd control. And there I was, stranded in a mountain town on the other side of the world.

The violence of the police reaction came as a shock, but so did the demonstrations themselves. In the short weeks I'd been away, Brazil had erupted with some of the largest and most resonant waves of protest in its history.

The catalyst was an innocuous march over a ten-cent hike in bus fares in São Paulo. Dissatisfaction had built like gas in room with a slow leak, invisible but dangerous. The unrest in São Paulo was the spark that triggered an explosion of pent-up demands. Within days, protesters were clamoring for better hospitals, better schools, less corruption, less brutality at the hands of police.

Back in Istanbul, I watched as videos showed Brazilian streets convulsing in city after city. Hundreds of thousands were joining these demonstrations that no politician, community leader, academic, or journalist had predicted. Even the protesters themselves were caught off guard by the strength of the movement, which wasn't even a formal movement. Although banners were soon raised, there was no political party behind the rallies, no singular issue or segment of society leading the charge.

I understood the frustration. This was June 2013. By then I'd been in Brazil for nearly three years, and knew about the terrible services, the corruption that drained public funds, and the venal political class. But those problems had plagued Brazil for generations. What new element suddenly made that old mix so explosive? And why were protests that started over the cost of public transportation and called for basic services so threatening to authorities they elicited this violent response?

The answers were rooted in the changes I'd observed since arriving. The country's economic outlook had changed since that cover of *The Economist* showed Cristo rocketing off his perch. The boom of 2010, when talk of Brazil was studded with exclamation marks and the economy grew at a China-like rate, had given way to three years of middling growth. But this wasn't the whole explanation, or even most it. This slowdown hadn't hit pocketbooks just yet. Employment was still strong, and inflation, the indicator that most worried Brazilians who suffered the instability of the 1980s and 1990s, was still within predicted parameters.

Watching videos stream over the Internet, reading and rereading placards and banners, what I saw were core middle-class demands: For a country without corruption! Stop the thievery or we stop the country. We want hospitals. Where are our taxes going?

There were polite ones—Sorry for the inconvenience, we're changing the country!—and those that went for laughs: There are so many things wrong in this country I can't fit them on this poster!

Not even the national passion was spared their fury; fans trying to reach Rio de Janeiro's Maracanã Stadium for the Confederations Cup, a test run to the World Cup, had to charge past clouds of tear gas and riot police trying to contain protests over the volume of public money spent on sports venues. Posters pointed this out as well: Forget stadiums, I want world-class schools. Call me World Cup and invest in me! one student's sign said, and another, I didn't vote for FIFA!

The author and her brother as toddlers on Ipanema Beach with an uncle and his girlfriend. The Dois Irmãos Peaks—the Two Brothers—loom in the background. *Personal archive*

LEFT: The author with her father, uncle, and younger brother during her first visit to Cristo, the statue of Christ the Redeemer that looms over Rio. *Personal archive*

BELOW: The author as a child playing outside her home with a shepherd's daughters in Basra, Iraq. *Personal archive*

Brazil's then-president, Luiz Inácio Lula da Silva, on a visit to a Petrobras offshore ship platform, shows hands covered in pre-salt oil from the Tupi field off the coast of Rio de Janeiro on Thursday, October 28, 2010. © *AP Photo/Felipe Dana*

Rio de Janeiro Mayor Eduardo Paes, left, businessman Eike Batista, center, and Rio de Janeiro Governor Sergio Cabral attend a ceremony in which Batista donated R$ 10,000,000 (around 4.5 million US dollars) to bolster Rio's 2016 Olympic bid on April 7, 2009. © *AP Photo/Ricardo Moraes*

Brazil's Lula is emotionally overwhelmed in Copenhagen on October 2, 2009, after hearing that Rio de Janeiro beat Chicago, Madrid, and Tokyo and won the bid to host the 2016 Summer Olympic Games. Note the missing pinky finger on his hand. ©*AP Photo/Claus Bjørn Larsen, Polfoto*

Cariocas celebrate on Copacabana Beach after Rio de Janeiro won the nomination to host the 2016 Olympic Games—the first South American city to do so. © *AP Photo/Silvia Izquierdo*

Sunbathers gather on Ipanema Beach in Rio de Janeiro during a hot September day in 2012. Rio boasts some of the world's most stunning urban beaches. © *AP Photo/Felipe Dana*

A vendor sells iced mate tea in one tank and lemonade in another on Ipanema Beach, on Saturday, February 2, 2013. © *Lianne Milton/Lianne Milton Photography*

A boy reacts with fear as firefighters work on a bus set on fire on Thursday November 25, 2010. During many weeks that year gang members erected roadblocks on major highways, torched dozens of cars and buses, and shot up police outposts, all to protest against a security program that threatened their hold on favelas where they would have held sway for decades. © *AP Photo/ Silvia Izquierdo*

An alleged drug trafficker aims a weapon within the Complexo do Alemão on Saturday, November 27, 2010. That day, armored vehicles were preparing to push past barriers into the favela complex as police increased pressure on drug traffickers believed to have ordered the wave of violence that had terrorized the city. © *AP Photo/Felipe Dana*

The author, right, conferring with her editor on the phone and with Flora Charner, in charge of AP Rio's video side, during the police occupation of Vila Cruzeiro. © *Austral Foto/Renzo Gostoli*

A woman holding a baby hides behind a door as an armored police vehicle patrols during an operation at the Complexo do Alemão. Alemão was the main base of the city's biggest drug gang when it was invaded by 2,600 police and soldiers on Sunday, November 28, 2010. © *AP Photo/Andre Penner*

Police plant a Brazilian flag at the highest peak in the Complexo do Alemão on Sunday, November 28, 2010, to mark their takeover of the sprawling conglomerate of favelas, an unprecedented accomplishment in their fight to secure Rio. © *AP Photo/Silvia Izquierdo*

Rio state Public Safety Director Jose Beltrame, second right, talks to the blue-clad officers of the Pacification Police Units, or UPPs in their Portuguese acronym, on November 6, 2010. Beltrame, the architect of the UPP program, was celebrating the creation of the thirteenth UPP unit in the Morro dos Macacos favela.

Rio would descend into chaos that month as armed men set up roadblocks and torched vehicles, and police responded by invading more than twenty favelas and engaging traffickers in massive shootouts. © *AP Photo/Felipe Dana*

A girl carries a bottle uphill back-dropped by a recently inaugurated cable car at the Complexo do Alemão on Monday, October 24, 2011. The gondolas were inaugurated in July 2011 and came at a cost of $105 million, yet only serve a fraction of the community. Installing the eye-catching cable car route required the removal of over two thousand families. Many residents remain in wait for essential services such as regulated water and electricity. © *AP Photo/Felipe Dana*

Two little girls in uniform walk to school past heavily armed police officers patrolling Alemão. The army remained there for more than a year after the complex of favelas was seized. The transition from soldiers to police officers happened around the time this photo was taken, on March 27, 2012. © *AP Photo/Felipe Dana*

Gustavo Nascimento da Silva, age five, flies his kite atop one of the roofs at the Santa Marta favela. In 2008 police stormed this favela, and it became the pilot in the UPP program, which intended to reclaim communities such as this one from gang control and bring government services. ©*AP Photo/Felipe Dana*

Customers get a haircut at Zé do Carmo's barbershop in Santa Marta. A consummate businessman, Zé do Carmo took advantage of Rio's improving economy and of the police presence to hike up rents on the houses he owns within the community. ©*AP Photo/Felipe Dana*

Leidemar Barreto stands outside her home in Santa Marta on December 17, 2010. Turning the favela into a model UPP unit improved safety and lowered crime rates, but it also raised the cost of living within the community, making life harder for single mothers such as Leidemar. ©*AP Photo/Felipe Dana*

An aerial view shows a neighborhood damaged by landslides in the town of Nova Friburgo, in northern Rio state, on January 16, 2011. Weary from days of steady rain and bracing for more thunderstorms, survivors of mudslides that killed around one thousand people carried food, water, and blankets to friends, neighbors, and relatives still stranded in remote villages. © *AP Photo/ Felipe Dana*

A family mourns after the burial of a landslide victim in Teresópolis, in northern Rio state, on Friday, January 14, 2011, surrounded by other freshly dug graves and drenched by the unceasing rain. © *AP Photo/Felipe Dana*

Garbage litters the shores of Guanabara Bay in this August 18, 2011, photo. The pollution resulting from decades of neglect and unplanned growth has long meant foul beaches and health hazards for local residents, but it became a matter of international concern as Brazil prepared to host the world's two biggest sporting events, the 2014 World Cup and the 2016 Olympics. © *AP Photo/Felipe Dana*

Kids play alongside a polluted river in the Varginha area of the Manguinhos favela complex in a photo taken Sunday, July 14, 2013. While the lack of sewage treatment and garbage collection affects all residents, those in poorer communities are often exposed to the greatest health hazards. © *AP Photo/Felipe Dana*

A woman sorting recyclables at the Gramacho waste site reacts as a dump truck pours out its load in a photo taken February 10, 2011. ©*AP Photo/Felipe Dana*

A group of trash sorters collect recyclable materials from the Gramacho landfill as vultures circle overhead, waiting their turn. Guanabara Bay stretches out in the background. ©*AP Photo/Felipe Dana*

The Rio 2016 Olympic golf course, seen here under construction on May 13, 2014. The golf course's location on a reserve has raised a number of environmental concerns. Gated communities, common in Rio's affluent west side, rise all around the proposed golf course. © *AP Photo/Felipe Dana*

Biologist Ricardo Freitas weighs a broad-snouted caiman before releasing it back in the water channel in the affluent western suburb of Recreio dos Bandeirantes on October 14, 2013. © *AP Photo/Felipe Dana*

Protestors march through downtown Rio and are reflected on a glass-fronted building, left, on June 17, 2013. In a 2012 poll, more than three-fourths of Brazilians said they believed corruption had infused Brazil's preparation for the World Cup. Their anger fueled widespread and often violent anti-government protests that sent more than 1 million Brazilians into the street during FIFA's Confederations Cup soccer tournament, the warm-up event to the World Cup. © *AP Photo/Felipe Dana*

Protests and clashes between marchers and police continued to erupt in Rio and around Brazil through 2013 and 2014, increasing tension in the months leading up to the World Cup. In this photo, police pepper-spray and strike protesters from the Pavão-Pavãozinho favela, on the mountains straddling Ipanema and Copacabana, after the burial of a young man from the community who they believed had been killed by police. © *AP Photo/Felipe Dana*

A woman bathes a child in the Favela do Metrô, just outside Maracanã stadium on Thursday, January 9, 2014. Residents from this community were forced from their homes, often without proper compensation or alternative housing, as authorities began to renovate the area for the 2014 World Cup and 2016 Olympics. © *AP Photo/Felipe Dana*

A man wearing a headdress and another wearing a ski mask sit on a windowsill on the site of an old Indian museum, within view of the Maracanã stadium, on Saturday, January 12, 2013. Police in riot gear had surrounded the site, which was an indigenous settlement of men and women living in ten homes, and prepared to en-

force their eviction. The Maracanã stadium was being refurbished to host the opening and closing ceremonies of the 2016 Olympics and the final match of the 2014 World Cup. © *AP Photo/Felipe Dana*

An indigenous man peers over the wall of an abandoned Indian museum building next door to the Maracanã stadium. The old museum had been remade into an encampment of indigenous people who needed a place to stay in Rio. Police surrounded the building, preparing to evict them. The streets around the stadium were undergoing a vast transformation as part of plans to

remake the region into a shopping and sports entertainment hub. *Personal archive/Christopher Gaffney*

A portrait of Luana, a sex worker and advocate for other *travesti* sex workers in Rio's bohemian Lapa neighborhood. She's shown in her office and pension, where she rents out rooms and watches over dozens of younger *travestis*. © *Núria López Torres*

Rio has thousands of sex workers, catering to all desires and budgets, and ranging from exclusive call girls who don't advertise, to prostitutes who walk the streets, to sex workers who paste explicit ads inside phone booths, such as this one downtown. The ads specify if the sex worker is female or a *travesti*. *Personal archive*

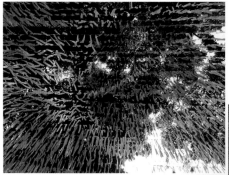

ABOVE AND RIGHT: After months of protests and clashes with the police, tension broke and Rio residents began to decorate streets in the national colors in the days leading up to the 2014 World Cup. *Personal archive*

BELOW: Brazil's national team leads fans in an emotional rendition of the national anthem before the World Cup semifinal soccer match between Brazil and Germany on Tuesday, July 8, 2014. David Luiz, right, and goalkeeper Júlio Cesar hold up the team jersey of injured Brazilian star Neymar as they sing. © *AP Photo/Matthias Schrader*

What I saw was that, with dinner on the table and democracy guaranteed, Brazilians wanted more—they wanted the whole package. The protests were the growing pains of a middle-income country with a middle class that had awakened to the reality that they paid taxes, they voted, and they wanted what was their due: decent services and elected officials who represented their interests.

After all, this was not the broke Brazil of yore that defaulted on international loans and cycled through so many currencies the Treasury had run out of historical figures with which to illustrate new bills—or so the joke went. This Brazil rested on a decade of economic stability and growth, and had enough oil reserves to pave its way to a better future. Watching the protesters with their banners, I saw a people who had long recognized the country's entrenched inequities, but who had only recently become aware of its potential. That was the Brazil they were chanting for on the streets.

There was a punch line Cariocas invoked whenever there was a massive failure of infrastructure: when a hard rain turned town squares into Olympic-sized pools, or when the commuter trains broke down in triple-digit heat, someone inevitably would pipe up, "Imagina na Copa!" Imagine during the Cup, when this city, already at capacity, will receive millions of visitors as the world watches.

Following the demonstrations on the news, the words came back to me. Imagine these scenes during the World Cup, or later, during the Olympics. Tens of thousands on the streets. Tear gas wafting into stadiums. Armed police bludgeoning protesters and journalists. I could see why the crackdown was so vicious. Authorities were desperate to stop this outpouring, by any means. They had sold the world a country that was democratic, stable, safe for investment. Angry protesters were not part of that picture.

Government officials had deeper reasons for worry. These were revolts born of higher expectations, and were likely harbingers of more upheaval. But they came at a time when the economic landscape was dramatically altered. Just when the population wanted more, Brazil's economy was stalling.

Dilma was also caught off guard. Approval of her government had plummeted from a peak of nearly 63 percent in March to 31 percent in June 2013, when collective frustration had reached a boil.

She addressed Brazilians directly on June 21, after weeks of protests. The goal was to connect with the population and reassure them she was listening, but her measured words sounded distant from the raw emotion in the streets. The determination she'd shown as a young militant had hardened into something unbending, unapproachable. Her hair was shaped into a lacquered helmet, her shoulders squared, all of her unyielding in appearance and tone. She met her electorate on television with cool caution, a Botox-smooth brow, and promises wedged between calls for restraint.

"As *presidenta* I have the obligation to hear the voice of the streets and to dialogue with all segments, but all within the dictates of law and order, which are indispensable to democracy," she said.

She did make three concrete promises: to develop a national plan for affordable public transportation, to invest the expected oil royalties in public education, and to expand the capacity of the public health network by bringing in foreign doctors.

Over the months that followed, the protests lost much of their initial force, but nonetheless persisted. Of the thousands that had marched on Rio's governor, a few score held on, camped out in front of his Leblon apartment. Cabral's approval rating sank to a dismal 12 percent. He would never recover, and he resigned before the end of his mandate.

Dilma, who had one year to go until the next round of presidential elections, got busy pushing through the measures outlined in her speech. A controversial plan brought Cuban doctors to underserved regions; Congress approved a law that dedicated the bulk of oil revenues to education and health. She met with social movements, but the population was largely unmoved. Her popularity remained a fraction of what it had once been, and Brazil was still gripped by a volatile sense of dissatisfaction. Small but frequent violent protests flared across the country.

Four months after the start of the demonstrations, she was back on television. This time the president would play her trump card, sharing with Brazilians a development that would bolster public accounts and allow the government to respond to their demands. This was the auction of Libra, the first of the deep-offshore oil fields open to exploration by foreign oil companies. In her own words, this would be Brazil's "passport to the future."

Trapped underneath a layer of salt deposited during the evaporation of a prehistoric ocean, these vast deposits are estimated to hold up to 12 billion barrels of light crude. Altogether they are the biggest oil discovery in the Americas in a generation.

Libra's contents, together with the 15.4 billion barrels estimated to lurk within the rest of the pre-salt fields, plus the rest of the country's proven reserves of 15 billion barrels, would be enough to hoist Brazil to new geopolitical heights. If these estimates proved true, Brazil could go from being the world's fifteenth-largest oil producer to one of the top ten, catapulting over China, Qatar, Kazakhstan, the United States, and Nigeria and landing somewhere near Libya, with its 48 billion proven barrels.

I followed the president's words on television, along with millions of other Brazilians. Coming from an oil family, I was more aware than most of the commodity's turbulent history, and the whiplash it had dealt Brazil not so long ago.

A mismanaged energy policy had been an important trigger in Brazil's downfall. In 1973 the country had been under the thumb of dictators but economically it flourished, feeding on cheap fuel from abroad to grow at rate of 10 percent a year. All went very well until October 16 of that year, when members of the Organization of the Petroleum Exporting Countries jacked up the price of a barrel of oil from $3 to more than $5 and pricked the balloon of the global economy.

At the time, Brazil imported 80 percent of its fuel. Faced with the sudden hike in price, the government chose to borrow money and push ahead rather than cut oil consumption and rein in the galloping pace of development. It worked in the short term. As other economies, including the United States, dipped into recessions, Brazil continued to borrow and grow. Debt soared, and so did inflation. By the end of the 1970s, interest rates on the borrowed money were ratcheted up, and Brazil was taking on new debt just to pay the interest on the old. Nineteen eighty was the last gasp in this mad race; that year Brazil still grew an incredible 9 percent. By 1982 the country was broke. Brazil defaulted on its loans. Inflation climbed from peak to peak until it reached a dizzying record of around 2,500 percent in 1993.

Now Brazil had its own source of oil. Deep within the complex geological formations of the pre-salt fields was the key to energy self-sufficiency and the solution to the country's most intractable problems, Dilma said. Having followed petroleum's bounty around the world during my childhood, I was keenly aware it was not always a blessing. For every Norway, with its generous social services, there were a handful of examples that showed the damage that mismanaged oil wealth could do. Sudden prosperity does not reform broken institutions or necessarily strengthen democratic channels. On the contrary, it often reinforces whatever social structures and power dynamics are in place. If these are corrupt and unequal, these traits can be exacerbated as well. It was still unclear how this revenue would play out in this shifting Brazil, but there were reasons to doubt it would do everything the president was promising.

The first problem was timing. Brazil had been celebrating this oil boom since November 2007, when the discovery was announced. The auction offering up Libra was momentous, but it came more than six years after the initial discovery. The excitement that followed the initial declaration had dimmed, muddled by political infighting among Brazilian states and the federal government about how to share the profit. As the years passed, Brazil's discovery was overshadowed by developments elsewhere, such as the exploration of shale oil and tar sands that had bolstered North America's energy potential and again tilted the global energy tables.

Lawsuits marred the run-up to the auction, and it took a task force of three hundred federal government lawyers to fend off the twenty-seven legal challenges. Protesters—from nationalist, it's-our-oil types to striking Petrobras workers—gathered at the beachfront hotel where the auction took place and clashed with soldiers sent to contain them, enveloping surfers and sunbathers in a nauseous mix of chanting and tear gas.

Then there was the way the auction was handled. With a focus on short-term gains, the federal government required participants to pay a mandatory signing bonus of $7 billion. This would bolster Brazil's primary surplus in the year leading up to the election, but it was steep, even by international oil company standards. This and other restrictive conditions scared off giants in the business such as Chevron, ExxonMobil, and BP. Of the more than forty companies expected to take part in the auction, only eleven confirmed their participation.[1]

The result: the jewel of Brazil's oil bonanza attracted a single

---

1 Private companies would also have to follow a host of stipulations during oil exploration. Brazil had switched from a concession-based system to a production-sharing one in which the fields remained in the hands of the government and the private sector partner got a share of oil for its participation. Under these rules, Petrobras would be the sole operator of the pre-salt fields and retain one-third of the control of all ventures. The Brazilian government would get a cut of at least 41.65 percent of the profit oil.

bid. It was a consortium led by Petrobras with 40 percent participation, China's CNOOC and CNPC with 10 percent each, France's Total and the United Kingdom–based Royal Dutch Shell, with 20 percent apiece.

Given the apparent lack of enthusiasm, Dilma's first job was to reassure the population that the sale had been a success. Indeed, the consortium was a solid and politically palatable mix of foreign and domestic, public and private companies. Together they had the cash and the experience to develop Libra, an adventure expected to cost about $400 billion, according to IHS, the largest consulting firm in the sector.

Also, under the terms of the agreement, approximately 85 percent of the revenue generated would revert back to Brazil, directly or through Petrobras. As promised, approximately $50 billion over ten years would be dedicated exclusively to two of the areas where protesters had clamored for investment: education and health.

Federal policy also dictated that up to 70 percent of all the gas ducts, supporting ships, platforms, and other equipment necessary to produce this oil had to be made in Brazil. This hamstrung Petrobras and other companies involved, but it promised jobs and investment, much of it in Rio.

But Dilma's post-auction speech did nothing to assuage concerns about its most debated aspect: the heavy hand with which her administration had shaped the process, imposing restrictions and costs on participants to bolster public coffers during a politically sensitive year.

This came at a time when investors were already wary of other interventions in the economy to keep up appearances. Inflation control was an example. By 2013, this old haunt was rearing its head again, though it remained just within the generous ceiling of 6.5 percent. The official inflation number was artificial, though, the result of price caps on costs the government could control, like fuel, electricity, and transportation. These fixed costs balanced other rising expenses. They also weakened some of the most important national companies, such as Petrobras and Eletrobras, by forcing them to sell their fuel and electricity at a loss.

Dilma's administration was increasingly reliant on this kind of intervention. It worked in the short term, but was unsustainable in the long run, injecting uncertainty into the market. How long would the price holds last? And when these expenses went up, as they would have to, what would they mean for household expenses, industrial costs, and inflation figures?

These questions, together with the sluggish growth of recent years, cast doubt on the country's direction and its long-term financial health.

The international scenario that had helped in the early 2000s, with its high commodity prices and great demand for Brazil's exports, was a thing of the past. The spending and credit access that had fueled the economy internally had run its course. There would be no new consumer run on televisions, cars, and washing machines. By the Libra auction, this growth model had played itself out, and it was starting to show. Two thousand thirteen was the third slow year in a row; Brazil was no longer a sure thing.

That impression was nailed home by news that the oil firm OGX, crown jewel in pop-star billionaire Eike Batista's coterie of companies, was filing for bankruptcy protection. It would prove the unraveling of his empire.

I'd watched Eike since my return. He was the country's wealthiest man, an inveterate self-promoter who put himself forward as the sun-kissed face of this can-do Brazil. He also identified closely with Rio, putting $11 million of his own money into the city's Olympic bid and contributing $10 million a year to the UPP program, among many other projects.

In a year and a half, he'd had gone from poster boy of the country's economic turnaround to starring in the continent's biggest corporate bust. His fall shook the oil world, but also reverberated

well beyond it, raising more questions about Brazil's economic fitness and the future of the city he was helping remake.

The tale had the contours of a telenovela, the prime-time soaps
that keep devotees entranced with hairpin plot twists and juicy
make-out scenes. Eike was a self-styled leading man, with a chiseled jaw, gray-blue eyes set off by a dusting of gray at the temples,
and a melodramatic lifestyle. He had been a powerboat racing
champion and husband to Luma de Oliveira, a *Playboy* centerfold
and actress who danced her way through the Carnaval parade one
year wearing nothing but sequins, towering platform heels, and
Eike's name on a choker. They divorced in 2004, but not before
bearing two sons named after Norse gods, Thor and Olin.

Brazil's superrich don't usually flaunt it, out of safety concerns
if nothing else. But Eike liked to traffic in superlatives. His private
yacht was often seen hugging Rio's sinuous coastline, and he had
another, a 177-foot converted cruise ship kitted out as a party boat.
A silver Mercedes-Benz SLR McLaren, one of his many cars, was
often left on display inside his mansion's living room.

Beyond the gossip-magazine material, what made his story
fascinating was the degree to which the billionaire's rise paralleled
Brazil's own. Eike also owed much of his fortune to commodities.
After trying his luck at several businesses and riding out a minor
boom-and-bust cycle with a gold mining project, he started an
energy company in 2001 and an iron ore firm four years later. Both
went public. But it was the pre-salt finds that Lula called "a second
chance for Brazil" that would be Eike's ticket to the top.

In July 2007, a month after Petrobras confirmed the pre-salt
discovery, he launched OGX with the intention of going after any
offshore fields Petrobras missed. He'd never worked in oil before,
but by then no one doubted Eike's golden finger. The firm's initial
public offering in 2008 was the biggest in Brazilian history and
raised nearly $4 billion.

Back then, Brazil was a party; investors who wanted to dance came to him—big names like BlackRock, Pimco, Mubadala, E.On, General Electric, ExxonMobil, IBM.

At his peak, he was inescapable. The man tweeted like a teenager, entertained celebrities, wrote a book of corporate advice, posed for photos, and regaled journalists with quotable bites spiked with his trademark hubris: "My companies are idiot-proof," or "The world belongs to the daring." When Charlie Rose asked him what he wanted in the next ten years, he replied, "I want to be the world's richest man."

Those who found his performance grating or his strategies reckless kept quiet, glad to be participating in the bounty. Critics were shunted out of sight.

Eike projected himself onto Rio, remaking the city he loved in his own, larger-than-life image. Beyond donations to the Olympic bid and to the UPP program, he had stakes in the Maracanã stadium and contributed to cleaning up the lagoon by Ipanema. With loans from the national development bank, he began renovations of the old Hotel Glória, a handsome building with an Art Deco façade and known for its traditional Carnaval costume balls, and bought a twenty-four-story building with commanding views of the bay to transform into a hotel in time for the Olympics.

His empire would come together at the super-port of Açú. Set in a remote corner of northeastern Rio state, it was, like everything he touched, meant to be better, bigger, grander. Its footprint was one and a half times that of Manhattan. Once it was completed and running the mega-operation would handle 350 million tons of goods a year and link Eike's logistics, shipbuilding, energy, and oil ventures in a self-contained loop that would feed itself and mint money.

When he hosted President Dilma and Governor Cabral in Açú in April 2012, the president put on the company's orange jacket and gushed: "Eike is our standard . . . Brazil's pride."

The plan behind Açú was brash and nakedly ambitious—pure

Eike. All of it rested on his collection of start-ups, especially OGX and its promise of oil.

So when, just over a year after the president's visit, OGX announced its wells were duds, what could have been a contained disaster in the hands of a more cautious man instead brought down his empire. He was overleveraged, running a business built largely on debt, charisma, and the promise of this new Brazil. When the bills came due, he couldn't pay. Investors fled and prepared legal action.

His projects around Rio were abandoned, visual cues of his spectacular crash: a UPP station was left, half built, in Batan. The Hotel Glória, which I biked past on my way to the Sunday farmer's market, stood amid abandoned cranes. The twenty-four-story building in Flamengo was deserted, and the sight of its gutted and weedy carcass reiterated the question: to what extent had Eike represented Brazil, and Rio in particular? More important, how much would they share his fate?

Lula, who'd famously said it was easy to help the poor, also said in 2010 that "it was rich people who made the most money during my administration," making clear that Brazil under the Workers' Party was very much open for business. Dilma had less compunction about making capital's needs second to those of the state. The über-capitalist Eike had been the fig leaf that covered this up.

Now Eike's empire had crumbled, the government's accounts were deteriorating, and investors scanning the world's economies for a place to put their money began to pull away.

Brazilians had noticed their buoyant economy was deflating, and that the years of plenty had not been used to invest in the economy or raise productivity. This was evident from the posters raised during the 2013 protests. As the tax burden grew and became one of the world's highest, at 36 percent of GDP, the population did not receive better services or infrastructure for it. They just got a bigger bureaucracy.

Transportation of goods, for example, was inordinately expensive because of poor roads, rail lines, ports, and airports; this jacked up the cost of living and made Brazilian products less competitive abroad. But the main federal program to improve infrastructure, the Programa de Aceleração do Crescimento, or Growth Acceleration Program, which was launched in 2007 and expanded in 2010, was very much behind schedule and over budget by 2013.

The number of federal ministries, however, had grown with each administration, going from 24 under Fernando Henrique Cardoso to 37 under Lula to 39 under Dilma. Each hung heavy with appointees and public servants. Together, they cost the taxpayer $27 billion in 2013.

Voters had marched during the Confederations Cup. They could do so again during the World Cup and the Olympics, transforming what had been intended as the country's moment to shine into a sharp-edged political rally.

So, was the party over? Perhaps, but this was not all that bad.

Eike's empire had rested on debt and his high-wattage smile. Brazil, in spite of its serious structural problems, had a solid economy with a flawed but functioning democracy. It had grown in ways that mattered, that started with the economy but went well beyond. The June 2013 marches may have unnerved the president, but they were a symptom of this maturity.

What the country needed most was, in fact, what the demonstrators had pointed out: painful, difficult, but necessary reforms. These included trimming government rolls, improving services and infrastructure, and tearing up the red tape that made running a business or renting an apartment so daunting.

The tax code could be simplified. The school system, which favored universities accessible mostly to the elite over elementary education or technical training, could be brought to better balance. None of these things were easy, and they would not gain the economy traction immediately, but would get the country in shape for steady, if unspectacular, progress.

So, in spite of Dilma's words, oil would not, could not, be Brazil's salvation. There would be no miracles.

But increased cash flow could help, if well managed. There were niches in the national economy and in Rio's landscape where this was already taking place. To understand the impact it could have, I visited Rio's port, deep within Guanabara Bay's embrace.

The old docks had been the city's engine for centuries. Smooth granite blocks, laid in the era before concrete, still lined the bay's oil-slicked waters. The port had anchored Brazil's naval industry through the late 1970s, when it was the second largest in the world, behind only Japan.

Back then, it had housed the largest shipyard in South America, the Inhaúma, from which sailed the greatest ships ever assembled in the country—hulks such as the *Tijuca*, which could carry 311,000 tons in its steel belly. In the 1980s, the economy collapsed and took the entire industry with it.

By the end of the 1990s, Brazil had stopped producing ships and oil platforms and the Inhaúma was abandoned. Bright orange blossoms of rust etched the picked-apart innards of the old yard and the vaulted ribs holding up empty warehouses. Only the long-limbed cranes remained standing, their spare bodies crumpling into themselves before the eyes of drivers on the overpass nearby.

Now, with the certainty of oil waiting just beyond the horizon and beneath miles of ocean, sand, rock, and salt, the shipyard began to stir again. In 2011 an old ship slipped past the pillars of the Rio-Niterói Bridge and into Guanabara Bay. It was the tanker

Titan Seema, essentially a bucket with a motor built in 1993 to ferry crude from port to port and retired two decades later, when its outdated engines made it too expensive to operate.

When this giant pulled into the Inhaúma, it was the meeting of two veterans. The shipyard hadn't built so much as a canoe in over a decade. And yet, it was tasked with transforming the *Titan Seema* into P-74, a floating industrial plant able to suck in oil from the deep, separate it from corrosive gases, water, and other gunk, store the fuel, and then offload it to ships in high seas, all the while keeping its position through storms, high wind, and the jostle of waves by relying on high-end computerized systems.

By late 2013, the transformation that would bring the shipyard back into shape was well under way. The manager, Alexandre Cruz, walked with me through the Inhaúma's innards and explained its complex and costly rebirth. Brazil's shipping industry had deteriorated to such an extent it was virtually being created from scratch, he explained.

Stocky and weathered by the sun, Cruz had close-cropped hair and a punctilious manner. He'd known the Inhaúma since the 1980s, when Brazil still had a fleet to be reckoned with. He worked on board Petrobras vessels and would dock there when the ships came in for repairs. Back then, the place had been alive with workers, he said; for every boat resting on the support pillars at the bottom of the Inhaúma dry dock there was another one waiting its turn outside.

The slow collapse of the place tore at him. The single company that continued to use the yard for basic repairs cannibalized the broken machinery for parts needed to keep a few essentials in working shape; the ground was littered with their remains.

When the commercial docks had died, they had taken the neighborhood, Caju, with them.

In the eighteenth and nineteenth century, Caju had housed gentry. Hand-painted, blue-and-white Portuguese tiles and granite doorways still decorated façades of the few colonial homes that stood. Once upon a time, not long after 1808, when the Portuguese royal family had settled in Rio, the emperor Dom João VI came to Caju for his medicinal ocean baths. The rest of the royals followed suit and started a fad, turning Caju into Rio's first beach resort. Through the early twentieth century, bathers would board trolleys and head to its beach for a day at the sea.

In the years that followed, Caju lost its shine and became an extension of the dock, the home of fishermen and stevedores. While the waterfront hummed with work, it remained vibrant, but when the country fell on hard times, the shipyard let its people go, and the neighborhood collapsed further into itself.[2]

For decades, decay wore down the little peninsula. Abandoned trucks lay beached on the sidewalks, their husks stripped of anything that could be sold. The trash company stopped making its rounds, and refuse piled; no one filled potholes as they appeared in the streets, and when the sewage system backed up, it spewed unmolested, turning manholes into foul fountains. A favela sprouted among the wreckage.

Now the shipyards and the docks at the heart of Caju were working again. Alexandre led me through a landscape of all-encompassing industry. Although we were by the water, not far from where small islands overflowed with exuberant greenery, we were battered by the screech of drills puncturing metal, the corrosive nose-feel of solvent, and the bustle of thousands of workers.

We finally reached the ship itself, nested inside a dry dock. Even by the vast dimensions of the shipyard, it was extraordinary—an empty shell the length of a hundred-story skyscraper laid on its side.

The race to reach the oil was such that the ship and the ship-

---

2 Highways also severed Caju from the city and increased its isolation: first Avenida Brasil, in the 1940s, then the Linha Vermelha, a highway linking the airport to downtown.

yard were being brought out of retirement at the same time, Alexandre explained. The six thousand welders, mechanics, painters, electricians, and others who hurried about, setting a frenetic pace, were evenly split between the two jobs. "We've already lost too much time as it is," he said.

The ship's guts had been carved out to make way for the platform parts and lay beside it, a mountain of contorted steel. Metalworkers had examined its cavernous insides, capable of storing 1.4 million barrels of oil, to see where it had worn too thin for use. On the great upswell of its hull there were shiny scars where plates had been replaced as well as X's, arrows, and circles drawn in chalk, hieroglyphics understandable only to the experts.

The ship-cum-platform was about ready for a coat of paint. After refurbishing, it would go to the Paranaguá shipyard in southern Brazil to be topped with three stories' worth of cutting-edge equipment before heading out to the pre-salt fields.

It was that vast oil discovery that made the Inhaúma's regeneration feasible, Alexandre said. Even now, the shipyard had an order to create four of these platforms for Petrobras.

We turned away from the ship and began to head back to the entrance. I noticed the safety signs were in Portuguese and Mandarin. It's because of the new cranes, Alexandre said; they came from China on board Korean ships. Three were already standing, red and white, vibrant against the luminous gray sky. Another was perched on a ship, about to be offloaded and then assembled by the Chinese crew that came with it.

I asked about the crumpled cranes that had dangled over the port for so many years. Their twisted shapes had come to stand in my mind for the desolation of the docks, and of Rio.

Alexandre stopped, looked to where they had stood. The cranes had been taken apart, he said. It was one of the first things he did.

"This is how I think about it: We've got this technical side. We have to get permits, refurbish, operate, all at the same time," he said. "But there's also the psychological side. We had to improve the way this looked. It impacted the morale of the workers, their productivity, our credibility. We had to show people things were changing."

After visiting the shipyard, I wanted to walk and think, to weigh the vigorous optimism of someone like Alexandre against the broader challenges facing Rio and Brazil. Since I was in Caju, and I'd always wanted to see the emperor's bathhouse, I went looking for the place. It still stood somewhere in this neighborhood.

Beyond the gates of the shipyard there were signs of improvement. Policing had returned when a UPP was inaugurated in early 2013; officers in their blue button-downs kept watch over narrow streets. Homegrown restaurants serving up rice and beans had sprung up to feed the workers who had returned. Trees had been pruned recently, and the piles of garbage were largely gone.

Abandoned trucks still hogged the sidewalks, pushing me into roads where the sparse traffic raised little tornados of dust. Although it was early evening, there were streets in which I was the only pedestrian. Low-lying colonial houses with chipped blue windowsills and tired once-white walls were boarded up, their planks splintering.

Of Caju Beach only the name remained. Landfill had pushed the ocean hundreds of feet away, and Praia do Caju was now the name of the street that lay where the bay once met the sand. Cobblestones paved the way to number 385, the bathhouse. Half a dozen palm trees stood guard before the modest whitewashed and green-shuttered house. The little plaza it faced would have been bucolic if it weren't for the busy Rio-Niterói Bridge arcing above. Cars sped by, nose to tail, creating their own winds and ruffling the mop tops on the palms.

The doors were locked. A sleepy-eyed man answered my knocks by opening a window. The bathhouse was closed. He didn't know why, *querida*, he didn't know when it would open, he didn't know who to ask. "Volta mais tarde, meu amor." Come back later. He just didn't know.

Not too far away, the Inhaúma was forging a part of Brazil's future. Standing by Alexandre, I had felt its frenetic energy and through it, the country's promise. Standing in front of the emperor's bathhouse on the cobblestones still warm from the afternoon sun, faced with the guard's eternal indifference, I felt the weight of Brazil's past. What had been achieved in the past decade and a half—the stability, the decrease in inequality, the strengthening of the middle class—was tremendous. But there was a legacy of centuries to be surmounted.

Two large, glossy cockroaches scuttled by my feet, resolute and innocent like windup toys. I turned to wave good-bye to the guard, but he'd already closed the shutters.

CHAPTER 17

FUTEBOL NATION

The idea was irresistible: the grandest soccer tournament in the world, hosted by the nation where "*futebol* is not only a sport, but a passion, a national passion."

With these words, Lula accepted the 2014 World Cup on behalf of Brazil. For once, the loquacious president was restrained. Ask Brazilians about soccer and you usually get breathless hyperbole. Other countries united around wars, raised their flag for myriad championships, annual independence parades, elections. Brazil waved its flag once every four years for the Seleção, the national team. The eleven men in canary-yellow jerseys were "the nation in cleats," in the words of Nelson Rodrigues, one of Brazil's best-known writers; their games were celebrated or mourned in great cathartic outpourings.

Soccer alone provided this continent-sized nation with a shared ritual and a common narrative. Over decades, this connection to the sport had become mythical; if culture is the stories we tell about ourselves, Brazil's story was spun around the ball.

There was that style, the *futebol arte*, a playful dance with the ball that was seen as quintessentially Brazilian, born of the racial and cultural gumbo of our origins. More than an approach to the game, it was held up as a representation of who we were and how we lived. Brazilians saw themselves as a people who fought harsh conditions not with bloody insurrections but with their wits, their irreverence, and the now-you-see-it, now-you-don't dribble of the street-smart hustler. There was a pinch of this *jeitinho* in the way they played the game, there was *jogo de cintura*, rhythm, spontaneity. Futebol arte was held in contrast to stereotypical European style: organized, professional, disciplined—in other words, stiff, planned, boring.

This way of playing took as much glee in showmanship, in leaving the opponent flummoxed and the audience delighted, as in driving the ball to the net. But it was also very effective. Between the 1950s and the 1970s, this style coalesced into three World Cup trophies in four tournaments. The 1970 World Cup was played during the worst years of the dictatorship. The national team won six of six matches, showing Brazilians that art could triumph even amid brutality, ignorance, and fear.

All told, Brazil had five World Cup trophies, more than any other nation. Soccer was a reliable mirror that always showed the nation at its best. This made it beloved during the long years in which we had little else on which to stake our national pride.

It also won Brazil much acclaim abroad. When the World Cup rolled around, the Seleção was nearly every country's favorite after their own national team. This fondness came through for me more times than I can count, earning me instant favor with a near-deaf cobbler in a small Greek town, a free lunch from an Algerian *bourek*-maker squinting over a deep fryer, an appreciative nod from a cantankerous parking lot attendant in a Rome. What would start as a stilted, wordless transaction between two people who shared nothing would tilt once I pointed to myself and said, "Brazil!" Along a broad swath of the globe, this would spark a smile and the inevitable response: "Pelé! Pelé!"

It was in this light that Lula welcomed the chance to host the

World Cup. The appeal was obvious; why not harness all this goodwill to a broader political project?

Brazil's Cup would have two burdens. The first was to show off recent progress, prove the country could manage the logistics of a major international event, and assert the nation's position internationally. The second was pure soccer: to reaffirm Brazil's primacy on the pitch and heal an old wound.

Two thousand fourteen would not be the first time Brazil hosted the championship. It had happened once before, in 1950. With Europe in tatters after World War II, FIFA had looked to South America. The war had been good for Brazil; industry and agriculture had prospered, and the country had assumed a leading political and economic role in the continent. For the young democracy trying to carve a global position for itself in the first years of the Cold War, the Cup would be a chance to spread a modern, progressive image. The sporting infrastructure would reflect Brazil's engineering and technological capacities, and Brazil's prowess with the ball would further its nation-building project.

This kind of dramaturgy deserved a stage to match, a stadium that was grand and contemporary, a reflection of the country's might and the promise of its future. There was fierce resistance to such extravagance from a segment that wanted schools and hospitals instead, but after much debate in the media and at city hall, the municipal government approved the stadium's construction. It would be the largest arena on the globe, and it would sit on the geographic heart of Rio like a giant buckle, connecting the wealthy south and the working-class north.

Raising the stadium for that first Brazilian World Cup became a patriotic affair; construction funds were complemented by thirty thousand families in exchange for rights to a seat for a few years or in perpetuity. It was officially named Estádio Municipal, and later, Estádio Jornalista Mário Filho, after one of its most vocal advocates, but Cariocas nicknamed it Maracanã after the river that flowed nearby. That's the name that stuck.

The project was beset by problems and delays. Even on the day of the final World Cup match, July 16, 1950, the public had to step around exposed rebar to find their seats. No matter. Even unfinished, the Maracanã was elegant and powerful, a double-tiered colossus in white concrete, and a fitting crown for the nation's certain victory.

Brazilians expected nothing short of glory. The country entered the 1950 World Cup a strong favorite, and reached the finals with the makings of a champion. After a 2–2 stumble against Switzerland, they'd trounced Sweden and Spain. This left only Uruguay— tiny Uruguay. The Seleção had a one-point advantage. Under the rules of the time, they only needed a draw in that last game to win the Cup.

Before the match, Rio's mayor addressed the team through the state-of-the-art public address system.

"You who will be consecrated within a few minutes as champions of the world, you who have no rivals on the planet, you who I already greet as winners . . ."

Brazil stopped to listen. The stadium could hold 170,000, but that day around 200,000 packed its stands, nearly 10 percent of Rio's population at the time. Among them were perhaps three hundred Uruguayan fans. Thousands of Cariocas encircled the arena to listen and be close to the action; millions listened on their radios at home.

". . . I have been true to my word and have built this stadium," the mayor concluded. "Now fulfill your duty and win the World Cup."

The moment was seared into the memory of twelve-year-old

Léo Rabello. He had followed every turn of the 1950 championship. When we met, sixty-four years later, he could still recite the
names of players, scores, and the tense moments in each game.

His father, a military man, had been among those who'd done
his duty and bought a permanent seat in the stadium. The exhilaration of the twelve-year-old soccer fanatic still rang in his voice decades later. Léo remembered the day of that final match in detail.

He took the tram with his parents and joined the throngs flowing into the Maracanã. The stands were packed; they found their
seats. The mayor spoke. Anticipation clenched his throat. Léo, his
parents, the team, all of Brazil hung breathless, together, waiting
for the shrill sound of the referee's whistle.

The game started. Over the next forty-five minutes, the public
had to swallow a tight, scoreless match. The tension rose; Brazil
could win with a tie, but it was too close for comfort. Two minutes
into the second half, Brazil scored: 1–0.

A collective exhalation rose from the crowd, then an explosion
of fireworks.

"We felt like everything was resolved," Léo said. "It was a sense
of total bliss."

The second half ticked by, each passing minute bringing Brazil
closer to victory. In the sixtieth minute, Uruguay scored. It was
1–1. This shook Brazilian confidence, but the end was near. Brazil
just had to keep the game tied. As the score held and the minutes
flew, FIFA's president, Jules Rimet, left to oversee Brazil's victory
commemoration. When he returned five minutes later, he was met
by a morbid silence. Uruguay had scored. Again.

"It was as if the world had ended," said Léo. "No funeral wake
has that silence, the silence of two hundred thousand people."

It is still possible to read the shock of the moment and watch it
crumple into sorrow on thousands of faces captured on the grainy,
black-and-white footage of the time. Brazilians of all backgrounds,
gathered as one, gave themselves over to grief. Perfectly coiffed

women in strings of pearls turned aside, trying modestly to hide their tears; working men in shirtsleeves raised thick-knuckled hands to their faces, eyes brimming over, or let sinewy arms hang, useless. Léo saw his father cry for the first time.

That day, Brazil lost much more than a game. Because of the buildup and the ties to national identity, the defeat was a blow to the core, a public deflation of the country's pride and its aspirations. It cast doubt on our worth as a people and as a nation.

The Seleção cast aside the white jerseys in which they had played that day; they'd never wear them again. The press, which had praised Brazil's mixed-race team and their unique style as a reflection of our best selves, now turned the myth inside out, singling out the black players, and particularly the goalie, as scapegoats for the disaster. Brazil wouldn't have another black goalkeeper for forty-five years.

"It was irreversible, that loss. We never recovered," said Léo. "Brazil might have won other times, in other places, but that loss was a wound that wouldn't heal."

He should know. Léo dedicated his life to soccer and made it his career. After rising through the administrative ranks to the top of his own his club, Flamengo, he recognized the market potential of Brazil's great players. These were men who could be geniuses on the field but often knew next to nothing about negotiating contracts and building a brand. Léo became FIFA's first licensed agent; his registration number is 001. Over the years, he shepherded generations of footballers from club to club in Brazil and around the world, and watched as the game he loved was profoundly transformed.

Players who were once locally grown and locally loved became global commodities; the sport moved billions of dollars. The Maracanã also suffered profound changes. Over time, it lost its democratic essence as a series of reforms wiped out the cheap standing-only section, installed VIP boxes, and destroyed all of the internal architecture. Its open, concrete bleachers were swapped for numbered chairs in molded plastic that held just over 78,000 fans, nearly 100,000 fewer than the original Maracanã.

The game and the stadium were much changed by 2014, but the symbolic weight of a World Cup in Brazil was still there. If anything, the burden on the Seleção was heavier. Sixty-four years after that traumatic loss, futebol was being called on, once again, to elevate Brazil on the field and beyond it. The final game of the 2014 Cup would be in the Maracanã. Brazil would finally have a chance to repair that old injury with a victory in what was still one of the sport's most hallowed grounds.

Irresistible, right?

No one, not the FIFA officials who handed the World Cup to Brazil, nor Lula, who accepted it, had thought the path to 2014 would be smooth. But the ride had been more harrowing than anyone anticipated, and from its start, the year of the Cup—the year that should have been all glee and giddy high hopes in the country of futebol—felt strained, dangerous.

A stagnant heat hunkered over the city in the first months of 2014, blocking the cool southern breezes and withering any clouds. The sun, relentless as a curse, baked the streets, strained the energy grid, and torched the vegetation. It was the hottest summer in half a century. There was no relief: the ocean's surface felt like a warm shower. A five-hundred-mile-wide mass of dead algae hovered just off the coast like a bad omen.

The stifling temperature left Cariocas on edge, and barbed everyday exchanges with impatience. But it wasn't just the weather. Aspects of life in Rio that had seen real improvement or that had offered well-founded reasons for hope just a handful of years ago—the economy, the environment, the feeling of safety when walking down the street at night—had recently suffered reversals or ended in failure. There was a sense of expectations pushed too far. What had been the punch line to a joke—*imagina na Copa!*—became a sarcastic mantra. Imagine during the Cup. What if Brazil fell apart as the world watched?

After years of sluggish growth, the economy was showing signs of real stress. The federal government's efforts to control the cost of living by artificially capping fuel and electricity prices were revealing themselves for what they were: *gambiarras*, makeshift solutions designed to get the country to the October presidential elections, leaving costs and consequences for later.

Petrobras, the state-controlled oil company, predicted it would have to spend $18.8 billion in 2014 to keep the country running on subsidized fuel. The electric sector stayed afloat with a $5.4 billion government-engineered loan, but this would have to be paid back through substantial rate increases in the years to come.

None of these mechanisms kept inflation from punching through the projected ceiling. Economists forecast another year of very low growth and floated ugly words like "recession."

Brazilians felt this as prices spiked in places that hurt: education, food, transportation, and housing led the list. As consumer debt hit record highs, banks raised interest rates, squeezing the new middle class. Each uptick pushed families closer to missing payments on their kid's braces, their teenager's English classes, the parents' new Volkswagen.

Even the traditional Carioca options for blowing off steam, soccer and the beach, were soaring out of reach. The first game I attended in the refurbished Maracanã set me back $30 for the cheapest ticket, about one-tenth of a month's minimum wage salary. A coconut from the beach vendor's cooler cost $3; a fashionable bikini went for a stratospheric $200. Even the bus fares had inched up once the protests of 2013 were a safe distance away.

Any careful observer picking up the newspaper could see the escalation of government spending, the lackluster stock market, and the unfavorable trade balance. By the end of summer, Standard & Poor's had cut Brazil's standing to its lowest investment-grade rating. No one was surprised.

Rio embodied this sense that Brazil's moment might be passing before it arrived. The city had been in dire need of investment for decades. Cariocas had high hopes that the international events that started with the Pan-American Games would bring measures to curb chronic congestion, pollution, and violence.

But they were learning, at great cost, that massive sporting events have short-term objectives and tight deadlines that do not mesh well with long-term city planning goals. In Rio, contracts bound resources to the needs of external organizations, creating a permanent state of exception that left no room or time for debate, consideration of broader needs, or the reform of flawed institutions. On the contrary, these pressures reinforced the existing hierarchies; the rush to kickoff or the torch lighting justified the further concentration of power and shortened decision-making processes.

Over four years, I'd seen this at work in the removal of favelas without due process; in the scrapped environmental reviews; in social cleansing policies that targeted street vendors, prostitutes, drug users, and the homeless; and in the further arming of a police force still lacking accountability. Gentrification worsened an already serious housing crisis even as favela-upgrading programs like Morar Carioca were cut off at the root.

With a couple of months to go before the World Cup and two years until the Olympics, many of the projects that were put in place were proving insufficient or poorly planned, with budget overruns, lapsed schedules, and unforeseen social or environmental costs.

Take transportation. Improved mobility was billed as an important legacy of hosting these sporting events, but one of the first projects to fall by the wayside was the bullet train between

Rio and São Paulo. Only half of the transit projects in the twelve World Cup host cities were delivered in time. Of those, one-third were incomplete. Many were abandoned, which critics pointed out was not all bad, as they had been terrible ideas from the start.

The undersupply of mass transit, the myriad construction projects, and the continued federal tax incentives for buying cars had tipped Rio's infamous traffic from frustrating to unbearable. To Cariocas, this meant time wasted and extra gas that cost drivers more than $13 billion in 2013 alone, according to Rio de Janeiro Federation of Industries, FIRJAN. No wonder motorists leaned on their horns, blasting out their anger.

The environment continued to suffer as more users were introduced to already overtaxed systems. Manhole covers exploded because of underground gas leaks; massive water mains ruptured, destroying homes and drowning residents; the sight of backed-up sewage pipes burbling in the gutters of my neighborhood no longer surprised me.

The push to clean up waterways was so behind schedule as to be practically abandoned by that summer. The promise had been to treat 80 percent of the sewage going into lakes and the bay, but Guanabara was still a toilet, while the state government acknowledged that less than 15 percent of the promised $4 billion needed to complete the sewage treatment plan was available.

Garbage was on everyone's mind—and nose—that summer. Rio's trash collectors went on strike during Carnaval, demanding a raise to their $360 a month salary. Mountains of refuse left to rot in the sun exacerbated the usual city-wide hangover and left entire neighborhoods gagging.

In the midst of the strike, the mayor was caught on camera tossing half-munched fruit over his shoulder during a political event. The message was clear: even the poster boy for the city's anti-littering campaign had failed to change his habits.

• • •

The scent wafting off the bay, the garbage bags rippling with flies, the rising prices, and the heat, the unrelenting heat—all this left Cariocas chafing. But perhaps the deepest disappointment concerned security. By the summer of 2014, several cases of explicit police violence had raised questions about the possibility of improving one of the state's most corrupt institutions.

After he took over as head of state security, Beltrame had pushed through reforms to make the police force more professional, more accountable, and less violent. By 2010, Rio's streets were safer than they had been in years. Crime had decreased, but perhaps just as important was the belief that improvement was possible. The experiment with Pacification Police Units within favelas left 74 percent of Rio residents feeling safer, according to a 2012 survey. This sense of safety, both real and perceived, was riddled with caveats: it was frail and it was unequal, hovering protectively over some people and some neighborhoods, eluding others. Still, it heightened expectations and fed demands even among those whom it did not reach.

These changes had started with real promise. In early 2011, during the months that followed the takeover of the Alemão complex, law enforcement faced some of its most glaring failings as investigations revealed corruption, murder, and cover-ups among rank and file as well as leadership.

The police chief, Mário Sérgio Duarte, had promised zero tolerance for the lawlessness that he called "a plague" within the force. During his tenure, he'd pushed out dozens of dirty officers, including heads of UPP units. Still, evidence of gruesome crimes by police continued to surface, and pressure mounted on the commander. He managed it all—until August 2011, when events took a turn straight out of mafia playbooks.

A state judge known for being tough on rogue police was shot twenty-one times with police-issued bullets in front of her house. Judge Patricia Acioli's murder was seen as a warning to the entire legal establishment. Eleven officers from the town of São Gonçalo were arrested and charged in her death. Among them was Cláudio de Oliveira, then in his first position of authority as chief of São Gonçalo's police battalion. His old friend from BOPE training days, Mário Sérgio, had nominated him for the job.

Police refer to purges among their ranks as "cutting our own flesh." Mário Sérgio had often taken that knife to others during his tenure. When he was faced with accusations against his friend and appointee, he turned the knife on himself. As chief of state police, all nominations were his responsibility. He took the blame and resigned. All eleven police officers were found guilty in the judge's murder, including the head of the battalion, Cláudio de Oliveira. As the summer of 2014 wound down, the men were sentenced to up to thirty-six years in prison.

Cariocas had last seen their police chief at the top of his game, addressing his troops from a *caveirão* and claiming victory on TV over the adversary in the hills. Now they watched the man brought down by the police corps' biggest challenge—the enemy within, the *banda podre*.

The case buried Mário Sérgio's career. The ambitious cop's cop took a job in the interior and spent his free time writing or helping his wife with their twins. With his chiseled features, ramrod sense of right and wrong, and unwavering loyalty to a fallen friend, he embodied the schizophrenic currents that coursed within state's police. Rio's criminals and cops were intimately twined, and the effort of pulling them apart could fray the fabric of the force to the highest levels; it could destroy even the most dedicated individuals.

The trust of Cariocas in the UPP program was also suffering under mounting evidence of dishonesty and brutality. One case came to represent its failures: the disappearance of a construction worker named Amarildo de Souza within the Rocinha favela.

After an investigation, twenty-five UPP officers were indicted as suspects in his kidnapping, his torture within their base, and his murder. By the summer of 2014, the state government issued a statement officially presuming him dead. The announcement would have to suffice for Amarildo's wife and seven children. They never got a body to bury.

In the face of the police force's weakened credibility, gangsters staged coordinated attacks against UPP bases across Rio that summer; shoot-outs shut down the city's main tunnel and left half a dozen pacification officers dead, four of them in Alemão.

That sprawling community was once again representative of the troubles afflicting the city as a whole. Shock troops reinforced strategic points; residents suffered searches and restrictions on their movement. Gun battles canceled classes for thousands of children and forced shut for days the gondola service that the president had inaugurated with pomp. Alemão's community health center was attacked, its computers and equipment destroyed. Doctors quit.

Its borders, which had grown porous to outsiders like myself, began to close down again. Walking through the alleys I felt that familiar reluctance of ordinary people to speak openly to a stranger. The attacks against the police, the uncertainty over who was the *dono do morro*, left locals feeling exposed.

"I was one of the people who stood here and waved a white banner out the window when the police first came," said one man, the owner of a hole-in-the-wall paper goods store. He shook his head, as if chiding himself for the naïveté of a few years ago. "Now, how can we trust them, if they can't even defend themselves?"

If anyone gained from the experiment, it was Diego, the Red Command trafficker who had turned himself in to face justice.

Ever the hustler, he remade himself even as the police chief who had orchestrated his rendition went down and the favela that was once his home slid into chaos.

The murder charge against him hadn't stuck; after a year in prison he walked free. He found a niche as a cameraman for a non-profit that worked rehabbing former traffickers and had discovered a talent for American football, which was growing in popularity. The young man who couldn't leave Alemão for fear of arrest or death at the hands of police now traveled the country as a middle linebacker with the Botafogo Mamutes.

His mother, Dona Nilza, still worried. Mothers will. Diego earned very little compared to his days as Mr. M; she wondered if he wouldn't tire of life on the straight and narrow. There was also the violence ripping through Alemão again. Would it reach her son, through a quest for revenge or sheer envy? Even as she continued to run the van service and cook for the drivers, she kept a close eye on her Diego. She had nine other children, she said, but this one needed her most.

Beyond Alemão, murders, street theft, and robberies in public transportation were up. Cariocas were back to swapping horror stories during lunch breaks and Sunday barbecues.

Street urchins in ragged shorts and flip-flops roamed in clusters again, new incarnations of that kid who'd once stuck a piece of broken glass against my ribs, holding me up for pocket change. There were many of these children, a little younger, a little older, mostly boys, sometimes girls, all hard-eyed, bony, and tough. Caring little for their own lives, they moved with a fearlessness that was heart-wrenching and chilling at once. I watched them hop-scotch through eight lanes of rapid-fire traffic with a maniacal grin to reach a promising target, and knock over a cyclist to steal his ride. Petty theft in my neighborhood went up more than 60 percent in a year.

Tension coursed like an electrical current under the rush and heave of the urban fabric. When it exploded, the damage was far uglier than anyone had anticipated.

Rio was once the sort of place where armed, off-duty officers killed homeless kids. The most stunning instance happened in 1993, when cops took potshots at the sixty or so kids sleeping in front of the Candelária Cathedral downtown, killing eight before they scrambled. The outlines of the children's bodies were spray-painted onto the sidewalk, creating a sort of anti-postcard of Rio, a portrait of the times: in the background, the soaring sanctuary, a symbol of our aspirations; in the foreground, a reminder of our worst sins.

When I returned to Rio, my bundle of expectations included the hope that cowardice of this sort was a thing of the past. The summer of 2014 brought it back, only this time it wasn't police. Cariocas began to catch kids suspected of street theft, or in one case, stealing food from a supermarket, and administer their own version of justice.

This particular strain of cruelty intersected with my daily routine on the last night of January. It came in the form of a young black man, a teenager still, who was beaten, stripped naked, and bound to a street sign.

Neighbors saw him, his fingers gripped around the arc of the bike U-lock that pulled his throat against the metal post. Someone called Yvonne de Mello. She lived around the block and worked with traumatized kids. She'd been a first responder to the Candelária massacre. More than two decades later, she was the one who sat with the young man and called the fire department for help. While they waited, he told her he was seventeen and came from the state of Maranhão, where the northeastern coast approaches the equator. The firemen had to use a blowtorch to get the lock off. The teenager was taken to a hospital for treatment, but escaped overnight, as if knowing what would come.

In just over twenty-four hours, a photo of the seventeen-year-old and details of the case had circulated widely through newspapers and social media platforms. As they spread, Yvonne began to get death threats. Neighborhood watchdog sites and online forums overflowed with comments, some calling for calm and others praising the vigilantes, inciting more violence.

"Wake up you idiots . . . people in Flamengo know he's a THIEF who robs elderly ladies and women every day. What they did wasn't enough, they needed alcohol and a lighter to 'sterilize' the delinquent," wrote one man.

"Too bad I didn't pass by with my Pit-bull to let him play a little. *Bandido bom é bandido morto*," wrote another.

This happened at the end of my block, a pretty residential stretch shaded by tall trees draped with orchids and bromeliads. This was the corner where I paused every morning, waiting for a break in traffic so I could dash into the park for a run. It was where I'd catch my first glimpse of the Sugarloaf's craggy face.

After that January, that spot on the sidewalk would be a daily reminder that among my neighbors were those who'd slip a U-lock around the skinny neck of a teenager and leave him exposed and bleeding on a public street. These were the same men who stood next to me in the supermarket line, chatting about prices and the weather, who jogged by me, nodding their good mornings.

This was Rio de Janeiro in early 2014.

CHAPTER 18

THE CUP OF CUPS

Brazil's World Cup felt like an impending disaster.

As the countdown to kickoff on June 12, 2014, went from months to weeks, strikes and skirmishes continued to break out around the country. São Paulo choked in its own traffic as subway employees went on strike and were repressed by police. Housing activists invaded the offices of construction companies to protest money spent on stadiums. In Rio, a bus driver stoppage turned violent, leaving nearly five hundred damaged buses. The northeast saw street cleaners in Fortaleza and public servants in Salvador walk off their jobs. Federal police threatened to quit, shutting down immigration and frontier checkpoints.

Passing through the terminal at Rio's international airport two weeks before the World Cup's first match, I watched as a great rectangular ceiling tile came loose and fell on deplaning passengers. In a cartoonish sequence, it knocked down a fence and revealed the startled construction workers behind it. The airport's refurbishing was two years behind schedule. Even the most essential equipment for the Cup, the stadiums themselves, were astonishingly late. The São Paulo arena was running so late that its test match would be the one for which it was being built—the opening game between Brazil and Croatia.

All this made FIFA officials very nervous. From the start, the Swiss-based organization had clashed with Brazil's slow-moving World Cup machine. FIFA's secretary-general, Jérôme Valcke, offended officials all the way to the president when he retorted in 2012 that the country needed "a kick in the butt" to speed up its organization. He later apologized, but FIFA officials and Brazilian leaders traded barbs throughout the fraught preparations. Dilma called FIFA officials "a weight" on her back; Valcke vented during a debate in Switzerland that he'd been "through hell" dealing with Brazilians.

Though they didn't want to hear it from others, Brazilian authorities were also worried. Many of them had staked their political futures on the World Cup's success. Their determination to make the competition go as smoothly as possible led to a rash of decisions meant to ward off foreseeable problems.

To ensure the free flow of tourists, VIPs, and teams, all sixty-four game days were declared full or partial holidays in their host cities. In Rio, the mayor canceled all non–World Cup public events and halted construction projects for two months.

Copacabana's homeless vanished before the tournament. They would reappear after the monthlong competition, and the state prosecutor would denounce their forced removal, but during the Cup the beach was free of panhandlers and ready to play the role of party central.

There would be no tolerance for disruption during the Cup— the message came from the president herself. To prevent protests, Rio's police arrested more than one dozen activists before the games started. Cops got new Kevlar-plated suits, helmets, gas masks, and belts loaded with a Taser, a pistol, extra ammunition, a nightstick, and handcuffs—twenty-two pounds of gear that turned a street cop into an intimidating Darth Vader look-alike. The federal government readied twenty-one thousand soldiers for action.

In spite of these preparations, there were plenty of signs that much could go unpredictably, embarrassingly wrong. Two weeks before kickoff, a bus carrying the Brazilian team to their training ground was surrounded by a mob of public school teachers on strike. The players, usually afforded the reverence of minor gods, stared in shock or covered their faces as police raised batons against teachers. Their banners called for more funds for education and less spending on stadiums.

In June, on the eve of the World Cup, a deep ambivalence pervaded the soccer nation. A Pew Research Center survey found that two-thirds of Brazilians were dissatisfied with the state of the country and the economy. Most felt the Cup had worsened conditions by taking resources away from essential public services.

For the politicians who'd bet on the success of the Cup, this was a nightmarish reversal. What if this dark, sullen mood lingered? And worse—what if millions poured into the streets and manifestations turned violent, with tear gas wafting into stadiums and frightened tourists hiding in their hotels?

Rather than just waiting to find out, the federal government went on the offensive with a national advertising campaign. Its goal: to promote the World Cup to Brazilians. It was ludicrous, unthinkable, but there it was. Pelé lent his image to a government-sponsored competition for the most elaborate street ornamentation. Posters in subway stations pictured happy children playing with soccer balls in streets festooned with green and yellow; a minute-long ad showed Brazilians drumming, dancing, and grinning like mad while touting the jobs, the tourism revenue, and the refurbished public transportation they would inherit after the competition. It ended with the campaign's slogan: "This is our Cup; it's the Cup of Cups."

The country had been building toward this moment for years; now that it had arrived, nothing, absolutely nothing, was as expected. Just as no one saw this coming, no one could predict what lay ahead. The effect was profoundly unsettling.

The ads only underscored the strangeness of it all. A Brazil that required an advertising campaign to jump-start enthusiasm for futebol was uncharted terrain.

The only reassuring element in this scenario was the Seleção itself: the majority of Brazilians still trusted that their team would make them proud.

The year before, Brazil had won its third Confederations Cup in a row. Brazil went into the World Cup with some of the most expensive defenders in international soccer. And there was the golden boy, Neymar. Lean and wiry, he was a dribbler with a light touch who'd been the Confederations Cup's best player. All he needed to climb the ranks of the sport to the top was victory on a World Cup pitch.

Even Coach Luiz Felipe Scolari, a gruff man of few words, overflowed with confidence: "We will be world champions." Sixty-four years was too long to marinate in loss. It was time to reclaim the Maracanã.

The first match was in São Paulo. Rain had burnished the gray city to a silver sheen and the winter light was clean, unfiltered, sharpening the edges of the angular new stadium.

For sports fans around the world, the Brazil versus Croatia match marked the beginning of four tense weeks; for Brazilians, it was the nadir of a long slog during which optimism had curdled into disappointment, into outrage at their own government and at FIFA, and even into regret.

Then, on that twelfth of June, this: the pristine stadium under a luminous sky, the buzz of the gathering crowd, the stands snapping with color. Croatia's checkered red-and-white jerseys popped like gingham tablecloths against a wash of Brazil's vivid yellow.

There was the Seleção lined up, shoulder to shoulder, arm in arm. The sun had set and the floodlights carved out each player's outline against the grass. The first strains of Brazil's national anthem lanced through the hum in the arena. Neymar lowered his head into his hand, overcome with emotion. When he looked up, his lips were a tight white line. The men strained for control. Some squeezed their eyes shut and turned inward; others looked to the sky for relief. Defender David Luiz enunciated each word with the zeal of a holy warrior; team captain Thiago Silva furrowed his brow, eyes closed against the battering emotions and the roar of tens of millions who sang along.

Theirs was a fraught task—to win before a nation that had widely questioned the idea of holding a World Cup and yet still expected the Seleção to win. Perhaps it was the raw sentiment stamped on the players' faces; perhaps it was the old habit of dusting off the flag and coming together for the Cup. But once the short, FIFA-regulation clip of the anthem was over, Brazilians in the stands ignored the rules and carried the next three stanzas in a thunderous a capella.

It was as if something unclenched inside the stadium. There had been protest, tensions, disagreements, violence even in the previous months. But this was the World Cup. In Brazil. The mounting dread of the past year dissolved as the hymn echoed in the stadium. There was the canary yellow against the green. All else dropped away. At that moment, and for the next four weeks, the world would revolve around a soccer ball.

The game itself started ominously. Ten minutes in, Brazil's Marcelo scored the first goal of the Cup—for Croatia. His mistake was met with a sepulchral silence; his eyes popped as they panned the crowd for one beat, two beats. The metaphor was there for the taking: Brazil, ever the country of the future, perennially unable to marshal its resources and fulfill its potential, was at it again, starting its Cup of Cups by undermining itself. This sentiment was reinforced when rows of floodlights blinked out minutes later, plunging nearly half of the $8 million stadium in darkness. For a few minutes, the prospect of disaster loomed again.

Then the lights came back on, Neymar snapped to life and tied the match with a shot that ricocheted off the post. Brazil muscled to a 3–1 finish; the tournament was on.

With each game, angst gave way to jubilation, because first and foremost, the World Cup was primarily about futebol . . . and the play was astounding. Tightly contested, fast-moving, high-scoring matches drove fans to delirium with dramatic finishes that often extended into overtime and penalty kicks.

With three, even four matches a day, lovers of the sport could gorge on world-class play. The round of sixteen was the longest in a World Cup ever: the eight games were packed with an additional two and a half hours of action. While the ball was rolling, soccer was the story, not the marches that failed to materialize or the heavily armed police that surrounded stadiums, in case protesters changed their minds.

Early on, surprising contenders emerged. Colombia. Costa Rica. Chile, which knocked out Spain. Mexico stood up to Brazil in a valiant 0–0 draw that felt like a win, thanks to an impressive performance by goalie Guillermo Ochoa.

There was brilliance, such as Tim Howard's sixteen saves against Belgium or Arjen Robben's breathtaking sprints, and pure joy like that of Mexico coach Miguel Herrera, who let loose in bellowing, fist-pumping, leaping celebrations that sent his tie and coat tails flapping. There was that holy-shit moment when Luis Suárez . . . did he really sink his teeth into that Italian? Fury or farce, the bite was dissected and debated for days.

Whatever the latest twist, the action was magnificent and magnetic. Even Brazil's toughest critic, FIFA's Valcke, conceded: "This is the best World Cup in terms of the soccer."

Beyond the stadiums, logistics functioned. The traffic flowed; the sixty-four strategic holidays took care of that. With a 15 percent drop in business travel, airports performed adequately. Expectations were low and easy to meet. Fiascos that might have been played up as disasters in another country were dismissed as glitches—the blinking spotlights in the opening match, the faulty Internet connections in stadium press rooms, the security breach that allowed nearly one hundred Chile fans to break into the Maracanã.

Even an overpass collapse that crushed two people to death in Belo Horizonte got little attention. The mayor brushed it off, saying "accidents happen," and that was that. Short of a catastrophic stadium collapse or a murderous rampage involving tourists, no one wanted to hear bad news.

In Rio, foreign journalists and visitors surrendered to the city's physical beauty and the charms of its ever-simpatico natives, with their inclusive street parties and penchant for striking up a conversation with just about anyone, particularly over soccer. The warm welcome (nearly) made up for the occasional canceled flights, picked pockets, or stratospherically priced hotel rooms with spotty Internet connections and a trickle of hot water. No one throws gargantuan last-minute bashes like Brazil, and the Cup at its best was a country-wide, monthlong Carnaval-meets-beach holiday. Who was going to gripe about the details?

The epicenter of this madness was Copacabana. Day and night, it swarmed with gleeful soccer fans in various stages of inebriation, dress-up—in national colors, mascot outfits, ridiculous wigs—or undress, as the visitors reveled in the balmy Carioca winter. Two weeks into this joyous mess it was clear Brazil's World Cup would be unforgettable. Not because nothing went wrong, but because while the game was on and the sun was shinning, it was the only place to be.

A sunburnt Brit I met in Copacabana summed it all up. I was walking along the ocean, scanning the crowd for friends. He was wading to shore. Cheery, chubby, with thin blond hair plastered to his head, he looked like a drenched duckling in dripping knee-length breeches.

He beamed at me. I smiled back.

"How are you liking the Cup?" I asked.

He raised the beer can in his hand, shook it to show it was empty.

"I'm here in the sun, right, up to my waist in water, drinking a beer, and watching football," he said. "What's not to like?"

Indeed. Minutes later, I'd found my own happy place in front of the giant FIFA Fan Fest screen, my back against a palm tree, my feet planted in the warm sand, ready for Brazil versus Cameroon. It was the first game I'd watched with a crowd, and the atmosphere was all there: the chanting, the happy Babel of accents. Behind us, a clutch of twenty-somethings hollered at the screen, threw their arms around each other, and bounced in delight anytime Brazil approached the goal, and all the while carrying on a flirtatious ex-change with an assortment of bemused Europeans.

By the end of the first half, Neymar had sunk two balls into the net to Cameroon's single goal. I gave myself over to the emotional swell. Brazilians cheer dramatically, elaborately, with grand dis-plays of sentiment. There were those who dropped to their knees, begged or thanked the heavens, weaving elaborate promises to a pantheon of saints. Others cursed and threatened and paced, turn-ing their back on unforgivable misses. Some walked away at crucial moments, unable to stand the pressure. Many just kept their eyes glued to the action, silent and entranced, as if they were person-ally responsible for the team and any distraction could throw the match.

Brazil scored twice more, sending Cameroon home. But the play itself was unsatisfying, flat. This was a World Cup of surprises, and the Seleção's performance was one of them. They had been Brazil's emotional anchor during the uncertainty of the preceding months. Now even as the tournament took off they remained uncoordinated as a team, clumsy, playing some downright ugly futebol. There was little creativity or elegance on the field; their victories had been laborious, even against Cameroon. Neymar kept scoring, but as a team, they were unconvincing.

There were also signs they were splintering under pressure. None had known the weight of playing a World Cup at home, and this one had dealt them an emotional whiplash from the moment their bus was rocked by angry teachers on strike. They hadn't brought the Cup to Brazil, but they were tasked with making Brazilians feel this foolhardy gamble was worthwhile. Was it too much to ask?

The next game, against Chile, widened the team's emotional cracks.

It started off well enough. Following another overwrought rendition of the national anthem, the team held their nerve and kept the game balanced for the regulation ninety minutes. The extra time was grueling, down to a last Chilean shot in the 120th minute that slammed off the crossbar, just inches away from knocking Brazil out. The players were quivering with exhaustion, but the game was tied at 1–1. It would go to penalty kicks.

As Brazilian goalie Júlio César prepared to take his place, he broke into tears. When he pulled himself together, it was the captain's turn to fall apart. Thiago Silva walked over to the coach and asked to be the last one to take a penalty. Then he turned his back to his mates, sat on the ball, bowed his head, and closed himself off—in prayer, in fear, or in denial. No one knew and it didn't matter. He broke down right when he had to come through for the team, and the team had to come through for Brazil.

As each man lined up to take his shot, apprehension played across his face.

David Luiz goes first, focused and furious, and knocks it in: 1–0. Chile misses. The Brazilian Willian is up; he misses and collapses sobbing on the grass. Chile shoots and misses again. Still 1–0.

Next is Marcelo, who redeems his own goal against Croatia: 2–0. Chile takes another turn, and it's a goal: 2–1. A Brazilian miss and one more Chilean goal tie the game again: 2–2.

Neymar is up. His face is taught. He takes a deep breath, lets it out, breaks into a loping run. Within feet of the ball he drops into a short, choppy shuffle. The sudden shift in stride and pace is disconcerting, but it works: 3–2.

Chile's turn. The stands heave. Fans chant goalie Júlio César's name. It's in his hands. But no . . . Their last penalty kick thunders off the crossbar.

Brazil won, but not without a glimpse of the abyss. The scenes that followed said far more about the state of the Seleção than the score. Game over, Neymar flung himself facedown on the ground, crying openly. Thiago Silva dropped to his knees, sobbing with the abandon of a child into the coach's arms. Team members crumpled into themselves or leaned on each other in a collective breakdown. These were not a few tears of mawkish patriotism; the men were unnerved, and dangerously so.

The penalty kick drama set off a mad chatter, with critics questioning everything from the Seleção's aptitude to their manhood. As if to prove them wrong, Brazil barreled into their next opponent, Colombia. It would be the most violent game of the Cup.

Colombia had been the leader in fouls; by the end of the match, Brazil would take that dubious title, having chopped into their opponents 31 times to Colombia's 23. The team was chasing the win at any cost—including a second yellow card for Thiago Silva, which suspended him for the next match.

I was watching this one with a group of foreign friends. I can't remember who first said it: "Someone's going to get hurt."

When it happened, it looked like just another tumble in a rough game: a Colombian player going for a high ball leaped up behind Neymar. As he came down, his knee went into the Brazilian's back. Neymar is a diver, known for going down at any chance. But this wasn't a calculated fall. Brazil's forward writhed on the grass, his limbs splayed at awkward angles, his mouth an O of agony. He'd fractured a vertebra.

Brazil beat Colombia, but it was a victory that left the country in mourning. The twenty-two-year-old had carried the nation's hopes with grace and a measure of composure. He was Brazil's top scorer, but he was more than good. As the Seleção struggled to victory, Neymar alone had flashed the old futebol arte. When he was carried out on a stretcher, he took that with him.

The bruiser with Colombia left two games between the home team and the trophy. Brazilians approached the semifinal with Germany much like a tightrope walker who keeps the balance by refusing to look down. Allow doubt to creep in, take a quick peek, and the illusion of being on firm ground is gone.

Maintaining this sort of magical thinking on a national scale required blind faith and confidence that with a little *jeitinho*, anything could be negotiated. In these categories, Brazil is gifted. This is a spiritual, superstitious country of many faiths, where the heavens have always been open for business: Catholic saints deal in promises and Afro-Brazilian gods take offers in the form of fruit bowls, flowers, candles, or the bloodier tributes left at crossroads. Even the severe Protestant God, who is making inroads and runs a strict monopoly, is receptive to prayer.

As the semifinal approached, questioning the team's chances or criticizing their performance was treated as sacrilegious and un-Brazilian, as if by voicing uncertainty, you were disrupting this

web of belief and allowing the unthinkable to pass from the realm
of possibilities into reality.

Walking to my sister's house to watch the game, I looked up at
the familiar profile of Cristo perched on the granite peak that rises
behind her building. Was it confidence in his charges or indifference to their fate that gave this ever-present Carioca his serenity?

The building's doorman was already gathered with other *porteiros* around a TV set up in a security guard's cabin, but he went
with me to the front gate, unlocked it, and pressed the button for
the elevator.

"So what do you think? Can we do it without Neymar?" I asked
as we waited.

"We are two hundred million. We can make it if we all do our
part," he said, earnest as a doorknob.

Right.

Up in the apartment, my sister's family was already arranged in
front of the television. Her three kids romped about, the twins in
matching yellow jerseys, oblivious to the strain we all felt. Goalie
Júlio César and David Luiz held up Neymar's jersey like a sacred
relic while they sang the anthem.

"This is too much, no? The man's not dead," someone said.

The team had been on a high-gear emotional feedback loop for
weeks. With Neymar gone, they'd reached a frenzied pitch that
brought to mind Léo Rabello's description of the Maracanã before
that long-ago final. The players, the public, the commentators
were all in the grip of that same blinkered obsession. This was our
Cup, the "Copa das Copas"; only one outcome was possible.

Kickoff. Brazil opened up with drive, but without much composure. Germany was flexible and well articulated, falling in and
out of formation with speed and precision. Within ten minutes

they scored. Minutes later, they scored again: 2–0. Everyone fell silent—the public in the stadium, my siblings in the living room. The toddlers looked up at the adults, aware of the sudden shift in tone.

Brazil could come back. There was still time. But with that second goal, the Seleção snapped, like a machine wound too tight. They went from functioning as a team to being elven terrified individuals stranded on the field, disconnected and alone in their fear.

The Germans tore into them, thrusting three fast goals into the net: one minute, two minutes, score; three minutes, four minutes, score; five minutes, score: 5–0.

My sister, down on the floor with the kids, turned to me, eyebrows flying high: "What? What was that? Was that a replay? Did that count?"

It counted. All of it. Just like that, the World Cup was over for Brazil: the agony of the wait, the fears and aspirations the nation had wrapped up in this Cup, our Copa. Finished. On the screen, the faces of fans flipped from confusion to shock to heartbreak. The camera closed in on a boy who wept alongside his father. Brazilians still dressed in cheery yellow got up and stumbled out of the stadium.

In my sister's house, two people left the living room and took refuge in the back of the house. If this were boxing, such pounding would have brought the match to an end: knockout, its over. But this was soccer. Brazil had to limp back out after halftime for another excruciating forty-five minutes.

As the pummeling continued, we began to revel in its absurdity. All the buildup, the chest-thumping, the billions spent on most expensive World Cup ever, for this? Brazil took another goal: 6–0. The humor that surfaced when we had nothing else came through. In the stands, desolate Brazilians began to cheer again—for Germany. In my sister's living room, we went from disbelief to the complete release of expectations.

The adults laughed nervously, unsure what to make of this. The twins playing underfoot looked up at the adults and giggled. In the stadium, too, fans gave in to the slapstick on display, raising a chorus of "olés" for each German pass around the hapless home team, who managed to squeeze in one goal before close: 7–1. *Sete a um*.

By the end we were disoriented and a little sick, like kids who'd been blindfolded and spun in circles. All our assumptions had been turned inside out: Brazil had pulled off the organization and the infrastructure for the World Cup, but our Seleção was an unmitigated disaster. A less spectacular defeat would have given us something to cling to, someone to blame, a way forward. This one wiped us clean.

Each of the players knew this. David Luiz spoke for them as he walked off the field.

"I'm sorry, everyone," he said, sobbing between words. "I just wanted to give my people something to be happy about."

Even for the Germans there was little joy in seeing the Seleção in tatters. Their celebration was muted and their after-game interviews bordered on contrite.

We sat and watched dumbfounded as each of the players and coaches came forward; we were hoping someone, somehow could explain what happened.

A defeat of this magnitude went beyond the game. It buried that most resilient of myths, of Brazil as the spiritual home of futebol and the Seleção as its finest incarnation. The country still exported more players than any other, but we were no longer the masters of the *jogo bonito*. The domestic league had suffered decades of corrupt, inept management, dire levels of play, and dwindling stadium attendance. Brazilians nostalgic for futebol arte at home made do by spinning stories from the past and looking for the old touch in players like Neymar. Brazil still had a huge talent pool, but playing at the highest level now also required training, strategy, professionalism, and funding. The 7–1 laid that bare.

The team had one more match, a sad, unnecessary coda in which the Netherlands beat them in a dispute for third place. It didn't matter. We'd lost all that mattered with that 7–1: the game, the Cup, our favorite fantasy. There would be no vindication of the 1950 loss; the Maracanã would host a final between Germany and Argentina.

The defeat also forced Brazil to face reality beyond the pitch without the comforting mantle of victory.

When talking futebol with Léo Rabello, I'd asked whether he was looking forward to a World Cup win in the Maracanã, something to ease the sting of that first, traumatic loss. He considered the question quietly for a few beats, hands clasped, arms extended toward me over the meticulous desk. His open laptop whirred.

"It would do great things for the business of soccer," he said. "For the people, it would be a beautiful moment that passes and leaves nothing. So, do I want Brazil to win? Yes. But more than that, I want soccer to stop being an excuse to sweep problems under the rug."

After the disaster of the semifinal, I thought back to what Léo had said. We'd produced a heart-stopping World Cup, there were no major disasters, and the festivities were fabulous. Despite the cost overruns and the delays, Brazil emerged with its reputation intact. If the country had also won the Cup, euphoria would have carried the day.

Instead, we got the 7–1, a defeat that didn't just lift the proverbial rug; it ripped it right off and exposed the gap between Brazil's aspirations and its ability to achieve them, on the field and beyond. The road to the World Cup had been littered with waste and squandered opportunities. We'd spent $11.6 billion—more than any other nation, more than Germany and South Africa combined. What did we get for it? Was it worth it? There would be no refuge from these questions in futebol.

In Rio, several projects that could have positively transformed the city had exacerbated economic and social inequalities. Their implementation raised questions about the tenor of our democracy and the society we were building. As with the sad state of domestic soccer, this had been unfolding for years. This monumental loss brought it back into focus.

At my sister's house, the party was also over. After the postgame interviews we had little to do but go home and digest those seven German goals. After the emotional upheaval of the past few hours, fear of renewed riots and demonstrations were not far-fetched. We said good-bye, went home, and stayed home, unsure what the night would bring. Commentators and journalists speculated.

The night went by quietly. The next day, Cariocas picked up their paper, with its tiered, all-caps headline—SHAME, EMBARRASS-MENT, HUMILIATION—stacked above a portrait of David Luiz on his knees, face buried in the grass. And they went to work. They slipped on their pumps, their work boots, their Havaianas; they boarded buses, walked into classrooms, boardrooms, factories; they turned on their computers, their taxis, their stoves, and went back to the business of everyday life.

We, Brazilians, had lost the game, the Cup, and our illusions. What did that leave us? Well, everything else.

For generations, we had had propped up our national image on that old tripod, samba-soccer-Carnaval. The central of those three pillars was gone, but perhaps it was time. We'd outgrown the old stereotypes. The 7–1 forced us to see it, for better or for worse, and to move on.

Most Brazilians remember only David Luiz's heartbroken apology, but the interview didn't end there. The team may have failed, he said, but there was strength in the way Brazilians came together.

"I hope fans, the people, use this, the Seleção, this closeness, to go after other things in life, not just those related to soccer," he said.

The protests of 2013 showed the population had heightened

expectations of their country. It was time to take up the questions they had raised. Brazil had state and national elections in three months. Rio would host the Olympic Games within two years. It was time to take up the discussion over governance, housing, transportation, security, health care, and education—to define the country we wanted, and outline our terms. Who were we, when we were no longer the *país do futebol*? What were our limits and our ambitions?

Brazilians had a lot of work ahead. The economy was faltering, the Seleção had crumbled, and Cristo remained as impassive as ever. There would be no miraculous rescue, not through Lula or Neymar, not through saints, side deals, or even our infamous *jeitinho*.

But that's okay. Brazilians are, above all, resilient. They get to work and save themselves. They're doing it now—slowly, daily. Saving themselves.

AFTERWORD

The World Cup stunned Brazil. But in the weeks that followed, the population's recovery from that most complete of defeats demonstrated a resilience of spirit—perhaps born from long experience with frustrated expectations—that salved the sting I had felt at the humiliation on the field and at the expense and folly of it all.

Brazilians can handle setbacks, I thought as I wrote the last chapters in this book. It was not the ending I had anticipated when I had started writing: the flat-lined economy, the burbling of corruption through public institutions, the homicide epidemic that grew even during the years of plenty. It was disappointing, but Brazilians are strong, I thought; they've been here before.

Those weeks after the 7–1 defeat, however, gave way to months that tested the limits of Brazilian endurance and of the sense of humor that keeps the national character supple. As it turned out, the soccer fiasco was nothing compared to what lay in store. The year that followed brought a stunning reversal of many of the positive developments of the past decade. By 2016, the effervescent mood I had found in 2010 had soured into a national hangover.

Just as when I returned home, the country had been soaring on a perfect confluence of factors domestic and global; political, economic, and social. Brazil in 2016 was being battered by a perfect storm. The country has seen its share of crises, but seldom, if ever, had it faced such turmoil on so many fronts. It was a conjuncture that would test the foundations of its institutions and the mettle of a people that had dared to expect more of their country.

First, there was the economy. During those six years, Brazil had gone from being an investment darling to a risky proposition. Ratings agencies such as Standard & Poor's and Fitch cut Brazil's sovereign debt to junk status. The currency lost one-third of its value relative to the dollar in 2015 alone. The stock market was in the dumps. Global prices for the country's commodities—iron ore, soy, sugar, oil—had plummeted and showed no signs of resurging. The unemployment rate rose to above 8 percent for the first time in years, and the economy shrank by more than 3.5 percent. Economists projected similarly dire numbers for 2016. They were right.

What did this mean for Brazilians? A lot of finger-pointing at the top, and a scaling back of plans big and small for the rest.

President Dilma Rousseff had won a second term by a very narrow margin in October 2014 on the promise she would preserve Brazil's social gains despite the worsening conditions. Immediately after winning, she surprised supporters with an about-face, pushing for fiscal austerity and budget cuts. Her popularity, already low, plummeted to single digits. Scrambling to jump-start the economy and demonstrate leadership, she cut government spending, including her own salary, and slashed the number of ministries in a bloated government from thirty-nine to thirty-one. This caused her to lose the faith of the Workers' Party and did not win her the support of the upper classes.

By the end of 2015, she was facing impeachment. The official charges were that her administration relied on accounting shenanigans to cover up overspending. But longtime Brazil observers felt her real sin, the one that could not be forgiven, was losing control of the economy.

The country was adrift, but Brazil's politicians were too distracted by other scandals to focus on governance. Prosecutors expanded an investigation that had started in 2014 around a money-laundering operation run through a gas station (and therefore known as *Lava Jato*, or car wash). Through 2015, they found mounting evidence that scores of politicians and business executives had used rigged contracts to siphon off public money through the national oil company Petrobras, its subsidiaries, and its contractors.

The public watched, riveted, as the most powerful men in the country were put under investigation: the Speaker of the House, the president of the Senate, dozens of other legislators. Even former president Lula was called in for questioning. The probe also extended to the nation's biggest construction companies—including those tasked with building Rio de Janeiro's Olympic venues. At stake were government contracts worth $20 billion and spanning several sectors, with $3 billions' worth in bribes and kickbacks. It was the deepest and widest corruption scheme ever uncovered in Brazil, and it would continue to unfold into 2016.

All this turbulence sparked the self-mockery with which Brazilians cope with their nation's flaws. When the former Workers' Party treasurer showed up to answer before Congress for his involvement with the *Lava Jato* corruption scheme someone released a passel of rats into the chamber, causing panic in the ranks and hilarity among the viewing public. The former treasurer was later sentenced to fifteen years in prison. President Lula's Workers' Party, which had been the source of so much hope to so many, was now fodder for sad practical jokes. As Cartola, a famous samba composer said, sometimes the only way out is *rir pra não chorar*, or to laugh, so as not to cry.

While all this was playing out in the news, the population felt the economic retrenchment clearly and daily. As inflation spiked, each trip to the supermarket was more meager than the last. My brother and his family had to move to a smaller apartment.

The visible stuff —the family car, the orthodontia, the new flat-screen TV—of the middle class's newfound prosperity was again retreating beyond the reach of many. Not only were the things themselves more expensive, but interest rates on credit cards sky-rocketed during 2015 to more than 400 percent per year. Suddenly, carrying debt could ruin a family.

Knocks in consumption and lifestyle mattered tremendously. A new iPhone or a tube of MAC lipstick have that magic fairy dust of global brands that heightens social status. But many of these new acquisitions had value that was more than symbolic; a home com-puter or English classes were rungs along the social ladder that many Brazilians had started to climb for the first time.

Many of the opportunities created over the decade of prosperity were also drastically reduced. Cuts in education funding together with inflation made for a particularly damaging combination. It meant mothers who could not afford a 15 percent increase in preschool fees had to withdraw their kids—at a cost to the child's future, and perhaps to their own. It meant low-income students had to give up on college after the government cut the number of loans (known as FIES, the Fundo de Financiamento Estudantil, or student financing fund in English) from 732,000 to 300,000, while doubling their interest rate. It meant that Brazilians pursuing doc-toral degrees at foreign universities had to return home without a diploma once the government withdrew their scholarships.

All this cast a shadow on Brazil, as if our World Cup defeat had been the harbinger of something broader. The 7–1 was not just a humiliating loss. It was a spectacular, public defeat on home turf, in our game, in the semifinal. It revealed something about ourselves that we did not want to see: our soccer had been weakened by cor-ruption and nepotism; it was now inarticulate and unimaginative. The country's boom of the last few years had rested far more than we wanted to acknowledge on legs that would not sustain us for long: the price of commodities, internal consumption, the hope of a fortune in oil lying just off Rio de Janeiro's coast. The structural reforms that could have been taken up in times of plenty had not happened. Now that moment was gone.

Dennis Novaes, an anthropology student at Rio's federal university, coined a phrase to describe those caught up in this whiplash: generation 7–1, *geração sete a um*. All those who were about to graduate with the first college degree in the family but had to drop out, who had their first job in the formal sector and lost it, who planned for a future that was no longer there, all those who believed they were just about to make it when the country they'd known for the past decade suddenly turned upside down and shook their dreams loose: it was his generation.

Dennis came of age in the can-do Brazil of the 2000s. He'd seized on a student grant to swing across the great divide that separated him from the life he was expected to live in Brasília to Rio de Janeiro, graduate school, and whatever else lay beyond. For the time being, he's hanging on, surviving in high-rent Rio with a grant that still appears like a small miracle in in his bank account. If this funding is cut, he'd have to push his PhD in anthropology to the back burner and get a job, he said.

"It creates a terrible uncertainty," he said. "All the other students are in the same situation: anxious, worried."

Worry about funding is only one aspect of this new reality. If he graduates, where would he get a job, now that federal universities have frozen new hires? And what of the country? Just five years ago it was growing, not just economically but socially, consolidating the benefits of policies that created more access to more resources for more Brazilians. Now the economy was shrinking, and it was also drawing down those windows of opportunity that had allowed people like Dennis to leap out of one world of possibilities and into another.

Even the symbols of 2010 Brazil had morphed into sad reminders of what we had hoped to become. Billionaire Eike Batista, who proclaimed to Charlie Rose in 2010 that he was on his way to becoming the world's wealthiest man, was disgraced and debt-ridden, running from photographers and creditors. The massive oil reserves in the deep waters off Rio de Janeiro's coast, once hailed as Brazil's "passport to the future," lost their redemptive sheen. Not only was Petrobras the radioactive center of the *Lava Jato* corruption scheme, but a plunge in global oil prices had crushed the prospect of expensive high-seas drilling.

And Rio . . . ah, Rio. By the start of 2016, most of what the world would see during the Olympic Games was ready. Unlike the mad rush to finish stadiums before the World Cup, most of Rio's sports venues were nearly complete, and test events had been held in many of them. Starting with the first event, beach volleyball in Copacabana, the stunning backdrop was certain to impress, as it has for nearly five hundred years. Rio was nearly ready to glitter on television sets around the world.

A closer look at the city and state, however, revealed strained systems that were close to snapping. Money was tight here, too. The venues might be ready, but even basic service suffered cuts.

In early 2016, state hospitals closed to all but the direst emergencies. Surgeries were cancelled; people with broken bones were turned away. The Getúlio Vargas hospital, where I'd taken refuge during the police action in Alemão, boarded up its entrance. Universities cut back on cleaning crews and maintenance. Public school students nearly lost their lunch when the state education department considered feeding them hot meals only four times a week. Thankfully, a memo from the state attorney general's office changed their minds.

Some of the headlines reminded me of the old *imagina na Copa* joke, when Brazilians would laugh off massive infrastructural failures by saying, "Imagine if this happened during the World Cup." The Rio municipal zoo was so decrepit that federal environmental authorities ordered it shut, and even Carnaval was on a budget in

2016, after the sponsors of street parades ratcheted down their support.

Infrastructure essential for the Games was also at risk. With the Olympics just a handful of months away, the subway extension that was supposed to ease the city's congestion was not finished—and would not be without an injection of nearly $250 million from the federal government. At the Maracanã, administrators fired three-fourths of the workers; at another stadium where Olympic track and field events would be held, the electricity and water were cut off as bills went unpaid.

By 2016, it was clear that key legacy projects would not materialize. Guanabara Bay remained a toxic soup. The urban improvements promised through Morar Carioca were long forgotten. There were shoot-outs in Alemão, Rocinha and other favelas, where residents still languished without services and gangs fought once more to reclaim their territory.

In Alemão, forty-four people were struck by spraying gunfire in 2015; twenty-two of them died, according to *Voz da Comunidade*, the community newspaper. Amid this carnage, sometimes a particular story seized the public's attention: the shooting death of ten-year-old Eduardo de Jesus by police led to protests, calls for justice and peace, and international news articles. Yet nothing changed.

The reports, like the thump-thump-thump of repeated fire, came with numbing regularity. An illustrator was hit on the leg while at work in a downtown building in front of the American consulate. He lived. A man shot in the head while leaving church with his wife did not. Neither did a two-year-old toddler, Ruan Bruno Gomes Nunes, after a stray bullet found him in his bed, asleep, in the UPP-controlled favela of Mangueira, within view of the Maracanã. His death barely caused a ripple—a small local protest and a couple of articles by local media. One of the articles devoted half its copy to the protest's impact on traffic.

The operating expenses for the Games, which had long overblown the original budget, were trimmed under the guise of fiscal responsibility: there would be fewer employees, more temporary structures, and more modest opening and closing ceremonies. This attempt to demonstrate fiscal responsibility did not mask the fact that the Olympics had by and large opened Rio's public coffers to finance projects that would benefit a small network of political and economic interests. Stop-gap measures would make Rio ready to welcome Olympic athletes, VIPs, journalists, and tourists. Eco-barriers and specially rigged boats would rake in the trash floating on the bay, and eighty-five thousand law enforcement officers would clamp down on the city, turning Rio into the safest place on the planet while the competitions lasted.

Rio's Olympics would be a grand party in the style Cariocas can throw like no one else—a moment as gorgeous as it is ephemeral. The city would burn bright, at great cost. And after the party, the cleaning crews in their orange uniforms would clean up and we would carry on.

This was not what I—what we, Cariocas and Brazilians—had hoped for. We didn't want an Olympic theme park built to shine for a few weeks. The changes we had believed were in store for Rio and for Brazil, and which had fueled the celebration when Rio was chosen to host the Games, were not just *para inglês ver*, a makeover for foreign eyes. The hope wrapped around that moment had been powerful, certainly, powerful enough to draw me back home.

And yet, at the start of Rio's Olympic year, I thought back to the questions I had brought with me: What city was being built here, and at what cost? Who stood to gain, and who would lose? The answers I'd found were hard to digest.

My return to Brazil had forced me to confront my own feelings about this place I called home. During the years I spent exploring the gaps between my expectations and reality, what I found was often astounding, frequently infuriating, and more times than I could count, left me feeling more foreign than ever. I could claim no other place, wanted no other home, and yet this one was so . . . maddening. This was particularly true of the city that was my window into Brazil.

What I learned is that Rio brooks no ambivalence. Over the years, it had exasperated and reclaimed me. I went from referring to Cariocas as "them" to speaking about "us"; the more I struggled, the deeper the tendrils of belonging had rooted me to this place. I owed some of this to my family, which had grown: I now had five nieces and nephews, little Cariocas who would always be of this city. But my relationship to Brazil no longer passed through family; I had my own ties, bonds forged as much in frustration as in long runs around the park in Flamengo, where I'd stop, stretch, and watch the play of light on the Sugarloaf's craggy face.

The indignation over inefficiency, corruption, and violence that sent me raging over the morning paper was borne of concern—I knew these stories, these people, these places. I arrived with a curiosity that was detached and journalistic; over time, I began to care in a way that was personal and subjective.

During my time in Rio, I'd met another in-betweener, a foreign professor who'd made Brazil his own through his work and activism during this turbulent period. After I finished writing this book, we married, and once again I bought a one-way ticket. This time it was to Zurich, where he had a new posting. This trip would be the opposite of the one that took me to Brazil: I had no connections in Switzerland, no expectations, no family or friends. The country was just a shape in the middle of Europe, a vague promise of mountains, an idea as pretty and empty as a snow globe.

As I prepared for the move, I considered the country I was leaving: a rich place daunted by its potential, so transfixing as it balanced there, on the brink—of what? Disaster? Redemption?

Even among the grim news, I saw good reasons for hope. Corruption was not new in Brazil. But an investigation as serious and far-reaching as *Lava Jato* was new and inspiring. That it had hauled in the rich and powerful for questioning, and still continued, untrammeled by political interference, said something about the strength of the institutions behind it.

The protests of 2013 and 2014 were also promising, with their calls for better governance and spending priorities in line with the population's needs. They had started with marches against an increase in bus fares and exploded into a million other demands, drawing hundreds of thousands to the streets. By January of 2016, new attempts to raise bus fares were fueling new protests in Rio, São Paulo, and other capitals. Would Brazil again burst into protest as the Olympics drew near?

As I thought about all this, I realized that perhaps I had been witness to significant changes after all. They were not within government or the economy, but among the people. The protests, the ongoing corruption investigation, even the fact that despite the brutality of police charged with her removal, there in Vila Autódromo, Penha was still holding on to her home: all this suggested that over these last few years, Brazilians long excluded from circles of power and money had heightened their expectations of their country, their awareness of rights, and their power to make demands. I'd noticed the spread of fresh ideas, of a stronger sense of agency, and of modes of communication that enabled new connections. The last decade had heightened expectations, and these would not be easily forgotten.

And so it was that even as I moved away, after all the years and frustrations, Brazil's hold on me was strong, stronger than ever: *volta mais tarde, querida*, later, darling, come back later. We'll be open after lunch, tomorrow, *amanhã*. Try again. One more time, one more stamp, one more day. Maddening, yes, but tantalizing. I had always come back. I always will.

Juliana Barbassa, February 2016

ACKNOWLEDGMENTS

My return to Rio has been a fascinating, at times infuriating, but thoroughly unforgettable journey; writing a book about the city during a period of intense transformation, when so much was at stake, deepened my connection to the place and proved to be one of my most rewarding experiences. I am deeply grateful to all those who made it possible, and all—from close friends and family to colleagues to complete strangers—who were endlessly patient with my questions, generous with their time, and always willing to listen. My name goes on the cover, but the effort and merit in this work is widely shared.

My first and biggest thank-you goes to my literary agent, David Halpern, who believed in this project from the moment I walked into his office with nothing but an idea. He's been an exceptional professional, a compassionate listener in moments of crisis, and always a generous human being, unstinting with his time, wisdom, and advice.

I also had the good fortune of having Michelle Howry as an editor, and the whip-smart team at Touchstone/Simon & Schuster on my side. Michelle's thoughtful suggestions improved the manuscript enormously, breaking up wordy chapters into readable chunks and guiding me smoothly through the production process. To the copyeditor, the book and cover designers, the mapmakers, and all those at Touchstone who have been so good to this book and who made the production process so seamless, my most heartfelt thanks.

Outside Touchstone, many attentive readers helped shape this book, improving it at every turn. I am most grateful to the lovely JillEllyn Riley, who walked with me through the hardest months, reading first drafts and second drafts, offering support, insight and a measure of calm, always ready to bridge the distance between New York and Rio through long Skype chats and terrible phone connections. Thank you for it all.

Other friends and colleagues lent their expertise and their time, reading over specific chapters and giving feedback. Thank you, foremost, to Joelle Hahn, a lover of all things Rio with a keen eye for language, for your time and good will; and to Maureen Gaffney, for your focus and your detailed comments.

It has been my extraordinary luck to write about Rio alongside a stellar group of correspondents. They were my companions and my teachers, and I relied on them in my work and in life, as friendships deepened over deadlines and drinks. Many helped me directly—thank you, Juan Pablo Spinetto, Tariq Panja, Julia Michaels, Arturo Lezcano and Tom Phillips for your comments, and Simon and Carol Romero, Jon Watts, Jenny Barchfield, Marcelo Lessa, Cecilia Olliveira and Andrew Fishman for advice on various levels. Taylor Barnes and Catherine Osborn did some of the research heavy lifting; those endless hours of interviews wouldn't have been transcribed without the untiring Lanna Leite and Zoe Roller. Manuela Andreoni was a dream fact-checker—a worthy journalist in her own right, deeply knowledgeable about Rio, and unflaggingly attentive to detail. Other friends—Alberto Armendariz, Javier Tovar, Laura Bonilla, Gerardo Lissardy, Flora

Charner, Felipe Dana and the rest of the AP team, *meus muito queridos* Daniel Silva and Diego Galeano—were essential parts of my life and helped shape the way I saw Rio. Thank you for being there, and for your warmth and friendship.

This book would not have been possible without all those who opened their lives and told me their stories. This includes the individuals whose stories are told here, but many whose voices were not included for simple lack of space; *obrigada*, in particular, to Otávio Júnior, Rene Silva Santos, Maycom Brum and Flávia Froes for helping me understand Alemão and what happened there. Inalva Mendes Brito has spent years working on behalf of Vila Autódromo and countless hours sharing that experience. *Obrigada de coração*.

A number of experts helped frame my understanding of specific aspects of Rio. Among those whose contributions shaped this book and who are not named elsewhere are Ignacio Cano, foremost researcher on violence in Rio; Theresa Williamson, tireless investigator and advocate of favelas; Mário Moscatelli and Marcelo Mello, biologists who have dedicated decades to improving Rio's natural environment; Carlos Amorin, whose knowledge of Rio's criminal history and the Comando Vermelho in particular is unparalleled; and Adalberto Megale and Cristina Pinho at Petrobras, who helped me delve into the connection between pre-salt oil exploration and the renovation of Brazil's ports. This book would have been far poorer without your patience and generosity.

I owe much thanks to my family—my parents, Rosa and Almir Barbassa; my siblings, Tatiana and Guilherme; their partners, Jaime and Luciana; and their children, the little Cariocas I love the most. They are my emotional tether to this beautiful and mad city, and the reason I care so deeply what becomes of it. They were steadfast supporters not so much of this project but of me, and that is what matters most.

Finally, I owe my greatest debt to Christopher Gaffney. He is my love and my partner, my sharpest critic, my keenest reader and my most devoted ally. His wit, his kindness and his moral compass were essential when navigating the rougher patches of this work and of life in a difficult city. Thank you.

GLOSSARY

Arrego: regular bribes paid to police to allow ongoing illegal activity.

Bala perdida: "lost bullet"; refers to stray bullets that hit unintended victims.

Banda podre: "the rotten half"; refers to the corrupt segments of the police force.

Bandido bom é bandido morto: "A good criminal is a dead criminal"; saying used to justify violence against anyone suspected of a crime.

Barraca, and barraqueiro: beach shack where one can buy drinks and rent umbrellas or beach chairs, and the person who runs it.

Cartório: registry or notary public's office.

Caveirão: the armored vehicle used by Rio's elite police squad, the BOPE; it is nicknamed *caveirão*, or big skull, because it is black and usually carries the squad's skull and dagger symbol emblazoned on the side.

Chimarrão: hot, strong, unsweetened *mate* tea traditionally drunk from a gourd in southern Brazil.

Chopp: a light draft beer, usually served extremely cold and in tall, thin glasses.

Cidade Maravilhosa: "the Marvelous City," nickname for Rio de Janeiro, based on a song written for the 1935 Carnaval that has become Rio's informal anthem.

Comunidade: "community"; often used in lieu of *favela*.

Condomínios: Gated residential communities.

Convivência: coexistence

Copa do Mundo: the World Cup.

Copa das Copas: an expression meaning "Cup of Cups"; the motto of an advertising campaign designed to promote the World Cup to Brazilians.

Custo Brasil: the hidden costs of functioning in Brazil, such as the poor transportation infrastructure or the high tax burden.

Deus dará: literally, "God will provide"; expression often used to describe circumstances that cannot be helped.

Favela: low-income communities that often started as informal settlements lacking basic services.

Futebol: soccer

Futebol arte: artistic soccer, used to refer to a particularly Brazilian way of playing.

Havaianas: a brand of plastic flip-flop sandals that are ubiquitous in Brazil.

Imagina na Copa: "Imagine during the Cup."

Jeitinho: a flexible approach to situations, held as quintessentially Brazilian, which bends the rules without breaking them.

Jogo bonito: "the beautiful game"; a reference to soccer.

Jogo de cintura: literally, a sway of the hips; it refers to being smooth, agile in interpersonal dealings.

Lanchonete: fast-food place

Mate: a tea that in Rio is often drunk ice-cold, with lemon and sugar. Beach vendors often carry twin tanks of tea and lemon and mix it at the customer's request.

Mensalão: an illegal campaign slush fund and a cash-for-congressional-votes scheme that broke out in 2005 and threatened to bring down Lula's government. Its nickname, *mensalão*, or the big monthly, came from the regular kickbacks paid to legislators in exchange for their cooperation.

Meu amor: "my love"; one of the many terms of endearment used even among strangers in Brazil.

País do futebol: the country of soccer; an expression used to refer to Brazil.

Porteiro: doorman

Querida/querido: "my dear" or " my darling"; common term of endearment.

Seleção: Brazil's national soccer team

Surdo: bass drum that is the foundation of samba.

Traficantes: traffickers

Volta mais tarde: "Come back later."

BIBLIOGRAPHY

Abreu, Maurício de A. *Evolução urbana do Rio de Janeiro*. Rio de Janeiro: IPP, Instituto Municipal de Urbanismo Pereira Passos, 1988.

Abreu, Sabrina, and Rene Silva. *A voz do Alemão: como Rene Silva e outros jovens ajudaram a mudar a imagem da comunidade*. Rio de Janeiro: Versos, 2013.

Amaral, Ricardo Batista. *A Vida Quer é Coragem: A Trajetória de Dilma Rousseff, a Primeira Presidenta do Brasil*. Rio de Janeiro: Primeira Pessoa, 2011.

Arago, Jacques. *Narrative of a Voyage Round the World, in the Uranie and Physicienne Corvettes, Commanded by Captain Freycinet, During the Years 1817, 1818, 1819, and 1820*. London: T. Davison, Whitefriars; and Howlett and Brimmer, Faith Street, Soho, 1823.

Arias, Enrique Desmond. *Drugs and Democracy in Rio de Janeiro: Trafficking, Social Networks, and Public Security*. Chapel Hill: University of North Carolina Press, 2006.

Batista, Eike. *O X da Questão*. Rio de Janeiro, RJ: Primeira Pessoa, 2011.

Beltrame, José Mariano. *Todo Dia é Segunda-Feira*. Rio de Janeiro: Sextante, 2014.

Brum, Mario. "Favelas e Remocionismo Ontem e Hoje: da Ditadura de 1964 aos Grandes Eventos." *O Social em Questão* 16, no. 29 (2013): 179–208.

Cano, Ignacio. "Uso da Força Letal pela Polícia do Rio de Janeiro: Os

Fatos e o Debate." *Archè Interdisciplinar Crime organizado e política de segurança pública no Rio de Janeiro* 19 (1998): 201–29.

Cano, Ignacio, Doriam Borges, and Eduardo Ribeiro, eds. *Os Donos do Morro: Uma Análise Exploratória do Impacto das Unidades de Polícia Pacificadora (UPPs) no Rio de Janeiro.* 1st ed. Rio de Janeiro: Fórum Brasileiro de Segurança Pública, 2012.

Cavalcanti, Nireu Oliveira. *O Rio de Janeiro Setecentista: a Vida e a Construção da Cidade da Invasão Francesa Até a Chegada da Corte.* Rio de Janeiro: J. Zahar, 2004.

Coaracy, Vivaldo. *Memórias da Cidade do Rio de Janeiro.* Vol. 88. *Coleçao Documentos Brasileiros.* Rio de Janeiro: Libraria José Olympio Editora, 1955.

Darwin, Charles. *Charles Darwin's Beagle Diary.* Cambridge and New York: Cambridge University Press, 1988.

De Paula, Marilene, and Dawid Danilo Bartelt. *Copa para Quem e para Que? Um Olhar sobre os Legados dos Mundiais no Brasil, África do Sul e Alemanha.* 1st ed. Rio de Janeiro: Fundação Heinrich Böll, 2014.

De Souza, Pedro H.G. Ferreira. "Poverty, Inequality and Social Policies in Brazil, 1995–2009 (Working Paper)." *International Policy Centre for Inclusive Growth* 87 (February 2012): 28.

Duarte, Mário Sérgio. *Liberdade para o Alemão: O Resgate de Canudos.* Rio de Janeiro: Editora Ciência Moderna, 2012.

Esteve, Albert, Joan García-Román, and Ron Lesthaeghe. "The Family Context of Cohabitation and Single Motherhood in Latin America." *Population and Development Review* 38, no. 4 (2012): 707–27.

Esteve, Albert, Ron Lesthaeghe, and Antonio López-Gay. "The Latin American Cohabitation Boom, 1970–2007." *Population and Development Review* 38, no. 1 (2012): 55–81.

Esteve, Albert, Luis Ángel López-Ruiz, and Jeroen Spijker. "Disentangling How Educational Expansion Did Not Increase Women's Age at Union Formation in Latin America from 1970 to 2000." *Demographic Research* 28 (January 2013): 63–76.

Ferrari, André Luiz, M. V. Serra, and Maria Teresa F. Serra, eds. *Guia de História Natural do Rio de Janeiro.* Rio de Janeiro: Cidade Viva, 2012.

Fischer, Brodwyn. *A Poverty of Rights: Citizenship and Inequality in Twentieth-Century Rio de Janeiro.* Stanford: Stanford University Press, 2011.

Freire-Medeiros, Bianca. "Selling the Favela: Thoughts and Polemics about a Tourist Destination." *Revista Brasileira de Ciências Sociais* 22, no. 65 (2007): 61–72.

Gaffney, Christopher. "Between Discourse and Reality: The Un-Sustainability of Mega-Event Planning." *Sustainability* 5, no. 9 (2013): 3926–40.

Gaffney, Christopher. *Temples of the Earthbound Gods: Stadiums in the Cultural Landscapes of Rio de Janeiro and Buenos Aires.* 1st ed. Austin: University of Texas Press, 2008.

Galvão, Jane. "Brazil and Access to HIV/AIDS Drugs: A Question of Human Rights and Public Health." *American Journal of Public Health* 95, no. 7 (2005): 1110–16.

———. *1980–2001: Uma cronologia da epidemia de HIV/AIDS no Brasil e no mundo.* Rio de Janeiro: ABIA, 2002.

———. *AIDS No Brasil: A Agenda de Construção de uma Epidemia.* 1a ed. Rio de Janeiro and São Paulo: Associação Brasileira Interdisciplinar de AIDS; Editora 34, 2000.

Garrido, Atilio. *Maracanazo, a história secreta. Da euforia ao silêncio de uma nação.* Rio de Janeiro: Livros Ilimitados, 2014.

Goldblatt, David. *Futebol Nation: The Story of Brazil through Soccer.* New York: Public Affairs, 2014.

Gomes, Laurentino. *1808: Como uma Rainha Louca, um Príncipe Medroso e uma Corte Corrupta Enganaram Napoleão e Mudaram a História de Portugal e do Brasil.* São Paulo: Editora Planeta do Brasil, 2007.

———. *1822: Como um Homem Sábio, uma Princesa Triste e um Escocês Louco por Dinheiro Ajudaram D. Pedro a Criar o Brasil—Um País que Tinha Tudo para dar Errado.* Rio de Janeiro, RJ, Brasil: Nova Fronteira Participações, 2010.

———. *1889: Como um Imperador Cansado, um Marechal Vaidoso e um Professor Injustiçado Contribuíram para o Fim da Monarquia e a Proclamação da Republica no Brasil.* São Paulo: Globo, 2013.

Green, James. " 'Mais Amor e Mais Tesão': A Construção de um Movimento Brasileiro de Gays, Lésbicas e Travestis." http://www.biblioteca digital.unicamp.br/document/?down=51350?.

Green, James Naylor. *Beyond Carnival: Male Homosexuality in Twentieth-Century Brazil.* Chicago: University of Chicago Press, 2001.

Instituto Brasileiro de Economia. *Rio de Janeiro: um Estado em Transição.* Edited by Armando Castelar Pinheiro, Fernando Veloso, and Adriana Fontes. 1a. edição. Rio de Janeiro: IBRE Editora, 2012.

Júnior, Otávio. *O Livreiro Do Alemão.* Rio de Janeiro: Panda Books, 2012.

Lage de Sousa, Filipe, ed. *BNDES 60 Anos: Perspectivas Setoriais.* 1st ed. Vol. 1. Rio de Janeiro: BNDES, 2012.

Lauderdale Graham, Sandra. *House and Street: The Domestic World of Servants and Masters in Nineteenth-Century Rio de Janeiro.* Austin: University of Texas Press, 1992.

Leitão, Miriam. *Convém Sonhar.* Rio de Janeiro: Editora Record, 2010.

———. *Saga Brasileira: A Longa Luta de um Povo por sua Moeda.* Rio de Janeiro: Editora Record, 2011.

Lemgruber, Julita, Barbara Soares, Leonarda Musumeci, and Silvia Ramos. "O Que Pensam os Policiais das UPPs." *Ciência Hoje* 49, no. 294 (2012): 34–39.

Levine, Robert M. *Brazilian Legacies. Perspectives on Latin America and the Caribbean.* Armonk, NY: M. E. Sharpe, 1997.

McCann, Bryan. *Hard Times in the Marvelous City: From Dictatorship to Democracy in the Favelas of Rio de Janeiro.* Durham, NC: Duke University Press, 2013.

Meade, Teresa A. *"Civilizing" Rio: Reform and Resistance in a Brazilian City, 1889–1930.* University Park: Pennsylvania State University Press, 1997.

Moura, Roberto. *Tia Ciata e a Pequena África no Rio de Janeiro.* 2a ed., rev. by the author. Coleção Biblioteca Carioca; Série Publicação Científica, vol. 32. Rio de Janeiro: Prefeitura da Cidade do Rio de Janeiro, Secretaria Municipal de Cultura, Departamento Geral de Documentação e Informação Cultural, Divisão de Editoração, 1995.

Osborn, Catherine. "A History of Favela Upgrades: 1897–1988." 2012. RioOnWatch.org. http://rioonwatch.org/?p=5295.

———. "A History of Favela Upgrades Part II: Introducing Favela-Bairro (1988–2008)." RioOnWatch. http://www.rioonwatch.org/?p=5931.

———. "A History of Favela Upgrades Part III: Morar Carioca in Vision and Practice (2008–Present)." RioOnWatch. http://rioonwatch.org/?p=8136.

Pereira, Júlio César Medeiros da Silva. *À Flor da Terra: o Cemitério Dos Pretos Novos no Rio de Janeiro*. Rio de Janeiro: Garamond Universitária, 2007.

Perlman, Janice E. *The Myth of Marginality: Urban Poverty and Politics in Rio de Janeiro*. Berkeley: University of California Press, 1979.

Samara, Tony Roshan. "Policing Development: Urban Renewal as Neo-Liberal Security Strategy." *Urban Studies* 47, no. 1 (2010): 197–214.

Schlee, Mônica Bahia. "Transformações na Paisagem e Seus Efeitos na Qualidade Ambiental da Bacia do Rio Carioca." *Coleção Estudos Cariocas*, no. 20030201 (February 2003): 1–46.

Serra, M. V., and Maria Teresa Serra, eds. *Guia de História Natural do Rio de Janeiro*. 1st ed. Rio de Janeiro: Editora Cidade Viva, 2012.

Sevcenko, Nicolau. *A revolta da vacina: mentes insanas em corpos rebeldes*. São Paulo: Cosac Naify, 2010.

Soares, Luís Carlos. *Prostitution in Nineteenth-Century Rio de Janeiro*. London: University of London, Institute of Latin American Studies, 1988.

Soares, Luiz Eduardo. *Meu Casaco de General: 500 Dias no Front da Segurança Pública do Rio de Janeiro*. São Paulo: Companhia das Letras, 2000.

Vidal, Laurent, and Maria Alice Araripe de Sampaio. *As lágrimas do Rio: o Último Dia de uma Capital, 20 de abril de 1960*. Rio de Janeiro: Martins Fontes, 2012.

Zaluar, Alba, and Marcos Alvito, eds. *Um Século de Favela*. 1a. ed. Rio de Janeiro: Fundação Getulio Vargas Editora, 1998.

DANCING WITH THE DEVIL IN THE CITY OF GOD

In *Dancing With the Devil in the City of God*, reporter Juliana Barbassa returns to Rio de Janeiro, the city of her birth, after two decades away. She finds this vibrant city, selected to host the World Cup and the 2016 Olympic Games, on the brink of change and ready to claim its place as a modern metropolis deserving of the world stage. But in order to succeed, Rio and its citizens must contend with long-standing problems of corruption, violence, poverty, and ill-considered development. Barbassa brilliantly charts the progress of the city and its colorful residents, their stumbles, and missteps, as they prepare for the largest events in Rio's history—and set its future course.

FOR DISCUSSION

1. How did the author's perspective as someone who had lived abroad for many years influence her writing about Rio de Janeiro? What aspects of life in Rio are most jarring or upsetting for her?

2. The gap between rich and poor in Brazil has shrunk to a fifty-year low. What factors played a part in this shift? How has the quality of life of Brazil's poor and middle-class residents changed? How has it remained the same?

3. What portrait emerges of the Cariocas, the residents of Rio? What characteristics of the upper classes and lower classes stood out to you? What makes Rio a "divided city"?

4. In what ways do crime and violence permeate the everyday lives of Cariocas? Do you think the steps the police and government took to fight the Red Command were warranted? How did the public's

response compare to the way Americans have responded to police violence in our own country?

5. Do you think that communities such as Vila Autódromo will be able to coexist with gentrification in Rio? How is the government's response to favelas such as Vila Autódromo or Metrô a barometer of progress?

6. Why would the program Morar Carioca have represented a significant step forward in how the government handled favelas? Why was the program abandoned? Contrast the failure of Morar Carioca with the success of the poverty-fighting program Bolsa Família.

7. Consider the condition of Rio's rivers and ocean. Why have its citizens and its government allowed them to become so polluted? Do they have the means and resources to do better?

8. How does the "state of exception" (page 218) invoked to meet the deadlines of the Olympic Games and World Cup shape building and development in the city? In instances such as the building of the golf course, what compromises are made?

9. What factors contributed to Brazil's progressive approach to gay rights? How do Brazilians' attitudes towards sex and sexuality differ from those of Americans?

10. What sparked the massive protests of June 2013? What reforms did the protestors demand? Did the protests have tangible results?

11. How is the Brazilian team's defeat in the World Cup emblematic of the disconnect between the country's "aspirations and its ability to achieve them" (page 280)?

12. In the introduction the author wonders whether the changes in Rio de Janeiro will be merely *para inglês ver*, "a nicety for foreign eyes" (page xxii). What is her conclusion? What is yours?

13. Of all the challenges that Rio faces, which stood out to you as the most difficult to overcome? Why?

A CONVERSATION
WITH JULIANA BARBASSA

How did writing your first book differ from writing news articles? Did you approach the reporting differently?

There is a moment during an interview that you always hope for as a journalist: when the person you are talking to relaxes into the conversation. That often happens after she is finished telling you what she thinks you want to hear, or has exhausted her agenda. There's often a break there—the person has run out of big, important things to say.

In the silence that follows is when the good stuff starts to come out: the chitchat about the kids, their jobs, the neighborhood, the stuff that keeps them up at night, and the minutiae of their daily lives. This is what makes that person real and not a stand-in for an issue; it fleshes them out, shows what makes them tick. It also reveals the contours of their world and where the tensions lie. By culling from these stories and observations the writer can turn a topic—say, the razing of favelas in Rio—into something the reader can connect with and understand. This is true of any good reporting.

But daily news has specific requirements—you work under deadline; keep your articles short and to the point. That's the nature of news. For me, it often meant having to leave an interview before that shift, before the good stuff; other times it simply meant leaving much of the nuance out of the final article for lack of space. My motivations for writing this book were many, but I admit that at the core was a very selfish desire to simply have more time to report, more visits to people and places. I wanted to bring the city to readers, but I also wanted to get under its skin. Covering Rio as a correspondent gave me breadth of experiences, thousands of interviews; reporting the book allowed me to return to the same person or place and see various layers. It gave me depth. And even that wasn't enough! I still found myself wanting more time, more visits.

One theme of the book is how modern-day Brazil often confounds your memories or expectations. What was the learning curve of living in Rio de Janeiro again like?

This process of trying to go home is always fraught, as knows anyone who has lived away from his place of origin and then tried to return years or even generations later. Over time, this place that is supposed to be home becomes flattened, static—a postcard. It becomes a convenient receptacle for hopes and expectations, far removed from the confounding and complex reality.

Confronting the disparity between the Brazil I'd known as a child and had carried with me and what I saw decades later as a reporter left me with a bad case of emotional whiplash. I often felt it would have been far easier to move to an entirely unknown country. At least there would have been no expectations of familiarity.

This move back home also tested my sense of self in unexpected ways. Being out of place in foreign country was a familiar feeling; I had felt that way for most of my life. But feeling out of place in what was supposed to be my home really knocked me off balance. I don't think this is an unusual experience; others who have tried to move back home often find it raises more questions than answers.

I also had challenges just trying to settle. I've known few places that are as immediately rewarding to the senses, as rich and as visually stunning, and as maddening as Rio. Setting up life and work there had me oscillating wildly between giddy pleasure at my surroundings and seething frustration at the traffic, the bureaucracy, the senseless violence, and the tremendous inequality that grate against you every single day. At the end of four years I'd found ways to navigate this, but I also felt a resignation creeping in, dampening the enthusiasm and the indignation that marked my first couple of years. It may be a necessary aspect of getting by in such a challenging place, but I am not sure it is a good thing.

The book weaves together many aspects of Rio's culture and the ways in which the city is changing. How did you choose what subjects to focus on? How did you shape the narrative?

Often as a journalist I felt I didn't chose the stories I worked on; they latched themselves onto me and I had no choice but to take them on, report them out, and write them down just to get them out of my system. It was the same with this book.

There are aspects of Rio that grabbed me from the moment I landed: the new favela occupation plan, the pollution of the rivers and the ocean, the economic upsurge that fed the growth of a substantial middle class for the first time in Brazilian history. These issues confronted me every day, every time I took a swim, walked past the heavily armed police officers at the entrance of a favela, or saw people who historically had lived hand-to-mouth sporting cell phones, dental braces, a new car.

The preparation for the upcoming World Cup and Olympic Games were also unavoidable. Big infrastructural projects tied to these events were physically transforming the city; favelas were being torn down and new transportation routes were being carved into the landscape, fostering new developments along their route. The city would live with the consequences of this change for decades, and all the construction was choking the city. This aspect had to be examined if I were to probe what this moment meant to Rio.

The real challenge was deciding what to leave out. I opted to focus on what was suffering immediate and clear change, and leave out longer term and more subtle transformations in areas like race and education. I also allowed the arc of my own expectations and curiosity drive the narrative, assuming the reader would share many of my questions. The economic downturn, Brazil's defeat during the World Cup, and my own readjustment of expectations gave the book a natural dénouement.

You describe Rio as both environmentally beautiful and rotten (page 129). What has allowed the environmental degradation to reach this point? Do you see any shift in the Cariocas' perception of the environment?

The poet Elizabeth Bishop, who spent eighteen years in Brazil, said in a 1965 article for The *New York Times Magazine* that Rio was "not a marvelous city, it is merely a marvelous setting for a city." This touched a raw nerve with Cariocas, or Rio residents, back then. In a rebuke, a Brazilian writer told her, "Monkey, mind your own tail!"

Cariocas are just as sensitive today to critiques of their *cidade maravilhosa*, but the truth is that Rio remains a poorly planned, chaotic mess of a city draped over an exquisite landscape. There is no integration between the metropolis and the more than one dozen other towns that make up Greater Rio, with its population of nearly 13 million. The planning and implementation of public transportation, garbage collection, and sewerage infrastructure is piecemeal and disconnected geographically and over time. This is, in part, what turned the city and the state into an environmental disaster.

Hosting the Pan-American Games of 2007, the 2014 World Cup, and the 2016 Olympics provided opportunities to at least tackle the problems that could interfere with the events, such as the perennially snarled traffic or the pollution in the Bay. Ideally, the needs of these sporting events would be harnessed to the needs of the city, and preparing for them would result in improvements that are useful to residents in the long run.

Instead Cariocas saw more of the same: projects imposed with no public consultation, unmarried to broader city-planning goals, and which served powerful but narrow constituencies. The city got, for example, several rapid bus transit lanes increasing flux to the wealthy west side, but no improvement in transportation to the mostly working-class north side, which has been historically underserved in all areas. New sewage treatment plants were installed where heavily polluted rivers empty into the bay, but the low-income communities upriver remain without sewage infrastructure. There are notable exceptions, but unfortunately I have not seen a significant enough shift in attitudes to force elected authorities to behave any differently.

Your reporting brought you into contact with Cariocas at every level of society. How do the opinions of Rio's future vary amongst the lower, middle, and upper classes? What unifies them?

When I first returned to Brazil in 2010, one of the most noticeable changes was in the decrease of extreme poverty. The narrowing of the great gap between rich and poor that I'd read about from abroad was clear. Don't get me wrong: Brazil was still a place of jarring social inequality, and highly stratified by class. But this was not the Brazil of the 1980s and 1990s, when hunger was a reality you could confront around the corner. For the first time in my lifetime, and I believe for the first time in the country's history, Brazil was doing well and it was the lot of the poorest that had improved the most (relatively speaking, of course).

This created a sense of possibility, particularly among lower-income Brazilians. This optimism overflowed from a segment of the population to the country as a whole. This socio-economic gap had always been Brazil's Achilles heel; the sense was that if Brazil could remedy that, then it could do anything. It reflected Brazil's potential. I remember going to the Cidade de Deus favela on the occasion of President Barack Obama's visit and hearing it from a resident, standing in front of his minuscule storefront: "The American president is here because we matter. It used to be that we had to go to them; now they come to us." For the first time, I saw pride in this new Brazil, in what it could accomplish.

The middle class and the upper classes also benefitted, of course, from the stabilization, the growing economy, and the investment the country was drawing at the time. It was hard to open a newspaper without seeing a new record broken: the lowest unemployment levels, the greatest number of cars sold, the astonishing number of Brazilians flying in an airplane for the first time.

In Rio, in particular, there were specific projects that targeted the city's most recognized challenges. These affected most directly the lowest-income Cariocas, but would improve the lives of all residents. The UPP project, which brought police presence to specific favelas, and was supposed to bring basic services in its wake, is one. Cleaning up Rio's polluted rivers and the bay is another. Morar Carioca, which would have brought basic services to all favelas by 2020, would have had tremendous impact on the quality of life in the city.

When the national economy took a nosedive and these Rio-specific projects failed to deliver or were cut off at the root, it was the lowest-income Cariocas who felt it the most. The better-off are affected by the worsening economy, certainly, but to a certain degree they are still able to shelter themselves from these failures and pay for safe housing, security, education, health, [and] distance from pollution.

In spite of the disappointments of the past few years, and the radically different ways in which these were felt, Cariocas of all classes come together around a stubborn, unstinting love of their hometown. No matter its flaws, nothing rankles laid-back Cariocas more than criticism of their *cidade maravilhosa*.

What has happened to the residents of Vila Autódromo since you finished the book?

They've been suffering increasing intimidation. First, all the trees in the community were cut down. Then the remaining residents began to suffer phone, water and power outages. Many families succumbed to the pressure and accepted compensation or the offered public housing. But as tickets for the Olympic Games went on sale, there were still about one hundred properties left. The mayor signed decrees declaring the site a public utility and calling for the immediate destruction of about half of them. This raised the specter of forced removal, with some form of compensation to be settled later by court. The residents continued to protest and question the need for their removal, pointing out that plans for building high-rent condos do not constitute a public utility.

The removal of this community, where many residents have titles to their land, to favor development of high-rent, exclusive gated communities is one of the starkest examples of how local government is using the preparation for the Olympics as leverage to push through a narrow set of economic interests. The deadline and the external commitments imposed by the Games allow authorities to invoke a sense of urgency and create a state of exception in which the usual legalities are plowed over. This is also clear in the development of the Olympic golf course on environmentally protected and sensitive land.

The extent of the protests in 2013 took the whole country by surprise. What effect did they have on the government? What events could precipitate more protests?

One immediate effect was leaving government officials fearful and increasingly willing to be truculent to maintain order. Many, from the president on down, had staked their political future on smoothly carrying off the games and projecting an image of Brazil as an orderly, up-and-coming country that is a safe bet for tourists and investors.

By the time the World Cup started, the president had vowed zero tolerance for disruption. Since Brazil's strategic plan for World Cup security had called for one billion dollars to be spent on public security—with states and cities contributing more—there was not only political will but also the cash to further militarize the police force and ready them to contain protests.

I'll never forget the sight of a Rio state military police officer wearing the gear they got before the World Cup: the black, Kevlar-encrusted body armor, the helmet with a face shield, the multiple gadgets meant for shooting, shocking, spraying, handcuffing, or beating. Keep in mind this is the police force that kills the greatest number of civilians in the world, according to the Instituto Humanitas Unisinos. In 2014, Rio police killed 582 residents—up from 416 the year before.

This strike-first approach was put into practice during the Cup. Before the games, police preemptively arrested alleged protest organizers and seized computers and cell phones. As the competition started, rows of these Robocop-like officers stood shoulder to shoulder, blocking streets and funneling fans into designated areas. After the games, the president signed a law allowing Municipal Guards—the guys who hand out parking tickets—to carry guns, and the Brazilian Senate began debating whether protests could qualify as acts of terrorism.

Protests were far more subdued during the Cup, as Brazilians were lulled by the irresistible combination of world-class soccer and loads of extra holidays, and turned off by the increasingly violent environment surrounding the marches. But in spite of heightened security, the unrest continues. Protests flared up again in March 2015, galvanized by the return of inflation, growing unemployment, an economic slowdown, and a vast corruption scandal that has implicated the governing Workers' Party, many of the country's top construction firms, and the national oil company Petrobras.

What these protests show is that various segments of the population have heightened expectations of their country. It is as if they got a glimpse of what was possible during the economic upswing of the 2000s, when the Workers' Party first came to power and Brazil hit on vast oil discoveries. The Brazil they glimpsed then—that's the country they want. And anything that stands in the way of the vision—a crumbling economy, another corruption scandal, overspending on megaevents like the World Cup or the Olympics—could spark another wave of protests.

How did the short-term objectives of planning for the World Cup and the Olympic Games undercut the city's larger goals?

The shortest answer has to do with allocation of public funds. Take the World Cup. After selling Brazilians on the idea that FIFA-standard stadiums would be constructed without a penny of public financing, Brazil spent $4 billion on what the NGO Play the Game has called some of the most expensive stadia ever built. Many of them were then handed over to the private sector. This is jarring in a country that still lacks adequate schools and health care. It was the same with the 2007 Pan-American Games, which were nearly ten times over budget and left a legacy of expensive-to-maintain venues (including an $8 million velodrome that was demolished by 2013; another one is being built for the Olympics). Many of the same people were in charge when Rio got the 2016 Olympic Games, so there is little reason to expect it will have different results.

Then there is the question of the particular projects put into place as part of the preparations for the games. Rio de Janeiro's transportation network, for example, was in dire need of improvement, after years with no significant investment. But instead of projects that fit into long-term city planning goals, Rio authorities threw a pet project into the Matrix of Responsibilities it signed with FIFA: a rapid bus transit lane connecting the international airport to the wealthy suburb of Barra da Tijuca, which serves neither the areas of greatest need nor the World Cup visitors. To carry out this and other projects, it was also given an exemption to Brazil's Law of Fiscal Responsibility (like other FIFA host cities), which allowed for deficit spending and emergency financing.

But the real pity here is the opportunity cost. By the time Rio has hosted the Olympics, it will have lived through over a decade of preparing for and hosting massive-scale, international sporting events. This process will have remade the face of the city, and residents will live with the consequences for decades to come. It is heartbreaking to consider what would have been possible to achieve if such monumental change had been implemented with long-term planning and real public consultation.

At the end of the book we see that the economic upswing has begun to swing back the other way. Where do things stand today?

The effervescent party atmosphere I found in 2010 has soured into a national hangover of continental proportions. Nearly all the positive developments that had led to such optimism have crumbled. Prices for Brazil's commodities—iron ore, soy—have tumbled. Inflation has spiked, the unemployment rate is the highest in years, and the economy is expected to shrink in 2015 after four years of near stagnation. The state-run oil company behind the oil discovery hailed as Brazil's "passport to the future" is embroiled in a corruption scandal that has involved the highest echelons of the Workers' Party and the nation's biggest construction companies. Brazil's currency, the Real, has fallen by about 50 percent since 2011. Even Eike Batista, the Brazilian and Rio resident who was once the world's eighth-wealthiest man, is now over $1 billion in debt.

The magnitude of the crisis has been recognized by investors: Brazil's credit rating has been backsliding, along with that of its state-controlled oil company, Petrobras. Now both are perched on the brink of junk. And it is also causing unrest in the streets. President Dilma Rousseff's approval rating fell to the lowest ever, 13 percent, after renewed protests in early 2015. So far, she has largely preserved the income redistribution programs that helped sustain the social gains of the previous decade: falling poverty rates, narrowing inequality, and increasing income among the poorest. But with a 2015 budget deficit that turned out to be, at $18.6 billion, twice as big as forecasted, it is unclear how long these programs can be maintained.

What do you think the legacy of the Olympic Games will be in Rio de Janeiro?
I feel I've already answered this question in other questions above, no?

ENHANCE YOUR BOOK CLUB

1. Set the tone for your reading group by playing some Brazilian music. Try the official song of Rio de Janeiro, *Cidade Maravilhosa*; or the classic "The Girl from Ipanema."

2. Bring Rio alive off the page by watching films set there. Try *City of God* or the documentary *Waste Land*.

3. Visit the website for the Olympic Games at http://www.olympic.org/rio-2016-summer-olympics to see photos and renderings of the construction and venues you have read about.

INDEX